FIRST EDI

# IT'S NOT THEM, IT'S YOU

How To Truly Lead A Company

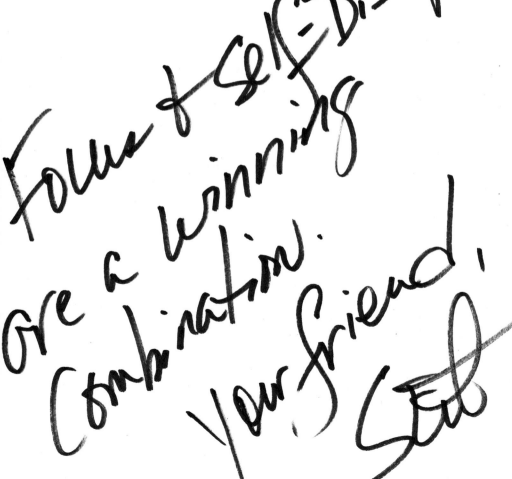

Focus of Self-Discipline
are a winning
Combination.
Your friend,
Stu

# IT'S NOT THEM, IT'S YOU

## How To Truly Lead A Company

### By Scot Ferrell

"The Rock Star of Personal &
Professional Development"

*Scot would like to express his thanks to his publisher, Leon Smith Publishing, for allowing him to "maintain his voice" in this publication! Working with Keith and Maura Leon has been a true joy for Scot, allowing him the ability to combine their strengths of publishing expertise and intuition with his knowledge of behavior and business. As a reader, you may find certain segments of this book that do not strictly adhere to "standardized" publishing rules. This is intentional by Scot Ferrell in order to emphasize his unorthodox, direct speaking and sometimes brutally honest approach to achieving the results he wants you to achieve in your life and business. Scot appreciates Leon Smith Publishing for allowing him this creative license in this book!*

ISBN: 978-1-945446-01-6

LEON SMITH
PUBLISHING

Printed in the United States of America.

"It's Not Them, It's You" is a set of guiding principles for you and your business which will systematically increase profits, boost employee and customer/client harmony, stimulate retention and upgrade the image of your company in the marketplace. If you "start with you," your employees and customers will have the finest in the ultimate experience with you and your company.

*"Never forget – You can never separate your private behavior from your professional behavior. Your decisions take on a whole new meaning when consequences have faces."*

Scot Ferrell

# *Dedication*

*To Shellie Hunt*

*The day I met you, I knew an angel had walked into my life. My life is forever changed because of you. You started out as a friend and became a sister. I will always carry you in my heart. Thank you for the guidance, friendship and love.*

# Acknowledgments

As a person who spends most of my life sharing with others the power of gratitude and appreciation, I would be at grievous fault not to include the very people who have been at my side throughout my life-whether in my heart, mind or still physically present with me, their influence and reach, in and through me, still carries magical power to this day.

Foremost in my mind are my two aunts-Aunt Frances Rogers and Aunt Norma Paige. These two strong women always believed in me, showed me kindness in dark hours and taught me the power of love. Without them, my fate would have surely been a dark one.

The strong and loving hand of my grandfather, Bob Earnhardt, lives in me, each and every day. There is not a day that goes by that I don't think about us fishing and having burp contests. Oh, how I still miss you and look forward to our reunion soon.

The two women in my life today, my "work wife," Chanda Livesay, and my "real wife," Patricia Ferrell keep me going with their dedication, caring, support and love for me. Thank you, Joey, for allowing your wife to help manage my career and for letting me love your daughter Camilla as my "unofficially adopted granddaughter." She has brought true joy and light to my life in ways I never anticipated.

To my dear friend, Cathy Lowther. You've seen me at every phase of my life and have continued to be a loyal, laughing and loving friend. Thank you for taking me in all those years ago. I will never forget.

I've been blessed to have Ryan Jones as my son. Of all of the people I've met in my life, I think he is truly one of the most gifted, creative and blessed individuals I've ever known. Everything he puts his hand to succeeds because of his intelligence, creativity and work ethic. How proud I am to call him my son.

My niece, Taylor Ferrell, is a warm, constant presence in my heart each day as I have watched her grow from a darling little girl to a beautiful young woman. I'm proud of you.

To James and "Mama" Ring-I have felt your love and friendship for the last thirty years. It seems like every time I tell a story from my past, it includes one or both of you. The question of "Do you know who I saw/did/heard this with for the first time?" in my house is always answered with the statement, "James Ring." You rock, brother.

To those who joined in this project with me: Dr. David Gruder, Lt. Col. Alan Tucker, Dr. Jeff Magee, Col. Steve Seroka, Aaron Young, Frank Tortorici, Dr. Sonza Curtis and Dr. Hank Sloan-you are a highly esteemed group of achievers who have done much to improve our world and mine. Thank you for your integrity, expertise and your friendship.

My life, thoughts and purpose have been forever changed by the power of these people-Gary Carter, Joe Hunt, Beverly Clayton, Ethel Rhodes, and Michael Pittard. How many lives have you touched and never even knew it?

Dr. Dennis Shaw is the man who taught me how to close my mouth, open my ears, watch and listen. His genius in the field of behavior and his ability to impart that genius to me altered the course of my destiny. He always expected excellence and taught me the power of that expectation. Your influence is all over this book and my life. Thank you.

I would be remiss not to include the "Men of Faith" and their presence in my life-Pastors Alan DiDio, Don Brock, Steve Goode, Robert Goode and my mentor, Bob Shank. I also want to thank Bruce Wilkinson for letting me follow him relentlessly and glean from his wisdom. I also want to acknowledge Steve "Big Poppa" and Gwen Jones for always opening their loving hearts and beautiful and relaxing home to us as we travel. The rewards this collective group has created (here and there) will be astounding to view one day, I'm sure.

My "East Coast, West Coast" connections, Shellie Hunt and Erin Saxton-where would I be without your wisdom and friendship? Life would surely be much more boring without the two of you!

To Berny Dohrmann, I want to say a huge "thank you." What this man has done for spreading the message of "cooperation, not competition" and the true meaning of an abundant life without scarcity or lack has changed millions of lives. Your courage to be different and stay true to your purpose is a true inspiration to me. CEO Space has become my family and one I love dearly.

My radio mentors, Joel Williams and Susan King, have been professional beacons of integrity and excellence, and have been true friends and sounding boards-thank you for your quiet spirits and listening ears.

My personal stylist and friend, Julie Baker, is a source of joy and laughter to me and has been a lifelong friend. Her talent is amazing and her laughter is infectious. Thanks for giving me (and my hair) a look worthy to live up to my media nicknames!

My "Vegas connection" friends Saville Kellner and Don Cote have been huge supporters of all of my efforts and for their belief in me, I am grateful. They have welcomed me into their hearts, homes and lives. It was a fateful trip that led me to meet the two of you!

To my agent, Bruce Merrin, who is a constant source of encouragement and support to me and my entire family. I am so glad that our paths crossed and am looking forward to many more years together!

To everyone who is anonymously included in this book, who met with me under the umbrella of confidentiality, thank you for your contributions. It took many people sharing their own individual stories of triumph, failure, frustration, joy and success to make this book come alive. Thank you for letting me share your stories, albeit anonymously! Your input in my writing is greatly appreciated.

To my "Rock Stars" who follow me wherever I go and whatever I do...Dave Vizzi, Kimmie and Skyelar Earnest, Donna Norman, Krystal "Squeal Weasel" Lipe, Shannon Pridmore, Robin Lee, Tommy Bahler, Bill Prater, Dave Phillipson, Chella Diaz, Renee and Christopher Mansir, Stephanie "Scooby" Hylton, Roger Blankenship, Dianna Donahue, Jasmine Smith, Twayne Hills, Jonathan Loudermilk and the baby "gingers," Cheryl Snapp Conner, Bridget Cook, Werner Berger and Heshie Segal, Dr. Dan Cook, Stephanie and Tonya Hartman, Gail Kingsbury, Dianne D'Andrea, Angie Mauck, Doug Hollandsworth, Robert Johnson, Dr. Dan Cooke, Tony Dietsch and Dan Liebrecht, Darren Mish, Chuck Boyce, Nick Nanton, Jack Dicks, Lindsay Dicks, Millie Weaver, Dr. Hallie Robbins, Lewis Lewis, Jacob and Ryan Cooke, and "Uncle Jay" - thanks for pouring out the love on me every day! Your texts and calls make my days "Best Days"!

# Table of Contents

# *Introduction*

*"It's not personal; it's just behavior."*

That quote is from one of my personal mentors who taught me everything I know about behavior. I couldn't think of a more appropriate beginning for a book on leading a company and business behavior.

This simple concept, if you can truly grasp it, will change your life. As a business owner, CEO or a high-level executive, this one concept will help you to become a sharper, more decisive, intuitive and less ego-driven leader.

In an effort for you to get the maximum benefit out of this book and every word on every page, I have provided research and suggestions and bonus sections in some chapters which features interviews with experts in other fields who can lend you their expertise in specific areas of business. Because I am a big believer in mastermind groups and the strategies that those groups can provide, I wanted this book to serve as your own personal mastermind strategy session about leading your company.

This book is a book about leadership, your behavior and its role in your results. However, it's not about behavior in the conventional sense. The book is more of an examination of behavioral approaches to life, love, business, values, vision, longevity and community.

As with each of us here on Earth, we are a combination of our environment, our experiences, and our senses.

When I began writing the chapters of this book, I examined

how I became who I am as a father, spouse, teacher, coach and business owner.

An honest look inside of my life revealed the heavy influence of my great-grandmother who grew up in the difficult "post-Civil War" era, grandparents who built their lives during World War I, an uncle who survived Pearl Harbor, parents whose lives were shaped by the Great Depression and a cousin and friends who were scarred by Vietnam, which landed me smack in between the Baby Boomers and the Generation X'ers.

As I child, I had the opportunity to observe short hair growing to long hair, street signs to peace signs, nightly body counts on the news, school integration, Watergate, that my bologna had a first and last name, that school houses could rock and Monkees could sing and dance, that Partridges could ride on a bus and not peck each others' eyes out, and the happiest place on earth was ruled by a mouse. I discovered that if I wanted to find the secret to life, I needed to ride in a Yellow Submarine, visit Palisades Park, become a paperback writer, walk down Penny Lane, make Ed Sullivan smile, ride a horse with no name, understand good vibrations, catch a wave, have a Coke and a smile, not be fooled again, listen to what two carpenters had to say, and, at the end of the week, Don Cornelius and Dick Clark would teach me how to be cool, spin the greatest tunes, and have the best moves in the club and if I did all of these things…I would know the Stairway to Heaven.

As these things shaped the man I would become, I discovered that chicks really did dig love, if you hide under your desk at school, you could survive a nuclear blast, platform shoes were a blessing from God, bell-bottoms really were ugly, cool jackets were for members only, authority figures were to be questioned and rules were for squares.

We, as combined generations, had begun to openly question government policy, religion, sexual freedom, social norms, the goals of parenting, the rules and philosophies of business society and anything that we thought would control or oppress our lives.

The combined generations began to question and examine any and all rules and behavior, decide if those had validity and, then and only then, did the generations agree to allow those rules to serve their lives. Historically, rebellion among younger generations had been common, but for some reason, during this part of history, rebellion was placed under a microscope by the media and could no longer be ignored by the public. The events of that day would change the trajectory of our country and our individual lives forever.

No longer would a behavior be tolerated just because it had been a norm in society or business. The generations were ready to blaze their own trail and make their own behavioral rules.

Sounds poetic and romantic, doesn't it?

For a while, it was.

It didn't take long to realize that sex, drugs and rock and roll, rebellion and peace rallies and gettin' smoked up at Woodstock wasn't going to pay the bills. Eventually, our frat and sorority days had to end, a suit and tie would be purchased, diapers would need changing, a station wagon would be bought, a house would be procured, vacations would be planned and a life of legacy would replace the "glorious revolution" of the summer of love.

It was easy to be a rebel with a cause when there were no consequences or responsibilities tied to that life. However, maturity and wisdom seem to shed light on the fallacies of idealism and fantasy. Ideas without measurement can always work in theory. Eventually, something must be proven to be valid. And that's the place where most glorious ideas fall apart. Regardless of situation, an idea must stand on its on merit based on proven results.

As a teenager, I wanted to be a part of the "glorious revolution." It made sense, since I was a gifted student, but three-time, rule-breaking offender. I decided that I knew best and the standard societal and behavior guidelines didn't need to apply to me. On a beautiful sunny morning, I was summoned to the principal's office. As my high school principal grabbed me by the back of the neck, he proceeded to launch into a lecture I will never forget. In an effort to get me out the door quickly, he used my head as the opener. The taste of metal still brings a smile to my face. It was his last attempt to knock some sense into me.

The lecture was about my behavior and why the rules he had in place were to protect me, not the school or him. He explained that the only person that could ever destroy me was me and that my behavior and contempt for rules was actually a reflection of my contempt for myself as a person.

He further explained that without rules to guide our behavior, we would have anarchy. He advised me that rules were guidelines that would help make me a success and that when I grew up, I would be able to make some of my own rules, but that I needed to be wise in my decisions regarding the choices I made. He also told me that as a leader, taxpayer and a businessman, I would have the right and the responsibility to vote for changes in rules and voice my opinion in a civilized, wise and orderly manner.

At the conclusion of the lecture, he decided to check my wisdom. He gave me a choice. I could choose two days of school suspension and thirty days of trash detail and graduation or not graduating and never being allowed to step foot on campus again.

It's amazing what a thirty-day 6:30AM trash detail can do for your life, behavior, and your outlook. Even though the garbage bag and the pick couldn't speak, their wisdom is still with me today.

Over the course of those thirty days, I learned that my principal was a man of wisdom and that he truly cared about his students, their lives and their futures. The bag and pick taught me that leadership and some rules were a necessity, that most people need guidance and wisdom imparted into their lives to mold and guide their behavior, that cooperation of ideas and resources was the key to success and that my success or failure in life was based on my application of my talents, ability to lead, cooperative resources and my hard work, drive and determination.

In the silence of those thirty days, I understood the power of thought. I was forced to spend one hour a day, thinking about my life. That's when I discovered…

Rules in themselves aren't bad or good. They just are. I began to analyze the rules that were placed on me and all of my behaviors – my personal life and my professional life.

I had a much deeper understanding that rules can be tweaked and adjusted and didn't need to be interpreted as being rigid. I also came to the conclusion that you could not separate who you are personally from who you are professionally. This idea also changed my idea of leadership.

This brings me to today and the reason why I wrote this book.

Some of today's existing business behaviors need to be re-examined. After the examination period, let's throw out the old, ineffective ones and bring in some new ones that emphasize common sense and results.

I always like to compare behavior rules to a fence. I ask people this question when discussing changes: before you take down a fence, do you know why the fence is there? Why was it put up? As a country boy, I know why you put up a fence – it's a form of protection.

Behavior guidelines work in the same fashion. Before you, as a leader, establish one, certain questions need to be addressed:

- Is it needed for protection?

- Does it provide the employee with the appropriate freedom to use their gifts and talents to do their job?

- Does it allow the employee opportunity to be rewarded for a job well done?

- Does it allow the employer an opportunity to measure and evaluate the employee's performance in a clear, just and objective manner?

- Does the rule provide the employer and employee an opportunity to grow the company and themselves?

- Who is allowed input on the guidelines that will govern day-to-day operations and functions?

If you approach business behaviors and results this way, these are the benefits that can be reaped by all:

- Leaders are allowed to flourish

- Employees are focused, productive and efficient

- Employees willingly take responsibility and initiative

- Businesses function with set standards of operation that allow them to stay focused on their mission and vision

- Guidelines are in place to objectively hire the right and fire the wrong people

- Profits increase

- Abuse of sick days dramatically decreases, employee turnover drops and absenteeism slows

- Employees, customers and clients enjoy a structured and harmonious environment

- Potential hiring pools expand to offer higher quality candidates

- Authentic and honest customer service becomes a part of your culture

- A cohesive unit is built on a fair, measurable and objective process

- A "productivity maximizing" environment is created for your employees

- Your customers and clients enjoy unforgettably positive experiences

- Community visibility and support of your company increases

The greatest benefit of a book like this is that it allows every person in your company to feel like they're a part of something special, dynamic and cutting edge that can change the world.

In looking at your current business behaviors, do your rules match some of or all of my suggestions? What were the criteria you originally used to create the guidelines? Are those rules productive and have they worked for or against you and your business? Have they been a success and produced great results and high amounts of revenue? Do you have a purpose, plan and direction to guide your daily decisions?

Over the course of this book, I'm going to ask you to take a good hard look at who you are as a person, who you are as a professional, your measurement as a leader, the security to surround yourself with integrity and expertise, your skills in building a cohesive unit, your talent in motivation and inspiration and your ability to appreciate what each individual in your organization brings to the table. I'm going to ask you the question: "Is it them or is it you?"

If you answer is "it's you," you'll be well on your way to creating profit, productivity and peace within your company's four walls.

Enjoy the adventure!

# *Preface*

## *What I've Learned About Behavior From the School of Hard Knocks*

Writing this section of the book reminded me of two shows that I really enjoy watching; the show "Dirty Jobs" and the show "Undercover Boss". "Dirty Jobs" is amusing because I get to go back and reminisce about a lot of the jobs that I had to do as a teenager and a young adult when I was working myself through school.

The "Dirty Jobs" show makes me laugh because 1) I hated those jobs, 2) they ARE dirty and 3), not many people want to do them and 4), it's entertaining to sit back and see what people do, how they do it, what they do for money and how much I have changed since I worked some of those "dirty jobs."

When you look at "Undercover Boss" it's about people who are really working hard on a daily basis and may be struggling financially, emotionally, personally, physically, but at the same time, they are still doing their jobs. They are doing their jobs the best they can and the CEO has an opportunity to be incognito in order to have a "rear window" view of what's truly going on in their companies.

Which makes me think back to when we were teenagers; chances are — you were like me. We got a job in some way — whether it was retail, fast food, restaurant, outdoor fishing or hunting. Whatever the job was; we were kids and we wanted to get paid, we wanted some adventure, and we wanted to stand on our own two feet and have some independence.

As we got through high school, we had to make an important decision about our future path. Eventually, we graduated (at least most of us did). The "career tracks" available to high school grads at the time I graduated were the military, technical school of some sort, college or nothing. Some folks decided to go ahead and start working right out of high school. There's nothing wrong with that choice; that was the path they chose.

Some picked the military. Military service helped so many people at the time. These paths helped them develop life, professional and communication skills that would prosper them at a later time.

Some chose technical schools. I love technical schools. There are so many things that need to be done in a technical world. We have to have people trained. Many people out there love this path because they are "hands-on" and I applaud them.

Then there's traditional four-year college. After high school, I spent eight years of wondering who I was and where I was going in life and then one day, my future became clear. During that moment of clarity, I visited several colleges and picked the one that best fit my needs. Even though I knew the exact degree – special education and behavior with an emphasis on autism and intellectual disabilities - and the path I wanted for the rest of my life, I still had to incorporate many "dirty jobs" to pay my tuition every semester.

Working a full time job and looking back on the previous eight years gave me a deep appreciation for the knowledge I was receiving as I pursued and procured my four-year degree. As I procured that degree, I was also allowed to take my love of sports and develop that love into a coaching and teaching career.

Human behavior has fascinated me ever since I was a child. I was interested in observing people and their behaviors. When I was a kid, I would stop people and say, "Why did you do that? What made you do that? What were you thinking when you did that? Why did you buy that?" I was a "why" kid.

It didn't change, once I became an adult, and as you know now, I added a degree to the question and answer sessions I conducted on the public at large. Even though the years have flown by, nothing has changed in my interest in peoples' behavior.

## PLANS CAN CHANGE

Naturally as we get older from the partying days of being a teenager and working lower level jobs, we get our education, go on and apply that education and become professionals.

When we left high school, we were on a certain trajectory. Many of us thought we had this completely planned out. As young people, we didn't fully understand that age and experience could change the tide of our lives and allow us to see new paths for our talents, our desires and our loved ones.

Does where you are now match where you thought you would be in your teens or your twenties? Maybe...maybe not. As I look back over my life, I always thought somehow, someway, I'd be in academia and I would always be an athletic coach. My sport of choice is basketball. Since I'm from the state of North Carolina, it's kind of like a religion for us. Between North Carolina, Kentucky and Indiana, we understand that one sport rules all – basketball!

Then one day, the parents of one of my students came to me for advice involving behavior. I assumed the advice was for their child's education and various issues that were taking place in their personal lives. I was right and wrong.

Yes, we did discuss their child, but the serious issues were actually taking place in the company they owned. After discussing the issues, they asked if I could help them. Little did I know that this would be the beginning of a brand new career for me.

I told them the only way for me to be a true asset was to be allowed to observe what was actually happening in the company on a day-to-day basis.

So they brought me in and I got an opportunity to observe everything that was happening in their business. They asked me to observe their employees' behaviors, record my observations, and express my thoughts on how to make the office run more efficiently and how to make the environment more harmonious. So I did.

They were just wowed at the results.

Then I said, "Let me just bring up a touchy subject while we are sitting here. There's a saying in educational world, "If you've met the child, you've met the parents or if you've met the parents, you've met the child." Now that I have observed your company and had your child in my class on a daily basis, I can say that is a valid statement."

I was able to help that family create a more profitable business and harmony in the workplace and their home.

That exchange happened a little over twenty-seven years ago. I've been doing this steadily since then. I liked both worlds; I liked being in academia and being with kids. I loved coaching, but I loved working with businesses. Those were my passions. I couldn't get enough of the excitement that both worlds provided.

Eventually, due to time constraints, I had to choose which world in which I would operate. I chose business. The classroom had become stifling to me and I enjoyed the never-ending challenge of helping business owners solve problems.

## IT'S NOT PERSONAL, IT'S JUST BEHAVIOR

One of my mentor's sayings always seems to ring true: "It's not personal, it's just behavior."

What in the world does this mean?

Basically, whether it's at home, in business or out in the community, we are the sum total of everything that we absorb — from birth to now. Everything we do, every habit we have, everything we say, every action we display is the sum total of everything we've observed, everything we've heard and everything's that's touched our five senses. And we're just displaying that on a daily basis. I always ask my clients: "Is it them or is it you?"

I get to see this acted out in the public arena. Begin to look at your customers in the same way. Watch how a customer reacts when something happens in your store. Let's say, they are in the checkout line and they are unhappy with either the price and they've started to argue with your checkout girl.

Do you think that that behavior is isolated to just your checkout girl or do you think that your customer displays that behavior at some other time throughout their lives, especially at home? Could this be a normal behavior for this person and this is the way they normally handle conflict? Behavior is basically a culmination of how a person acts on a daily basis and their observable behavior is the outward display that tells you how they are going to try to settle conflict.

So, whenever you have a difference of opinion, a customer complaint; whatever the situation may be, remember: it's not an isolated event aimed just at you.

That's what my mentor meant when he said, "It's not personal, it is just behavior."

The displayed behavior is going to take place whether you're involved or not. A person is going to react the same way with their spouse, their kids, or a family member as they act with you, or as they would at a community baseball, basketball, football or other social event. It's still going to be the same.

Now, think about your employees. There's a situation at work; one of the employees gets angry. Do you think that is the first time that that employee has ever displayed that behavior? No. Chances are, they displayed that behavior as a child, as a teenager, as a young professional, in college or military or that first job, with their spouse, with their kids and now with you. It is the sum total of who they are.

People will demonstrate their habits, sights, sounds, smells and tastes and everything that was implanted into them. It just so happens that your disgruntled customer is displaying it in front of you now.

So if your employees and your customers are the sum total of all their senses, what they absorbed as a child and everything that has impacted their life since then, how about yourself?

Have you ever wondered why you do the things you do? Why you have the habits? Why you have the thoughts? Why you have the feelings? Why you have the actions you do?

Have you ever been in a Board meeting or in a meeting with your staff and you just explode on somebody? Is that the first time you've ever done that, or can you honestly look back objectively and say, "Oh man, this seems to be a pattern throughout my life"? Again, is it them or is it you?

So many people have told me, "Well, my dad had an explosive temper, and my mom had one, so I inherited it."

I hate to break it to you, but that's simply not true.

That explosive anger is an observed behavior and you've learned to mimic the behavior. You didn't receive it in your genes or inherit it. It's not in your DNA.

So let me ask you these questions…are your behaviors creating productivity in your employees, vendors, customers and company? Are the behaviors you're demonstrating conducive to your clients' satisfaction? Are they going to increase sales? Are they going to increase the harmony in your office? Are they going to enhance your business? Are they going to enhance your standing in your community? If any of the answers are no, it's time for those behaviors to go.

Here's my point: your employees, your clients and you are a bunch of displayed behaviors on a daily basis. Chances are that the things that you act out within the business arena aren't personal; it's just to get the job done. The same could be said about your employees and about your clients.

One of the reasons that I enjoy behavioral rules and guidelines is because they help to nullify the negative behaviors. Appropriate rules don't respond to emotion. They only respond to facts and what's going to be beneficial to the business. Rules aren't based on opinion; they're based on a standard. If you measure everything by a standard, personal feelings don't get in the way and then you've already got a pre-prescribed business plan of standards and rules that will be beneficial to your company.

It's just like dealing with your spouse. If you "pre-argue" before you argue (as I encourage my marriage clients to do), is it conducive to your marriage? Sure it is. You sit down and you map out every single thing that you could possibly argue about in your marriage and you go ahead and solve the problem ahead of schedule. Once that's done, you automatically put into place six or seven rules that you use to disagree.

Are you going to disagree in your marriage? Of course you are. It's not a marriage if you don't.

The same thing works for your company.

Sit down; look over every single thing that could possibly be a problem with your Senior Vice Presidents and your prominent department heads within the context of your business. Work out a solution.

Next, without emotion (and as a committee, I normally recommend), sit down and begin to write out your own company rules. Let's say you've got a board meeting and there are five of you. Is there really an opportunity for people to air their opinions about a policy that's put into place? If it's a company that is genuinely based on rules, everybody gets up and has the opportunity to speak their minds and offer suggestions. It's not personal and you will go with the recommendation that's most conducive to profit. Everybody wins.

Your leadership and the rules you establish are built on fairness and objectivity when it comes to your company. They're not based on how you feel, your parents, how you were raised, all the emotions you brought in that day and the fact that it's raining, you were in traffic and you and your spouse had an argument this morning.

Basically in a nutshell, with business, it's all about behaviors, behaviors, behaviors and how they impact business. It's not personal. It is just business.

And at the end of the day, it is just behavior. It's not personal.

Create, use and keep the rules, the fairness and the objectivity in your company and many issues will work themselves out to bring your company increased productivity and profit!

# CHAPTER ONE

# IT'S NOT THEM, IT'S YOU

During my first face-to-face visit with a potential client, I sit down with the decision makers and I ask two questions:

Why did you call me?

What are the problems?

Once the decision makers and I discuss the issues, our next discussions determine whether or not I'll be working with their company. If I feel like I'm not the right fit for what the client needs, I will recommend someone I have confidence in that I know can handle their company issues.

Once I "sign on" with a company, we start the vetting process of why the problems are taking place; who needs to be involved and what changes need to be made. I normally work with CEOs and/or owners because they are the individuals who create the policies, make the financial decisions, decide the direction of the company, and set the tone, the energy and the vibration in and for the business.

The next thing I do may be considered a little unorthodox for a person who consults with companies. However, unorthodox does not mean unnecessary.

Since a company will normally reflect the personality and values of the CEO/owner, I express a very simple, yet sometimes

1

overlooked idea. Maybe it's not the company, the product or the employees – maybe the problem is you.

If you have any doubts about the previous statement, watch any popular reality show connected to business. A one-hour show has now allowed the casual viewer to "armchair quarterback" all of the decisions of a business owner or CEO.

Even though this type of show is scripted to a point, the production demonstrates that many business owners are in way over their head because they've entered an industry where they had little to no experience. Many of the individuals featured on the shows have no real understanding of who they are, what they want and have no true concept of their life direction.

The reality genre has also been able to show how difficult running a large (and small) company can be and that one CEO cannot be all people and in all places at one time. Many of the CEOs observed on these shows are loving, caring people who want what's best for their employees, their clients and their company. This format has allowed the average person to gain a deeper understanding of the tools and values a person needs to be a leader and direct a company on a 24/7 basis.

In order to direct a company on a 24/7 basis efficiently and profitably, the leader needs to know exactly who they are and why they have chosen their current position.

This generally leads me to the next part of the conversation process. The rubber really meets the road during this segment of our discussion.

# THE TWO IMPORTANT QUESTIONS AND THE FOUR REASONS

This is where I ask two important questions: "Why are you with this company?" and, "Did you choose this profession?"

I normally receive one of the following four reasons in response to those questions:

1. Money

    a. Pure and simple – it's about the dollar bills. Individuals saw a way to make a lot of money and money was the only factor in the decision. In "millennial terms," it's all about making fat stacks of Bennies and bringing Benny home!

2. Family

    a. There's a reason why family-owned businesses have that title. Family members work in the business. Many CEOs vocalize that their position was based more on parental pressure than their actual desire to work within the family business. They were "chosen" to lead the company and weren't given any other options by family members. The combination of guilt and expectation are extremely powerful.

    b. The parents decided the college course of study and applied pressure and expectations that that course of study would be completed so that the eventual outcome would be entering into the family business. At no time, did the parents ask if this course of study was a desire or dream of the individual now working in the family business.

c. The leader has married into the family and there was an expectation of him or her working for the family company.

d. There was a genuine desire from childhood to take over the family business.

3. Chance

a. A person goes to college and ends up with the "right roommate." The roommate's parents own a huge company and they include that individual in the business.

b. Someone starts out working for one company and a chance meeting takes place with an individual from an entirely different industry. That meeting starts a whole new career for that individual.

c. A personal need began a new profession for an individual.

d. A guidance counsellor gave the individual a "career test" their senior year in high school and on this basis, a career was chosen.

e. A summer job in college turned into a profession.

4. Desire

a. A passion swells in the heart of an individual and the career is a reflection of that passion.

b. A dream from childhood — an individual never had any doubt that this was "their path."

c. A person, filled with an original passion from

childhood received training, combined with degrees and decided this was not the correct career path for them, set out a new course and is continuing on that course at this time.

## *MONEY*

I don't meet many people, especially business owners, who <u>don't</u> want to make money. Most business owners want a good lifestyle, they want to make money, they want to be profitable, they want to take care of their family, and they want to take care of the next generation of family, and they want to leave a legacy.

Why else would you go into business? Nobody goes in business, outside of government, that is, and plans on losing money. As a business owner, it's all about the dollars. There's nobody to bail you out; you have to make a profit or you go under.

So many times I've sat down with business owners and asked them how they started their career. Normally, it started in high school, when they dropped by a guidance counselor's office, sat and chatted and went over some form of career review sheet.

Then, the counselors suggest three careers the student should probably pursue based on a career interest test. The test is supposed to match a career with what the student has an interest in and might want to do for the rest of their lives. For many, a career path is chosen because he or she checked a box on a generic questionnaire.

Sometimes, the student didn't have the natural inclination, skill or aptitude for the career. Why? There weren't basing their choice on a burning desire to do a particular job or develop a skill set — they were basing it on a preconceived notion they needed a pay check and that job was the fastest path to that pay check.

Now, I'm not picking on guidance counsellors here; the counselors are doing what they feel will help the student the most. However, the average guidance counselor is in charge of at least 400 students and knowing the ultimate desire of each student is physically impossible. Of course, when a counselor looks at a career for a student, future financial responsibilities are a factor.

For many, money is usually the driving factor when deciding a career.

Many individuals never seem to connect to their earthly purpose and the task they can perform for the world. So many times, their extraordinary blessing to the world is connected to a dream or desire that was possessed during childhood.

I have talked to a lot of attorneys who started out to be attorneys for the money, but have ended up driving trucks or owning restaurants in the end. It is very interesting; in the end, they wanted to do anything but practice law.

Several of my personal friends went to medical school, got disillusioned by the profession, and again, picked alternative professions because they couldn't take the long hours, time away from family, ever dwindling compensation and insurance headaches anymore. They did it for the money and the money was drying up. Since the money was drying up, their entire reason for the profession dried up also.

But the real question is: Why did you get your degree or certifications, get a career and end up staying in that unenjoyable career/profession for an extended period of time?

M – O – N – E – Y.

As the money gets better and better, you get married, you grow your family, live in the house of your dreams, take exciting vacations, drive sweet rides, place the kids in private school, and you enjoy the trappings of the successful family.

You may not necessarily love your job or career, but you love what the profession has provided for your family and the allure of financial "security".

Again, all of this for the sake of a dollar — a dollar that you may not have enjoyed earning for many years.

And where did it all start?

It started the day you let your childhood dreams and fantasies go.

The "real world" was calling and you decided to "grow up." Growing up meant choosing a path that provided greener pastures and hopefully, streets of gold.

So many times, the pastures are wastelands and the streets aren't gold, but asphalt, and growing up wasn't all it was cracked up to be. Many took a job or began a career straight out of high school or college, with temporary mentality, but as time passed, it became a permanent reality. How sad.

I'd like to say I didn't do that too, but I did. However, I changed my course, went back to college, changed degrees, and went into a profession I loved, ending up as a high school basketball coach and special education teacher, and stayed with that for over 20 years.

But during all of that time, I never stopped working with businesses. I was the blessed one. I had two careers (inside and outside of academia) that I dearly loved, and was able to do both for many years.

For many, money is the main factor in pursuing a career. However, after many years of interviewing business owners on the radio and after examining my own life, I see a much more important factor in pursuing in a career — time.

Our time on earth is limited, and it does have an expiration date.

I keep an hourglass in my office. I look at it every single day, and then I walk over and turn it over. It reminds me that every single second that I have on this earth is a blessing, and not one of those seconds is guaranteed.

Since our lives have an expiration date, let me ask you this: If you could walk away from your job tomorrow, would you?

If you are working solely for money, isn't there something else you could do and excel at that would provide for your life and remove some of your stress and misery?

If you own the company, why don't you sell the company and move on and do something that you love?

If you are a CEO, why not move to a different company? Here's an even better idea: Why not take the money you've made as a C-level executive and create something you really love that will fill the void in your life; instead of watching the sands in your hourglass slip by, second by second?

Please don't assume that you have all the time in the world.

You don't!

Think about that while I go on to the second reason why people stay in positions that drive them to the brink of insanity.

## FAMILY

Many of the CEOs and business owners tell me that the profession they are in currently was their parents' dream, not theirs. I can think of five owners right now that I interact with on a daily basis that are doing a job they don't necessarily love because it was a responsibility handed to them because they were 2nd or 3rd generation family and they were chosen to pick up the mantle of the company and carry it on.

I have friends who tell me things like, "My grandpa was an attorney, my dad was an attorney, I'm an attorney and my son (or daughter) is going to be an attorney."

I remember sitting in high school talking about this very subject. When we would discuss our futures, my friends would say stuff like, "Dad is a doctor, I'm going to be a doctor" or, "My dad is a CPA, I will be a CPA. My Dad said I need to take over the family business."

Many of those same people did pursue those degrees and since that time, have changed professions or sold their family businesses.

But I ask you this question. On the day of your birth, were you christened as "an attorney, a doctor, a CPA, a teacher" or did they christen you with your name?

If you were christened with a name and not a profession, doesn't that mean you have an opportunity to choose?

As a behavior consultant and coach, I watch families, many times, choose the college their kids attend. The child does not get to choose their actual desired school.

I have talked to many people that confirm this fact in their own lives. For fun and information, I walk through shopping malls and randomly ask people, "Did you pick the college you attended or was it picked for you?" So many times, the individual will say it was picked for them. Personally, I got to pick the college I attended. Many don't.

Have you let someone else make these life-altering decisions for you, now or in the past?

I express a sobering thought to 2nd or 3rd generation family business leaders and owners: "If you haven't melded into your own company, your employees won't either."

Your employees aren't stupid; they know if you don't want to be there. I can walk into a company and know immediately if the owner is into it or mentally disconnected. So can your employees!

All a person has to do is look around. Are the details handled? Do the employees realize when the owner isn't there? Do the employees ask: What does the owner do all day? Does the owner let time pass (as in watching the clock and play Solitaire) or is he or she a contributing factor to the business? Heck, can the employees even find the owner when he or she is needed?

I have one company in particular that I go into quite frequently and I observe the owner's behavior. The owner isn't doing his job, he is not living the life of his dreams, and he is watching time pass and the employees know it. They can smell it and sense it. They scrutinize everything he does because THEY KNOW!

That is a very dangerous place to be. If you don't want to be doing what you're doing now, more than likely you won't be motivated to do anything that's in this book, so we <u>absolutely</u> have to start here. It's not them, it's you.

Let me ask you this, if you were forced into a career by your family, why would you want to continue that behavior and force it on your children? Don't you want your children to be happy? Do you really want to force your behavior upon them when it comes to their career? But most people do exactly that.

When I started doing research for this book, I actually sat down and talked to twenty different attorneys. I wanted to know why they decided to practice law. At least eight out of twenty told me it was because of their family. Some of them were third generation attorneys, at the very least. Some even went farther back than that.

And then I asked, "Do you have a fourth generation coming?"

"Yes," was their answer.

"Are they going to be an attorney?"

"Yes, of course."

"That's an assumption, correct?"

"Yes."

"Have you ever asked your child that question?"

"No."

Hmmmmm…

Why would you force a career on your child that you didn't particularly enjoy and tomorrow, if I gave you a financial way out of that miserable career, you'd leave? Why would you do that to your own child?

I'll come back to the point that your time on earth is limited and it has an expiration date. Why continue on a path for money or because your family wants you to do a certain job?

I strongly encourage you before you get any farther into this book to examine how you feel about your career and why you're doing it.

If you're not completely bought in, you're not fooling anyone.

Since your company is a reflection of who you are, you're going to be leading an entire company of people who don't want to be there any more than you do. Always remember: it's not them, it's you.

That's no way to run a company.

Maybe this is the weirdest way ever to start a business book — by encouraging the owners and leaders to change their careers, but it is a major problem I see in many of the companies I work with. The leaders are there for the wrong reasons.

They can't lead because their behavior tells everyone that they don't want to be there and they can't hide their true feelings.

It's not them, it's you.

So, if you're in that unique position of not wanting to be where you are right now, take comfort in the fact that transitioning careers and responsibilities may not be as difficult as you think it is. It may not have to be an extreme change at all.

If you're a CEO and you don't like the company you're with, chances are, you have amassed an amazing amount of experience in running a business. Someone will be lucky to have you, once you leave the company you hate. Or you could take the money and run and create a new company that you have always dreamed about when you were a kid.

Structure your responsibilities in a way that offloads the stuff you hate to do and free yourself to be the captain of your own destiny.

Maybe you could stop being a CEO and become a consultant. If you love "fixing companies", you can show your magical skills, fix the problem and then pack your bag and go home. My father-in-law did this very thing and is much happier being a consultant than being a Senior Vice President for a major banking entity. He's still consulting, well into his eighties, and is busier now than he was when he left the bank — and MUCH happier.

If you are the owner of a company and hate the business, here's an option. Hire someone who is passionate about the job and the company, and minimize your contact with the business as much as you can. If it's financially feasible to get rid of all of your responsibilities tied to the company, do it. If not, simply get someone to run the place for you, oversee them on a high level and then start doing what you want to do with your life!

If you hate what you're doing and you hate going to work every single day, hire a CEO to take your place, let them handle all the responsibilities and stress of the company, and remove yourself (other than financially) from all the decision making and let someone who is extremely passionate about the business handle it. This is especially important in family businesses.

I like to think of the movie "Sabrina" (the updated version with Harrison Ford). It is one of my favorite movies. It goes beyond a typical love story because it takes place inside of a family business.

Linus, Harrison Ford's character, in one of the last scenes of the movie, says that he never had a choice in what he did in his career. He was basically selected by his father to take over the family conglomerate. And although he'd done an amazing job, he had never really enjoyed what he was doing; he was just good at it.

He says in the movie, "I didn't have a choice — it was made for me. I never got an opportunity to choose."

If you've seen the movie you know that in the end, he does choose and he hands the company's leadership over to his younger brother, gets on a plane, and the movie closes with him reuniting with Sabrina, the love of his life, who has shown him that there is much more to life than work and money.

Will your story have a happy ending? Can you be the Linus who sees the final credits?

It is your decision. Time is ticking and every single day you wait, you lose momentum, opportunities and the joys of life.

What's it going to be?

In some cases, selling the business is the best idea. Sell the business, split the proceeds up between all equity partners and move on with life.

Need I say more?

When I say every second is precious, make sure you understand why. Everything can be temporary if you choose for it to be. You don't have to do this for the rest of your life; you do get to choose.

You can be Linus and make that choice.

Every day you get out of bed, you make a decision; it's your turn to choose what you want.

The time is now — **it's not them, it's you!**

## CHANCE

Many people have arrived in their current profession based on chance, or what people perceive as chance or "karma" or "cosmic energy."

Financial services and financial planner, Andy McClung, a great friend to my radio shows in the past, decided to go into his field of study because he could not find someone to answer his questions about financial planning for his son's college. That was over twenty-seven years ago, and he has become a financial planner with a loyal following and a very successful track record for his clients.

As told to me by a business associate, the company Lens Crafters was started because the founder's wife broke her glasses one day and the glasses company told them that it would take ten to fourteen days to get her glasses fixed. His question back to the glasses company was, "How is she going to see for the next ten to fourteen days?" His profession at the time was advertising, not eyewear manufacturing and distribution.

Maybe you showed up on the first day of college and ended up with a magical roommate whose father owned a huge company and wanted you to be a part of it.

Now, many years later, you own multiple franchises in multiple states and you're cranking in the cash.

Chance doesn't necessarily mean you aren't making money or you don't enjoy the career—it just means that the stars had to align to place you where you are right now.

But, I have to go back and ask you again, are you really enjoying the job or are you just punching the clock and earning a salary, even if you are there by chance?

## *DESIRE*

The fourth reason people give me for being in their current profession is desire. These blessed individuals have consciously chosen the profession that they dreamed of as a child. They picked a profession that they really enjoy.

My godson wants to be a doctor. He has impeccable grades in high school and he's getting ready to move on to his undergraduate work and progress to medical school. I have absolutely no doubt he will not only graduate from medical school, but he will be one of the finest doctors that this country has ever seen.

Understand this; my godson has wanted to be a doctor ever since he was a little boy. His entire life from a very young age has been consumed with his preoccupation with this choice.

Are you beginning to see how important childhood can be in your professional choices?

I have another associate of mine who wanted to be a doctor ever since he experienced growing up with his father who was critically injured in a work related accident. He became obsessed with finding answers for his father who lost his hearing due to nerve damage in a work-related accident.

His own grandmother pointed him toward chiropractic work because she knew it "did something with nerves." So he decided to hang out with a chiropractor and then a surgeon. That surgeon mentored him, guided him, and helped him to pick his medical career path, almost 30 years ago.

My associate has been in the medical profession for a little over thirty years, has a thriving practice, does radio, lectures all over the world, writes books, and has his own nutritional line, all because he is doing what he loves. He got creative as a kid, attached himself to a mentor that was in the profession he loved, and now every single day he gets up with a burning desire to do what he was purposed to do, all sparked by the love for his father.

He started his dream as a child.

Are you starting to get this now?

Always keep in mind; desire is the fuel of life. You're not going to get through life without fuel.

Maybe that desire has allowed you to create your own genre in business. Look at Steve Jobs and Apple Computers. Some would say he basically recreated the computer world in everything that he did. Right after his death, he was called the modern day DaVinci by several magazines. As a casual observer, I might have to agree with that being an accurate statement.

In our family, we have an uncle that started a food supply business in the back of his car by delivering chickens to schools and nursing homes that were in out of the way places in the mountains of North Georgia. Basically, he started a food company in the back of his car by packing the trunk with ice and chickens. He went on to make his company one of the most successful food companies in the United States and years later, sold it for a very nice profit.

All of his activity was based on desire—a burning desire to succeed and the conscious choice to work hard and be the best to satisfy a need that no one else was supplying.

He started as a teenager.

The power of desire has magic unto itself and that magic can generate the energy it takes to have an exceptional life that touches the world.

## PERMISSION GRANTED

Once we establish why the CEOs or owners are sitting in their office and how they got there, then we can start the fun part of the process.

Many desire something to change in their lives and companies, and up until now, have never given themselves permission to make the change or just don't know how to go about the process.

Sometimes an "outside voice" is exactly the mechanism needed to start the change process. My "outside voice" always asks CEOs or owners the following:

What do you want from your personal life? Are you receiving what you wanted?

What do you want from your professional life? Are you receiving what you wanted?

What drives you to get out of bed every day? A pure love of life, your spouse hitting you with a bat, or obligations and responsibilities?

If you could sell your company free of guilt, or resign tomorrow and pursue your dream, would you?

Most look at me and ask, "Aren't you here to help me with my business, not my personal life?"

I follow up that question with, "Your business is a mirror of who you are inside." Your thoughts, your feelings, your desires and your values are played out daily in your personal and business behaviors and decisions. Many times, our family members, associates and clients can see who we truly are, but for some reason, the mirror is not showing us a true reflection of reality and our true selves.

Time is an amazing thing and something that is taken for granted and many times, underrated. So many people live a daily life assuming there will be opportunities to right wrongs, repair relationships, bring in new business and perform extraordinary wonders for the world. When would now be a better time to devote our lives to excellence, extraordinary performance and above all, being an extraordinary human being? Since the mirror doesn't lie and there is no guarantee of the future, wouldn't you agree now is the time to change your program and make extraordinary part of every fabric of your being and give that mirror a new, exciting reflection?

## THE TIMELINE

Unfortunately, I sit with many business owners, CEOs and higher level executives who would quit today if they could, and understand they are currently filling a role due to family pressure, guilt, financial obligations, spousal pressure, apathy and a perceived notion that they are too old to start something great. All reasons I completely understand and would be 100% valid if time had no limits.

However, time on this earth does have limits. Death will knock on our door eventually; tomorrow has no guarantee of coming and "someday" seems to always be in the future.

The most effective way I've found to explain this to individuals is by using a timeline.

According to insurance actuaries who keep track of the statistics regarding life span, most people in the United States will live to be approximately seventy-eight to eighty years old. These statistics vary from firm to firm.

So, for most people, that gives them seventy-eight to eighty years to work, build a life and legacy here on Earth. For illustration's sake, I start the timeline at age twenty-five. I picked the age of twenty-five because most twenty-five year olds have completed some form of degree, have entered a profession, found a love interest, and many have either married or started a family.

When I discuss the timeline with CEOs and owners, I do so because I want them to understand the hourglass and how quickly the grains of sands run out. I also want them to realize how quickly they can move off track, either with their company, their careers or their lives.

Since so much attention is given to the "1% of society" in any given topic, I use 1% and 99% as a way to illustrate how quickly someone can realize or destroy their dream life.

As it's repeatedly stated in the media, 99% of individuals have one type of life and the 1% has a completely different type of life. Just so we are clear and you, as the reader, understand where I'm coming from, when I explain the timeline, the 1% has a completely different life because they planned, struggled, stayed focused and overcame obstacles to live a life and a lifestyle that few are willing to make the sacrifices to create and enjoy.

Let's discuss the 99% first.

On the timeline, let's say you are twenty-five years old, fresh out of college and ready to kill it in life. You've got your degree, your idealism and your new career. After about two years, you're already disillusioned with your job, the world and your finances because life isn't turning out the way you thought it was going to. You think to yourself, "Maybe if I find that special person, life will turn around."

So you get married…

…to the wrong person.

By the ages of thirty to thirty-five, chances are, you are unhappy with your job, more than likely your spouse and now add to the mix, one or two children.

You are completely stressed out, running on fumes, confused and disenchanted with the entire "real life" scenario. You get up each day wondering when the fun part of life starts, thinking to yourself, "How many more years can I take this?"

Guess what? You still have many more years to go on your timeline.

By age of forty, more than likely, if statistics are true, you will be divorced. Now that the ink is dry on your first divorce, you decide that "special person #2" can bring meaning and happiness to your life. In addition to being the same person who got the first divorce and the fact that you haven't changed any of your prior behaviors, you also have half the money you used to have and less time with your children because of the first divorce. You've got more financial pressure and a higher level of stress than ever before. Add to that the emotional baggage you have to sort through – not just your own, but your "special person #2's" load of baggage also!

By forty-five or fifty, you have probably experienced a severe and potentially devastating career change due to a lack of vision on your part. You may have been laid off, downsized or just "replaced by a younger model." Your employer has explained, "You're not what you used to be and a change needed to be made." Combine that change with increasing health problems that now have the potential to completely debilitate or kill you if you don't make some serious lifestyle changes and you have the makings of a midlife crisis out of control.

In the meantime, your biological children and stepchildren have decided you are less desirable as a parent and they basically can't stand you; you are wrapping up the never-ending custody battles, ever increasing child support is still due and you still haven't made the necessary behavioral changes that can improve your life and change your circumstances. Now, chances are, your parents are aging or dying, you may be assigned as caretaker and your "special person #2" has just walked out on you. Ain't life grand?

During the ages of fifty to sixty, you begin to contemplate your own mortality and currently death seems to be the only way out of this hell you call a life. You continue to ignore health problems; you take jobs that just pay the bills because no one in the marketplace values your knowledge or experience.

You have several acquaintances that suddenly die from heart attacks and/or cancer. At this point, you'll probably have lost one or more of your parents and are now stuck straightening someone else's mess of a life, after they're gone. Your children are creating their own lives and futures and don't call, email or text.

Keep in mind, you created this life by choosing not to have a vision and a direction for your life, thus giving others complete control over your life.

From the ages of sixty-five to seventy, you've officially entered the "Retirement Zone." But you can't retire. Due to a succession of bad decisions, you've lost most or all of your savings and your daily life revolves around coupons and "early bird specials." If you have any significant conversations with anyone, they revolve around your medical ailments, medication comparisons and complaints about how awful your children treat you.

Your life continues in a downward spiral, with you having no clue how you got there and no one to stand beside you to love you, support you or care for you. Loneliness, regret and lost opportunities haunt your every waking (and sleeping) moments.

From the ages of seventy-five to eighty, you are placed in a nursing home, suffering from the effects of a lifestyle of carelessness, neglect and indifference. Your weekly highlight is when they serve chocolate pudding on Wednesdays. If you can process coherent thought, you still wonder what happened to that bright, hopeful twenty-five year old who was going to change the world.

At eighty, you pass away. There's no one to grieve your death. No one comes to the memorial service, which your children resentfully host while they wait for the will to be read in hopes that there might be something, anything of value that they could sell to help pay off your debts. There are no flowers, no loving tributes, no tears and no one to miss you.

…all because you chose wrong timeline.

Ebenezer got three ghosts and chances are, you did too. But you chose to ignore them.

But what about the 1%?

What happens to them?

Here's the life of someone who is on the 1% timeline:

Since you had parents of vision and they allowed you to be an individual and choose your path, at the age of twenty-five, you receive the degree that you worked so hard to achieve. That degree is a living part of the vision you have for your life and your intent to follow that vision. Since following that vision allowed you to work in the profession in your teenage years, you know exactly the types of experiences you're going to have when you begin your career. You have your ideals about your profession, but you're still realistic about what to expect. You even have a few new ideas on how to make your profession better. You know your exact purpose for your life and each new day is validation that you have something special to offer to the world.

Approximately between the age of twenty-five and thirty, you meet "that special someone" that makes your heart pound with excitement and your dreams flow without end. After dating and discovering that your mutual purposes in life blend together in a powerful way, you decide that this is the person who can walk down the road of life with you. You marry, surrounded by happy friends, families and co-workers who all comment that you are "made for each other."

From ages thirty-five to forty-five, you and your spouse begin a family. In addition to beginning a family, both of your professional careers blossom. Your personal and professional success is a combination of combining your individual vision and dreams with daily lessons to your children on how they can identify their special gifts and use them, at any age, to benefit not only themselves, but also the world. You and your entire family pick exciting ports of call, learning about life first-hand and experiencing the most amazing places, events and happenings.

From ages forty-five to fifty, your children are creating their own futures, having identified their own purposes and are moving on to college, starting their own businesses and are finding their own "special people." They are filtering their dates through the same set of criteria that you used when you selected your "special person." People comment on what wonderful children you have, you actually enjoy spending time with your family and you are excited to see what their lives will produce. In the meantime, you and your spouse have launched additional companies to reflect changes in your profession and industry and may have added a non-profit component to help deserving young people in your profession with their personal and professional training.

From ages fifty-five to sixty, you and your spouse are still healthy and fit, due to a healthy lifestyle of integrative medical treatment, exercise and proper diet. You have limited health issues, an active sex life and still have amazing energy to continue your work, inside and outside of your profession. The highlights of your day include seeing your grandchildren who adore you and fight to see who gets the most hugs from you. Your focus begins to shift towards creating a legacy, not only for your family but also for your industry, companies, co-workers, community and the world.

From ages sixty-five to eighty, you are still working towards creating miracles for your family, friends and other business associates. You give generously to your church or synagogue and other deserving organizations.

In your late eighties or nineties, you die peacefully in your sleep, with your children, grandchildren, friends and family all around your bedside. While they are sad to see you go, they know that you have truly had a wonderful life and count themselves blessed to have been a part of your life. Five generations of your family continue to tell stories and train their own children how to identify their purpose, choose the right careers and mates and to give back generously to their family, friends, church, community and the world.

By now you can feel the intense difference between the two timelines and the lives those two timelines can create.

Which one will or have you chosen?

What do these two timelines have in common?

The power of choice.

Every single decision that is made during the each stage of both timelines matters and can be life altering. Those decisions not only have a ripple effect in your life, but in every single life that touches yours.

There is no such thing as an isolated decision.

Your life now and your legacy that lives on will be based on the results of your choices.

Choose wisely.

# PROGRAMMING, BEHAVIOR & THE FUTURE

Chances are, that sometime today, you will log in to a computer or use a cell phone. Most days, those activities take place without much thought on why the computer and cell phone are able to complete your desired functions. It's very simple. Someone programmed your computer and your cell phone and the devices are doing what they have been designed and programmed to do. The devices cannot perform a task that has not been pre-programmed into them to execute.

Your life decisions and habits operate the exact same way. You are the sum total of everything that has been programmed into you since birth. Have you ever wondered why you enjoy certain foods, speak certain languages, wear certain clothes, enjoy certain activities, repetitiously do things on a daily basis and make certain personal and business decisions?

In order to make sense of how you've arrived at your current destination, I have three charts that explain certain stages that program and develop your life, which explain who you are, how you act and how you make decisions on a daily basis.

The first chart covers the ages of birth to five. At this time in your life, you can only absorb information. You do not have the ability to block out anything. Anything that touches your life touches you and impacts your programming.

| Developmental Age | Who & What Influences You | Ability to Make Choices/Filter Information |
|---|---|---|
| 0 – 5 Years | Parents, Grandparents | Everything that is heard, felt, seen, tasted or smelled is absorbed into you like a sponge. During this period of time, you do not have the ability to block out any information. The information received during the 0-5 period is the cornerstone to your programming and will dictate your actions, behaviors and habits for your entire life. |
| | Day care | |
| | Baby Sitter/Nanny | |
| | Friends & Parents of Friends | |
| | Pre-School | |
| | Teachers | |
| | Extended Family | |
| | Church/Synagogue | |
| | Sports/Coaches/Teammates | |
| | "Play Dates" | |
| | Languages You Hear | |
| | Foods You Eat | |
| | Aromas in Your Home, Your Extended Family's Homes & Day care or Frequented Public Places | |
| | TV Shows That Are On While You're in the Room | |
| | Any Sounds That You Would Have Heard (example: music your parents or guardians listen to) | |
| | Anything you touch or that touched you will generate an feeling or emotion (example: favorite fabric or blanket) | |
| | Medical Issues (Personal or Connected to Family or Friends) | |

This second chart covers the ages of six to eleven. You now have the ability to filter information, however your environment heavily affects your decisions and behaviors.

| Developmental Age | Who & What Influences You | Ability to Make Choices/Filter Information |
|---|---|---|
| 6 – 11 Years | Parents, Grandparents | Beginning around the age of 6 or 7, you develop the ability to discern information for yourself. You are no longer a sponge that absorbs information without question. Even though you have the ability to make your own decisions, you are heavily influenced by the environment within which you spent the most amount of time. |
| | After School Care | |
| | Baby Sitter/Nanny | |
| | Friends & Parents of Friends | |
| | Events Attended (example: sporting, musical and/or social/ societal events) | |
| | Teachers | |
| | Extended Family | |
| | Church/Synagogue/ On going Social Activities | |
| | Sports/Coaches/ Teammates | |
| | "Play Dates" | |
| | Languages You Hear | |
| | Food You Eat | |
| | Medical Issues (Personal or Connected to Family or Friends) | |
| | Death of Someone You Love | |
| | Music That Is Heard (example: my love affair with Led Zeppelin) | |
| | First "Crush" and/or First Kiss | |
| | Spending Time with Parents at Work | |

| | Sleepovers | |
|---|---|---|
| | Nickname Assigned to You by Other Children & Has Been Rhymed Into a Song | |
| | Family Moves | |

The third chart covers ages eleven to eighteen. You are now able to make your own decisions, process information and progress past the concrete world to the abstract. Even though you have the power to filter information and make your own decisions, environmental impact will still shape many of those decisions.

| Developmental Age | Who & What Influences You | Ability to Make Choices/Filter Information |
|---|---|---|
| 11 – 18 Years | Parents, Grandparents | You are starting to make your own choices and decisions. As the chart outlines, many of those choices and/or decisions are heavily influenced by your relationships and environments. Many of the decisions made during this time period will dictate the outcome of the rest of your life. |
| | Friends & Parents of Friends | |
| | Social Activities (example: school dances, musical performances, dating, first job, learning to drive, high school sporting events) | |
| | Teachers – many people start to identify with select teachers during this time period | |
| | Extended Family | |
| | Best Friend or Close Circle of Friends | |
| | First Love or Serious Relationship | |
| | Nickname Still Haunts You & The Song Still Rings in Your Ears | |

| | | |
|---|---|---|
| | Physical Changes (example: get taller, gain & lose weight, boys & girls begin to develop) | |
| | Academic Pressures & Issues are More Prevalent | |
| | Pressure to Make Life Decisions (example: future plans, sexual activity and educational choices) | |
| | Experimentation with Alcohol & Drugs | |
| | Death of Someone You Love | |
| | Divorce of Parents – Remarrying of Parents | |
| | Church/Synagogue Routine has Been Replaced by Questions & Debate | |
| | Sports/Coaches/Teammates – Normally, at this stage, a coach will impact your life and be part of the rest of your life | |
| | Languages You Speak | |
| | Foods You Have Decided to Enjoy | |
| | Hormonal Adjustments Are Taking Place Which Lead to Confusion, Moodiness and Irritation | |
| | Medical Issues (Personal or Connected to Family or Friends) | |

| | TV Shows & Movies Watched | |
| --- | --- | --- |
| | Music Listened To | |
| | Family Moves | |

No list is all-inclusive. The lists are provided in order to give a general idea of many of the things that have influenced and shaped you throughout your life.

In order to clarify, let me sum up the charts:

- You are programmed by everything that touches your life from birth to five. In a practical every day sense, what does that mean? The way you act and the decisions you make every day were shaped during that time period. Much like your computer, you are acting out a program that was hard-wired into you by your parents, extended family, friends, neighbors, and every sight, sound, touch, taste and smell during that time period. The daily and weekly repetition of your environment has set you on a course and placed you where you are today.

- From the ages of six to eleven, in addition to your initial programming, your daily environments progressively shape you. You are beginning to process information yourself, but the desire for conformity and fitting in heavily sways your choices and decisions. Does your "Nickname Song" still echo in your ears from time to time?

- From eleven to eighteen, in addition to your programming and your desire to fit in, you add in hormonal changes, feelings of love, an ever-increasing questioning of the world and what you end up with is a hot mess. Most kids by this stage of the game are confused, pissed off, indecisive, feel unattractive, and question the future from every angle. Unfortunately, there are casualties at this stage of the game, whether it be physical, emotional or permanent. As you pour that first cup of coffee and think about your day, do any of those memories and thoughts run through your head? As you progress through your day, most, if not all, of the decisions you will make today are based on those first eighteen years, especially the first five.

For most, the charts help identify an observable pattern of behavior (habits) that has been displayed over many years. Hopefully, this has shed some light on: why you relate to your spouse in a certain way, your relationship with your children, how you view your employees, why you may have outbursts at staff meetings, why everything in your life has to be a certain way, why things in your company never seem to change, why employees choose to stay or leave your company, or why that smile, at times, is so hard to muster up.

Programming is an amazing thing and so much of our lives are lived running a program we neither enjoy nor understand.

Since prior personal programming is a mystery to so many, I like to keep the conversation casual and light. "Casual and light" means discussing wants and desires and not jumping straight into "hard-wiring" and "programming." Sometimes a flip chart and a laser pointer just won't do the trick when discussing this subject.

I deal with a lot of 2nd, 3rd and 4th generation companies and family businesses. Keeping it casual and light comes in the form of me asking them, "What do you want?" and "What do you really want?"

In my experience, I've talked with many business owners who took over a company when a parent passed away. The company and the responsibilities usually weren't what they really wanted. They just felt the burden of responsibility of having to take over the company and take care of the family business. You can imagine the other emotions that accompany that-guilt, anger, resentment, irritation, duty, etc.

So now, I'm sitting with that same owner, they are ten, twenty, thirty years into it and these owners still don't know who they are, what they want, or have any security or assurance of what they are doing.

That's very troubling considering that a lot of these companies have twenty-five to five hundred employees that depend on them every single day for a pay check, vendors who expect prompt payment and customers who depend on them to deliver their services and goods.

But they're sitting behind their desks in their office wishing they had different lives and different occupations.

That's why I say, "What do you want?"

After they give me a bogus, non-emotional answer, I ask them:

"What do you really want?"

"Why are you here?"

I mean, why are you here on planet Earth? What is your life about? Who are you? What's your purpose? What's your direction? What's your plan?

And then I'm quiet and I wait for them to answer.

So many people, especially CEOs, look me dead in the eye and say, "I don't know. I never really got an opportunity to make that decision myself. It was made for me."

Whether you're involved in a family business or you're a high-level executive in a company, this question is critical to your professional success.

If you don't know why you are here, why do you get up every day?

The thing that frightens me the most is that I've had way too many people say these scary words to me, with tears in their eyes;

"I just don't know."

"I don't know why I get up."

"I don't know why I do the things I do."

"I don't know who I am and I don't know what the future holds and that makes me very afraid."

And I always follow with the next question. "If you could get up tomorrow and quit, would you?"

I've heard many, many people say, "Yes. Immediately."

If you'll notice, I'm not talking of profit and loss statements, sales figures or operational budgets. I've yet to ask one question about their company, **because the company itself isn't the core issue or problem.**

Several years ago, I sat across from a friend of mine who owned several companies, and I looked at her and asked, "Are you where you think you should be? Are you where you thought you would be as a child at this point in your life? Are you happy with the decisions you've made with your career?"

"No" was the answer to all of the above.

My next question was even more difficult for her.

"So, are going to sell your companies and get your freedom back?"

Obviously, to her, this was a shocking and thought-provoking question.

When I went back six months later, the companies were in the process of being sold, and the one thing I finally got to see was a smile. That smile had been absent six months prior because to her there was nothing for her to smile about.

And then I asked her this question, "Did you trade your childhood dreams for an illusion, the call of duty and the obligation of family?"

Mentally, I always like to take my clients back to the place when they were children.

Once upon a time, most of us were innocent children, filled with hopes and dreams.

When we were kids, we would sit and play for hours in an imaginary world, there were no limits, there was no judgment, only excitement. I used to play on the floor with boxes more than I did the actual toys at Christmas time because I could make that box a fortress, a kingdom or a castle. It could be anything that I declared it because I was the King of the Realm.

I grew up in a farming community where we would lie out in the field at night, just look up the stars, and talk about all the really cool things we'd do when we grew up. Well, we all grew up; did we do any of those cool things we talked about as kids?

It's very stressful being an adult and looking back and having to say, "Man, if I was that 6-year-old kid again, I would kick my own ass because I didn't do any of those things I said I was going to do as an adult. I followed a pattern of something I didn't want to do."

Why?

Programming.

When you are the leader of a company, CEO or business owner, you have to make the decision to change your flawed programming.

Basically ask yourself, "Am I going to change my flawed programming or am I going to keep it and have a less prosperous and harmonious environment at home and inside my company?"

You have to make that decision because it starts with you.

Now that you know what is sabotaging your life and your company, you have the power to create a new life and by creating a new life, you create an entire new situation for your company, your staff and your clients.

## THE PREAMBLE TO THE SOLUTION

Before I provide solutions, I always like to do a quick review and/or provide pertinent information in order to make sure everyone is on the same page.

Just so we are clear on one thing, I want to restate something I said earlier. Every single decision you have made up to this point in your life has determined your place in life at this time.

Basically, your actions have produced your current outcomes.

The following is a quick illustration of what I mean:

As stated earlier, the average person begins making independent decisions around the age of six or seven. For this illustration and for the ease of the numbers, let's start at the age of ten and go to age thirty. That span of time is twenty years. I realize you may be younger or older than thirty, however, my illustration will allow you to adjust the numbers based on your age.

If you started making your own decisions at ten and you are currently thirty years old that means that for twenty years, your decisions have determined your actions, thus determining your outcomes for that period of time.

Let's break this down even farther.

Many psychology journals and research models state that the average human has anywhere from 12,000[1] to 70,000 thoughts per day. Yes, this data does change based on research populations, conductors of research and search engine reliability, but for illustration's sake, let's keep this conservative: I will use a baseline of 12,000 thoughts per day.

Usually, there are 365 days in a year and most business people work the majority of those days. All people continue their thought patterns and processes on every one of those days. Thought does not take a day off, as illustrated below:

---

1 The National Science Foundation states that the average person has 12,000 to 15,000 thoughts per day.

*12,000 thoughts per day*
*X 365 days per year*

---

*4,380,000 thoughts per year*

*4,380,000 thoughts per year*
*X 20 years*

---

*87,600,000 thoughts per 20 years*

Many of those same psychologists also state that somewhere between 70% and 85% of those 87,600,000 thoughts will have a negative slant for the average person. Of course, these figures are approximations. There is no way to research every human on the planet.

*87,600,000 thoughts per 20 years*
*X 70% negatively slanted thought percentage*

---

*61,320,000 negative thoughts per 20 years*

If the psychologists are even remotely close in their calculations, which would mean that the average person will generate approximately 4,380,000 thoughts per year and over the course of twenty years, a thirty year old will have produced 87,600,000 thoughts.

However, again, if the stats are even remotely close, that means that 61,320,000 of those thoughts have a negative slant, which will produce a negative emotion, which will produce a negative and undesired outcome.

If you are like the majority of people in the world, right now, you may be saying to yourself things like:

"I had no idea."

"No wonder I am so unhappy."

"I finally understand why I haven't been able to get to the place I want to be."

Once you sit down and begin to process this information, at first, it may be overwhelming, but the math doesn't lie and the numbers can be quite sobering.

I didn't say each thought produced a decision; I just wanted you to understand that your mind continuously produces thought in some form. What if those 87,600,000 thoughts required a 1% decision rate? Then, what if those psychologists are right and 70% of the decisions made had a negative slant?

*87,600,000 thoughts per 20 years*
*X 1% decision rate*

---

*876,000 decisions per 20 years*

*876,000 decisions per 20 years*
*X 70% negatively slanted thought percentage*

---

*613,200 negatively slanted decisions per 20 years*

That means, on average, your current life was produced by those 876,000 decisions you have personally made over the last twenty years; 613,200 of those decisions having a negative slant.

## AND YOU WONDER WHY YOU DON'T HAVE THE LIFE YOU'VE ALWAYS DESIRED, YOUR LIFE LACKS DIRECTION AND FOCUS, AND YOUR PROFESSIONAL LIFE IS EMPTY?

The good news? The solution doesn't take 365 days to happen, 876,000 decisions, a special decoder ring, high-fiving someone in a workshop, hopping on one foot while you say the alphabet or any other wacky trick that may have been tried in the past.

All it takes is one decision.

The time span of that is less than one second.

The effect can reach eternity.

**Before any transformation can take place, you must make the decision right now to change your life.**

**Nothing will ever happen in life without a decision being made first, then following that decision with action.**

Just so we're clear; the decision to change must be made before anything else can be done. You are either in or out. You can no longer sit on the fence, be indecisive and blame someone else for all the ills of your life and your business. Yes, your programming may have flaws, but now you understand where your flaws are located and the following will show you how to reprogram your thoughts, feelings and actions.

Now that you have made the decision to make an immediate change in your life and you are willing to do whatever it takes to produce the desired results, we will discuss methods that will not only change your life, but change the lives of the people you love.

If you're anything like me, when you are learning something new, directions or steps are an easy way to get started and integrate the new system of operation into daily life. So here goes...

## THE SOLUTION

Before we start discussing new ways for your life to change, I want you to know that once upon a time, I was also acting out a script or running a program that had been programmed into me since birth. Once I discovered my programming was flawed, everything finally made sense. Nothing was changing in my life because I was continually acting out the same script. If I wanted my life to change, it was up to me to write out the new script or program and change my programming to respond to the new "hard-wiring" I was installing. By responding to the new programming, my life changed.

Just so you won't think I'm going all "woo-woo" or "wackadoodle" on you, let me give you a quick science lesson on what I'm talking about.

There are some universal facts and laws that you must consider before we go any further. I'm going to cover the facts first.

The first fact is that the power of thought is one of the most powerful forces in the entire universe.

As we've previously covered, each thought carries with it the power to negatively or positively affect your life on a daily basis. Every thought you have will get you closer to or farther away from your desires.

Have you ever wondered about the speed of your own thoughts?

I did wonder about the speed of my own thoughts and a research group from John Hopkins answered that question for me. The speed of your thoughts is around 300 milliseconds. That's how long it took a volunteer to begin to understand a pictured object. Add to that another 250 to 450 milliseconds to fully comprehend what it was. Total speed of thought: between 550 and 750 milliseconds.[2]

Combine the speed of your thought with your flawed programming, a misunderstanding of who you are and it equals a supersonic mess.

If you don't know, crystal clear, what you want, every single decision you make from this day forward will be the wrong decision. So, if you don't decide what you truly want, you have the wrong thoughts leaving your brain at the speeding through the universe, every single moment of your life; projecting out all the wrong thoughts **guaranteeing** that you will receive all the wrong results.

Just so we're all 100% on the same page and understand why I'm hammering this so much, let me go over the research one more time: Remember, psychologists have verified that, on a

---

2 May 25, 1998, Proceedings of the National Academy of the Sciences, John Hopkins Team Leader, John Hart

daily basis, 70% to 80% of the thoughts you think are negative, redundant and **do not support your desires.**

Previously, I worked out the math on how many total thoughts you produce yearly. For this example's sake, I'm only going to use your waking hours. If you're awake sixteen hours a day, that means you spend on average, **twelve hours a day** *repetitiously thinking negative thoughts.*

So, is it really a surprise that you're not achieving your dreams if you spend a majority of your time focused on the negative in your life?

What would happen if you reduced negative thought time to...

60%?

50%?

40%?

Would the results in your life change?

Of course.

In order to understand how to change the percentages of negative thoughts you have on a daily basis, you need to understand the relationship between energy and your thoughts.

A quick science lesson is needed, but I promise to make it enjoyable. Relax; I've had lots of practice. I used to teach high school physics classes and I know how to keep you from being asleep with your eyes open while I explain this.

I remember how I used to see the "light bulbs" come on as my students began to grasp that they could control their own destinies using this information I'm about to teach you.

My students came into my class expecting to learn information to help them pass a test. They left understanding that regardless of the test that life presented, they could find all of the answers they needed using these concepts.

The fact that you have to accept is this: Our entire world and everything in it, is made up of energy. Energy cannot be created nor destroyed. Simply stated, when energy changes from one form to another, the amount of energy stays the same. This rule is called the "conservation law of energy."

All energy that ever was, or ever will be, is 100% evenly present at all places at the same time. This explains why God (or the Creative Source) is who He says He is…omniscient (the capacity to know everything), omnipresent (to be present everywhere at the same time), and omnipotent (having unlimited power).

Everything is energy. What do I mean by everything?

Every person you know, every animal you see, every building you walk in, every plane you fly in, every car you drive, and every plant you see, is energy.

Because everything is energy, you also have to understand that everything is actually in motion, all the time. Even though it doesn't appear to be moving to your naked eye, everything all around you is actually vibrating — your body, your furniture, plants, animals, everything. Stop staring at the couch…it's not going to move (according to the naked eye)! If it is moving, put down the hashish, crack pipe and peyote, and understand it's time for more hugs, not drugs!

I am going to make this as simple as possible for you, so I am going to give you a quick, basic meaning and why it's important and move on. Now I'm going to cover some of "The Laws."

A law is a rule or a guideline of how everything in our world works.

According to the Law of Vibration, one of "the laws", everything vibrates and moves and nothing sits idle. Everything is in a constant state of motion. For example, put your hand right in front of your face and hold it perfectly still. While you are holding it still and unable to perceive any motion in your hand at all, know that the electrons that compose the hand are moving or vibrating.

Your hand appears still to you. But in reality, it is in a constant state of motion. Of course, although such motion is invisible to the naked eye, under a high-powered microscope, it would be very apparent. If you shake your hand, you are actually increasing the vibration rate. So, if we can increase the vibration rate of your hand, then it is also true that you can increase the vibration rate of your thoughts. If thoughts are vibrations, and you know how to increase the vibration level of your thoughts, you can actually make your thoughts more powerful…more about this in a moment.

Just to make this perfectly clear, let me give you one more example to help you understand vibration. If you take a drop of water from your tap and place it on a microscope slide, you see nothing. You see clear liquid on a glass slide. No movement, no nothing.

However, if you place that same slide under a microscope, you would be amazed at what you would see. Under examination, you would see many organisms, dashing back and forth, apparently by magic, moving with rapid motion.

So, just because you couldn't see it before you looked through the microscope, does that mean that the organisms aren't moving around? Of course not. It simply means that you didn't have the correct tools to be able to recognize that movement happens.

This is how the entire universe (made of energy) works. I can see you nodding your head. You're starting to get this now.

Along with vibration, I need to explain frequency. A very simple definition of frequency is how often an event repeats itself over time.

Like a radio playing music on an unseen frequency, you can't see the frequency, but you can "fine-tune" the radio to the correct station so that you can hear the music, and once you are listening to the music that you like, you can relax and enjoy it. This is actually an easy concept to understand and as you're reading, you're already grasping it. This is the key component to changing your life, so pay attention!

Everything vibrates and how often the vibration occurs, is called frequency.

Since everything is energy and everything has a vibration and frequency, you may be asking if there is a way to "dial in" the vibration into the frequency that you want.

The answer is yes. The "fine-tuning" button for your frequency and the rest of your life is your thoughts.

Let me reiterate one more time that thoughts are one of the most powerful forces in the universe.

Thoughts transcend all time and space.

You now know that all energy cannot be created or destroyed. In addition, you know that all energy is in motion, all of the time, even though you may not be able to see it moving.

Let me 'splain again…

1.  All matter (plants, animals, inanimate, animate objects) is energy.

2.  Energy vibrates.

3.  All matter vibrates at a different level.

4.  The rate at which matter vibrates is called frequency.

5.  The higher the frequency, the more power it has.

6.  Thoughts have the highest frequency.

7.  Changing your thoughts will change your vibration.

8.  Therefore, thoughts are one of the most powerful forces in the universe.

9.  If thoughts are one of the most powerful forces in the universe, and you are able to control your thoughts, then you have the power to control your own life with your thoughts.

10. Repetition of thought is how you were programmed.

If this is bringing back bad memories from science class in high school, relax. This is science you'll be able to use the rest of your life. The only way your life can change is if you understand and operate from these universal facts and laws.

Now you know, without a doubt, that if you change your thoughts, you change your feelings and if you change your feelings, you change your actions and if you change your actions, you change your outcomes.

In an effort to make this clear, easy to follow and applicable to your life immediately, I will put the method of rewriting your software in step-by-step form.

*Before we even start this process, I want to get a few things straight: I know you may currently feel overwhelmed, you work endless amounts of hours per day and are worn out, you have multiple tasks to do, I don't know you personally and don't know how complicated your life currently is, and if you have to add one more thing to your plate on a daily basis, you're going to scream — all is duly noted and acknowledged. Since life isn't going to stop for you to change, my steps can be integrated into your current life and that way, all excuses are handled.*

## STEP 1: GRATITUDE

Begin the day with the right "vibe," man.

If you want to change your life immediately and change your thoughts immediately, the best place to begin is by establishing a positive vibration with thankfulness and gratitude. Beginning your day with an "attitude of gratitude," as some would say, will place you in the right mental state and get you well on your way to having the right "vibe" to have a super day and build a extraordinary life.

## *PROCESS*

Upon waking every single day, begin the day by being thankful. Options for "gratitude time": You must adapt this time or "gratitude time" to fit who you are, your routine and your personal lifestyle. The following are different methods that people use:

A. Before getting out of bed, verbally express ten to fifteen things you are grateful to have in your life or that you love.

B. Place your feet on the floor and verbally express the ten to fifteen things.

C. Get up, begin your "morning process" of toilet time, brushing your teeth and showering and integrate into this process your verbal expression of gratitude.

D. "Windshield time" – many people have plenty of time in their cars in the morning to verbalize their gratefulness. I live in a major metropolitan area and windshield time normally means verbalizing profanity at a high rate of speed! I've just given you a way to get rid of your potty mouth and be thankful at the same time!

There is no right and wrong way. Just pick a process that fits you best. The key to this entire process is to begin your gratitude time as quickly as possible at the beginning of the day. If you want the right "vibe," you have to start the day immediately in the right vibe. Your beginning vibe normally dictates your thought process for the remainder of the day.

## STEP 2: REWRITING THE PROGRAM

You arrived at your current destination through all of your thoughts and decisions. Your beliefs, assumptions and perceptions have been programmed into you. Since all that you are was programmed into you through repetition of thought, it only makes sense to reprogram yourself through repetition of thought. On a daily basis, you're going to think 12,000-15,000 thoughts anyway, why not choose what you think, how you think, how you feel about you think and the actions you take based on what you've been thinking?

This is where the magic happens. If you change your thoughts, you can change your beliefs and by changing your beliefs, you can change your perceptions and if you change your perceptions, you can change your experiences.

Let me give you an example: My mom and dad were raised during the Depression and one thing I heard in our house every day as a kid was, "Money is hard to come by and hard to keep." That was a true statement in our home at the time. I had absolutely no reason to doubt that what my parents were saying wasn't true, therefore, I developed a belief that money was hard to come by and difficult to keep.

I went into my adult years with that belief and that belief was leading me to nowhere jobs and limited opportunity and empty pockets, thus reinforcing my programmed perception about money. I finally met an older gentleman who introduced me to a new thought process that helped change my belief system, which changed my perception, which changed my entire life.

Yes, my dad was right when he would say so many times, "We aren't the Rockefellers." However, he was wrong by not understanding that each individual gets to choose his own destiny, beliefs, perceptions and outcomes. My dad wasn't a bad man or trying to hurt me. Actually, he was trying to protect me. My dad was running a program that was passed down to him from his dad and grandfather.

One older gentleman helped me rewrite a program that had survived for generations in my family.

Once I understood that the program could be rewritten and my life could change, I had to decide what the change was going to be and what direction I wanted to go. I had to sit down and analyze my talents, my purpose, my vision for life and the gifts that I had to bless the world.

Chances are, if you've been running a program passed down to you, you've also been living someone else's life and dreams and reaping the outcomes. Before we get to the actual thought process, we need to take time to sit and think.

Since you understand that a new program for your life can be designed, let's design a program that you want in place for the rest of your life. That process starts with you deciding from this day forward what your purpose will be, your vision for your new life and all the desired outcomes.

## STEP 3: YOUR PURPOSE

Let me guess. You have been down this road before. You can probably look to the left or to the right and see on one of your bookcases, a book that addresses purpose or a book connected to the concept of purpose. I can probably also assume during the last several years, you have attended a workshop or seminar that has addressed purpose in some form. How did it work for you? Since you're still reading my book, we will operate from the assumption that work still needs to be done.

I don't want this to be complicated, pointless or a dreaded task by you. The cool thing is: If you will take the time to knock this out now, you really can have the life you've always dreamed of.

Look, I have shown you why dreams are possible. Thoughts are things and outcomes can be changed. So please, don't try the "I don't have time" excuse on me. Why bother to take the time to reprogram yourself and change your thoughts if you have absolutely no idea of the direction you're going to walk in next?

Next time you get on a plane, ask the pilot if he minds randomly picking a destination, without a flight plan, and taking off without any idea of where the plane and passengers are going. We both know after he or she stops laughing at you and asks you to sit down, or calls Security, they will communicate with the tower, review the flight plan and proceed to the destination printed on your ticket. If it's good enough for the FAA and every pilot connected to a major airline, the same concept is good enough for you to get to your destination.

In order to find your destination, look inward. Relax and enjoy the process.

## THE PHASES OF FINALLY FINDING YOUR PURPOSE

A. Understand that God or a "Creative Source" created you and acknowledge that you're not a random thought, but designed to do something outstanding during your time on Earth.

B. You possess amazing gifts and talents.

    a. Identify your gifts and talents.

        i. Write out all the things throughout your life that you've excelled at doing.

        ii. Write out all the things you enjoy and would do professionally for free.

        iii. If you have a spouse, ask your spouse what he/she sees as your natural talents and gifts.

iv.   Ask your five closest friends (whom you trust) what they see as your natural talents and gifts.

v.    Look back at all the awards and commendations you've received in elementary, middle and high school, college, from service groups and professionally. Write down the talent or gift that is connected to the award.

vi.   Ask your mentors what they see as your special talents and gifts. Either have them write them down or you write them down.

vii.  Think back to all of those times as child when you sat under the stars, played in a box, charged the fort, redesigned a wardrobe and had no fear. Write out all of those "left behind" dreams that had no limitations and endless possibilities.

viii. Play back the musical memories and the songs that you've always loved and the feelings the songs generate in your heart. Write down the emotion and value that those notes and words bring to your soul.

ix.   Relive the heartbreak of love's past. Feel the deep emotional pain that has been a burden and let it go. Understand that freedom came from the ending of that relationship and the letting go of the emotional bondage that has held on to you since that day. You do this as a way of showing yourself why it had to end, who you were then, who you are now and how those experiences have allowed you to pursue your ultimate purpose at this point in your life.

C. Place every list made in Step B above on a table in front of you. Read every list. Once you have read every list, then compile a list of the reoccurring talents, dreams and gifts that are listed. Step viii and ix help because many times, the music or the emotions you experience will trigger a memory that is connected to a talent or gift that you possess and possibly activate a hidden desire or forgotten dream. Roman numeral i, ii and viii can be combined if it helps you activate the emotion needed to honestly compile your list.

D. Take the compiled list and identify the ten things that really excite you now in your current position in life.

   a. On your lists, circle the ten things you've identified or if you're like me, you will write out the ten things on a new list.

   b. Narrow the ten things to five things.

   c. Narrow the five things to three things.

   d. At this point, you can narrow the three things to one, but you don't have to. The three things may funnel into one big, overall purpose.

E. Now that you have three gifts or talents that you excel in, without any doubt, you can decide your vocational destiny. As a business owner or CEO, you have already displayed your ability to make money. Now you have the opportunity to combine money making, with desire, with a dream and build an extraordinary life that brings fulfillment and enjoyment to you, transforms your family life and unleashes a powerful unstoppable force that fills a void in the world.

Tears normally flow freely once you put meaning and purpose to what was an empty, uneventful monotone life. Deep emotion, combined with expressed excitement and sorrow, can create a desire and passion that can propel you through the next several years of your life.

Now you have the basis for why you were created and placed on this Earth for this time in history. There is a void out there waiting for you to fill it. The entire world is waiting on you to step up, claim your purpose and get the job done.

## STEP 4: VISION

I'm going to keep this very simple.

What do you see happening in your life during the rest of your time on Earth that is connected to your purpose?

Maybe the previous sentence was too nebulous. Why don't we make this even easier? Just answer this question: How do you want the rest of your life to play out and what does it look like?

This is your opportunity to write the fairy tale with you as the main character and the star.

Your vision is your road map to the future. If you're thirty years old, think about the next fifty years and how you want each single year to play out. In order for your vision to come true, you must combine your purpose with planning, focus, hard work, unwavering desire and a crystal clear picture in your mind of exactly what you want out of your life. Heck, you gotta relax enough to get the ball rolling and believe enough that what you write down on paper can and will happen.

## WRITING IT OUT

A. Decide what your God-given purpose is and make a decision to live your purpose on a daily basis.

B. Get some "alone" time and put some honest thought to where you are right now and how you want your life to continue until your last grains of sand run out. This session doesn't have to be written, however, you need the thought process time as a way to open up the door to a belief that you actually have a purpose that God or a Creative Source really cares that you accomplish this purpose. Recognize the fact that once you have a new programming system, dreams and desires become possible. Basically, throw on some smooth tunes, get a beverage, and find a comfortable, relaxing place and think.

C. Write it down. Don't make this complicated! Just write down what it is you see in your head and that you want to come true. Manifestation comes after imagination — dream it, believe it, and act on it!

D. There are various ways to get this done. Methods used by many:

   a. Write down an overall vision for the next fifty years. You may be asking, "Man, what's that look like?" as my wife did on our first date. Yes, believe it or not, this is what the two of us did on our first date! I take my work seriously! I needed to know what her dreams were in order to know if she was someone I was going to continue dating. It worked out pretty well; we've been married for several years and she is not only my business partner, but also my best friend.

i.   Some people prefer a blanket vision that includes their personal, financial and professional all in one statement or sentence. If this works for you, that's great! For example, my wife's original vision from our first date was: "I want to create a life where I work with my husband and son, inside and outside of our businesses, creating the schedules we desire and being the masters of our own destinies." No, it's not perfect, but it's a great start and it was written on a napkin from a coffee shop. Remember, at the time, she had no idea that we would marry and that she and I would be involved in businesses that would take us to exciting cities all over the world. Now, years later, her rough draft on a napkin is her day-to-day life. Since that first date, I've never seen her waver in her belief that her vision would come true. Trust me, as we all know, and have lived, our marriage hasn't been perfect, nor easy at times, but her faith, desire and commitment allowed her vision to become reality.

      ii.    This method worked for her and now she's on to bigger napkins and visions. Actually I splurged and got her an eight and a half by eleven sheet of paper! I know, I'm a giver!

  b.  If you're more like me, you may want to do it this way:

      i.    Write an overall vision.

      ii.    Break that vision into categories such as personal, financial, professional, etc.

      iii.    Make a chart that contains the overall vision, each "broken out" vision and action steps for each category.

      iv.    Each day, I combine my overall vision with my "broken out" visions and I plan every day of my life around those visions. All my goals, whether they be daily, weekly, monthly or yearly, originate from the visions. I'm fanatical about the way I plan things and I have spreadsheets for everything I do because I want to make sure my actions always match my visions.

As you can tell, my wife and I have two entirely different approaches to this process and there is nothing wrong with that at all. The goal is to live your purpose and your vision, not to design it in a way that makes everybody happy. My wife is a social butterfly who loves fun and her vision is a reflection of her desire to have way less structure and more creativity. I, on the other hand, crave structure and I like to see everything in black and white in a neat, orderly fashion.

So have some fun with this and only design this vision to make you happy. Don't worry about grammar or how it sounds. Your high school English teacher is not coming by to grade this, nor am I coming by to make sure you're doing it right!

This exercise is your roadmap to the future and your way of staying on course to making all of your dreams come true.

## STEP 5 CHANGE YOUR PROGRAMMING

As you begin this process, keep in mind the following three things:

1. Just because you've had a limiting belief for a long time doesn't mean that it takes a long time to change it. This is as easy as changing the software on your computer — you "uninstall" one and install a new one.

2. Changing old behaviors and thought patterns isn't difficult or painful unless you want it to be.

3. You don't need to know the cause of the problem in order to change it. The only thing you need is your destination, not your former "stop-offs" along the way. The past can't be changed, so leave it there.

You were programmed through repetition of thought. The repetition designed the original software that was installed in your mind. So now, it's time to uninstall the original software and install the new software that will allow you to be in a freethinking, life-loving profession – enjoying showing your assets to the world.

How do we do it?

The exact same way you were originally programmed.

Repetition of thought.

Remember every day when you get up, you're going to think 12,000-15,000 thoughts a day. Prior to this exercise, many of those thoughts were random, unfocused, undirected and 70% to 85% of them were negative. Time to change a flawed and broken thought process!

Before we begin, I understand that life is not going to stop for you to change your way of thinking, your behaviors or your habits. I'm not asking you to change your daily life, create a special schedule, get up any earlier, or add a "special time" to an already jam-packed exhausting day.

I know you have meetings, you have a routine for getting coffee, you have commitments that may span six months ahead already, you have kids to pick up, functions to attend and you've got a life that's busy as hell. For many of you, your only "alone time" during the day is when you go into the restroom and, for some, that's not even an opportunity to be alone.

Everything I recommend can be integrated into your already out of control schedule. My philosophy is to meet people where they are and allow them the freedom to make the changes when they are ready. Your current schedule and life is based upon your current thought process. Once you begin to change your thought process, your schedule and life will change. The following are ways to integrate change into your life and change your programming without having to add any time to an already impossibly busy schedule. If you do these exercises on a continual and daily basis, your life will automatically change.

1. Start your day with your gratitude time. This sets your tone of vibration and starts your thinking process in a positive and focused direction.

2. Since this is a beginning stage for you, let's keep this simple. Keep a version of your purpose and vision with you at all times. It can be in the follow forms:

   a. Written
   b. Electronic
   c. Text
   d. Picture
   e. Music
   f. Short movie — Powerpoint with music or a picture-based one to two minute short film

   The key is: Making the method match your needs. This **has** to fit you or you'll do it for a couple of days and then say it doesn't work. Your flawed programming took thirty years, one thought at a time, to develop. I think you can give your reprogramming one thought at a time for a couple of months so you can receive the life that seemed impossible fifty-two pages ago.

How do you eat an elephant? One bite at a time. How do you control 12,000 thoughts? One thought at a time. Things are going to happen that will push you towards a negative thought every minute, every thirty minutes, every hour and every day. You already know the negative triggers in your daily life. Those triggers may be people, phone calls, smells, sounds, clients and employees or anything else that just gets on your damned nerves.

The great thing is: You know that those negative triggers are going to be there every single day, and you could probably tell me the exact time those triggers will appear. For example: most offices have a guy that we normally call "Mr. Irritating." He shows up about the same time every day with the same stories and annoying behaviors. Every time he shows up, you experience feelings of irritation, exasperation, negativity and an overall desire to punch him in the face, set him on fire, run over him with a car or throw him off of a very tall building. Since everyone in your office probably feels the same way, no one would say anything if you did it. However, HR tends to frown upon these types of behaviors in the workplace, there's a huge section on employee conduct in the company manual and even though the manual doesn't outline those specific behaviors, you know you'll be in deep yogurt if you do it. Plus the police would have to show up and it would add one more thing to an already busy schedule! So you do what everybody else does. You think those things and for the next hour and a half, you're pissed off, in a bad mood and you just produced 2000 negative thoughts that got you farther away from your desired life.

The great thing is: you're the boss; fire his ass. Everyone hates him and nobody's going to miss him anyway. Plus, you just gave yourself a huge endorphin rush and you've removed a negative trigger from your life. Felt good, didn't it? You just changed your negative thought process to something that brought joy and energy to your day. Taking action can be a great endorphin rush!

The reason you keep a version of your vision with you is to combat the negative triggers that will always appear in your life. Re-reading a statement or looking at a picture that is based on your vision allows you to control your thought process and keeps you focused on your desire for your life. Keep in mind; whatever you focus on will materialize in your life. Every day brings 12,000 focusing opportunities. In order to change, you have to make those 12,000 opportunities work for you instead of against you.

Here's how I want you to do this: Every time you experience a negative trigger, look at your vision. In the beginning, this could be every five seconds! It won't always be this way. This is the beginning of retraining yourself to think and focus differently. Throughout your day, every single time you experience a negative trigger or thought, look at your vision and instead of focusing on what you don't want, focus on what you do want. No, you can't control every thing or every person that you encounter throughout your day. However, you have complete control over your response to things.

Thoughts and behaviors survive the exact same way everything else does in this world. They must be fed to stay alive. Once you stop feeding negative thoughts and behaviors, they will die.

It works the exact same way with things you desire. Start feeding only the things you want to live.

You have the opportunity to feed 12,000 reasons to feel great about life on a daily basis. Make those 12,000 reasons grow and multiply in your life.

1.  End your day the exact same way you started your day with gratitude and focus time.

    a.  Express gratitude for all of your blessings today.

    b.  Express gratitude for all of the people you love and that love you.

    c.  Express gratitude for having a vision for your life and having one less negative thought today.

    d.  Express gratitude for being able to control your thoughts and your destiny.

    e.  Express gratitude for all the wonderful things

that are taking place and will take place in your life.

f.  Re-read your vision, accept your vision, express gratitude for your vision and feel the deep emotion that comes with knowing your vision is unfolding in your life as you speak.

g.  Since you have spent a few minutes in gratitude and have focused on your desired vision, you will go to sleep completely focused on exactly what you want in life and that life will be delivered to you.

Everything starts with you. Your family, your leadership of your company, business performance and your employees' and family's futures will be decided by your programming, your thoughts, your behaviors, your habits and your outcomes.

You now have the beginning tools to reshape your life, your thoughts, your perceptions, your habits and your desires. As your outcomes change, so will your relationships, your opportunities, your social network, your community and your vision of the world.

You are the leader of your life, the master of your destiny, so seize the moment, take control, stay focused and change all the lives around you for the better.

**The mirror doesn't lie.**

**Your business will mirror you.**

**You had better make sure that what's in the mirror is worthy of reflecting.**

# BONUS

When I think about leadership, I think about integrity. When I think of integrity, I think of Dr. David Gruder. His nickname, "America's Integrity Expert" is not just a label, but a lifestyle and an example for all to follow. What follows this section is my interview with Dr. Gruder about leadership and integrity.

## *DR. DAVID GRUDER*

Psychologist Dr. David Gruder, PhD, is a thought leader, integrity expert, Collaborative Culture Architect™, Entrepreneur MacroMentor™, speaker, trainer, media guest, and 8-award-winning author.

Dr. Gruder is a specialist in the psychological skills necessary for individual success, team collaboration, positive culture change, and sustainable business profitability.

Throughout his three-decade-plus leadership career, he has provided keynotes, training programs, consulting, and mentoring worldwide on emotional intelligence (EQ), collaboration intelligence (CQ), spiritual intelligence (SQ) and integrity intelligence (MQ-moral intelligence). He has done this with businesses, helping professionals, educational institutions, nonprofits, politicians, and World Trade Organization Ambassadors.

An entrepreneur himself, Dr. Gruder is founder of Integrity Revolution, LLC, and Special Counsel to the Chairman and Board of CEO Space International, a business development organization helping members create sustainable profitability through integrity, collaboration, and social responsibility. A multi-faceted talent, Dr. Gruder's broad range of experiences enriches the benefits he brings to audiences, organizations and leaders.

*Scot:* *The first question that I had was: What is your definition of integrity?*

*Dr. Gruder:* Well, my definition of integrity is an unusual one because it is the only one that I know of that views integrity and sustainable happiness as inseparable. Because what I have found in studying people who are sustainably happy versus those who are intermittently happy is that sustainably happy people report all three of the following things:

- They report that they feel they are being who they truly are, which means they feel *authentic*

- They report that they feel bonded with people around them that are important to them, so they are *connected*

- They feel they are a positive influence in whatever their chosen spheres of influence happened to be, and that is *impact*

So, authenticity, connection and impact—people who are sustainably happy—report that they are living in the intersection of all three of those drives, if you will; that they are authentic, they are connected and they are impactful.

Integrity is three-dimensional. Authenticity is about self-integrity. Connecting is about relationship integrity. Impact is about collective integrity, whether the collective is a family of community, of country, or of planet — whatever it happens to be, a business, as well. So, my definition of integrity is three-dimensional. It is one-third self-integrity (authenticity), one-third relationship integrity (connection), and one-third collective integrity (impact).

*Scot:* *When I walk to an owner or CEO's home and then go into the office with them, how would I see integrity played out in their behavior?*

*Dr. Gruder:* The way that you can see integrity, or integrity deficits, playing out in their behavior starts with the extent to which they leave their authenticity behind, or they bring their authenticity with them. Meaning that there are a lot of people in leader roles who are promoted prematurely and have been trained to believe that they have to wear a particular mask. They have to wear a particular version of a so-called "false self" in order to live effectively in that role. Of course, those of us who have been around in the leadership development field for any period of time know when a person or a leader is leading from their mask. They end up being perceived as fake, untrustworthy and unfollowable — even if they are charismatic enough to have fooled people for a limited period of time. Sooner or later it's going to come out.

One way integrity plays out in a leader's life is: how does a leader behave when their back is against the wall? What happens at home happens at work. So, if a leader really doesn't know how to navigate conflicts, disconnection, hurt feelings or broken agreements in a centered, collaborative, teachable, humble and leader-like way at home, they sure aren't going to magically know how to do that at work. Any of us can be at our wonderful best when things are going well. But where the rubber meets the road, how do we show up when things aren't going as we had hoped or wanted?

In our personal lives, we live at the level of our wounds, not our wishes. And that's exactly how that shows up for leaders in a work situation; a re-framing of that principle happens at the work setting: Leaders build business at the level of their psychological limitations instead of their entrepreneurial intentions.

*Scot: Let me talk to you further about this question because it's such an important theme in this book. Why is it so important for CEOs, owners and business leaders to have integrity? What are the effects that it has on their ability to lead, their businesses, employees and their clients?*

*Dr. Gruder:* Integrity is all about walking your talk. And in order for me walk my talk; I've got to be really clear before I actually start walking or even talking. I want to be clear about my own personal life vision, mission, values, passions and things along those lines. I have to be clear about what my ultimate life goals are. I have to be clear about what my current life balance commitments are on my way toward achieving my ultimate life goals, because all of that clarity directly feeds into the career that I choose and the rules that I play by, whether I am in an employee role or in a leader role, working as an entrepreneur, or working as an executive in a large company.

If I'm not clear about how my personal mission gets to be expressed through the role that I fill in the job that I occupy, if I'm not clear about the role's true value to the business, if I'm not clear to the businesses through value to its customer in a specific society in general, then I can't have an integrity alignment inside myself. I need that integrity alignment to be my "true north "it's—the compass that guides me in my decision-making in business, because executives have huge responsibilities:

- The leader's first responsibility is to be the steward, the voice for and the overseer of the company's manifestation of each mission.

- The leader's second responsibility is to be responsible for how they "sell" their role in moving the company toward more fully manifesting its mission. They need to be passionate and juiced by the fact that what they are doing in their role on behalf of the company's mission. They need to feel like their role enables them to express important portions of their personal mission, because if they don't have that integrity alignment, they're not going to have the motivation, the passion, the "Stick-to-it-tive-ness" or the drive for excellence that will keep them maximally engaged in fulfilling their role.

*Scot: Why is integrity such an important part of the longevity of the company? And can a company stay in business with longevity, out of integrity?*

*Dr. Gruder:* Longevity without integrity? No. Some businesses with significant integrity deficits do stay in business for a period of time. But do they remain able to sustain profits over the long haul? No.

Companies water down their integrity due to their arrogance, their disregard for social responsibility, their mistreatment of their employees, their mistreatment of their vendors and their neglect of their customers. Often times, the company gets confused about their own mission, and takes on new opportunities and new business directions that really aren't are in integrity alignment with their core mission. I've watched this harm companies over and over again.

I've also watched businesses attain initial success through high levels of integrity, only to become so successful that they decided to go through an IPO (Initial Public Offering). They become a publicly traded stock and as soon as that happened, their integrity with their own mission got axed because the shareholders' priorities in a publicly traded setting are not uniform. The company becomes most concerned about maximizing profits, no matter what gets sacrifice in the process. Companies regularly end up sacrificing their integrity because they work solely for profitability; they are pursuing greed. We pursue greed when we carry a faulty definition of happiness — one that is not three-dimensional like the definition I offered toward the beginning of our conversation.

*Scot: What are your own favorite quotes to tell to business leaders and individuals related to integrity and leadership?*

*Dr. Gruder:* My favorite quote regarding integrity is from Bishop Dickie Robbins: "Too many people are allowing their talents to take them to a place where their character cannot sustain."

The good news, of course, is that we can do something about this!

# Chapter 2

# Leadership

When I started writing this chapter, I was channel-surfing and ended up watching a show called "The Walking Dead." I was familiar with the title of the show because the series is filmed in the Atlanta area, where I live.

I'm very late to the party concerning this show. Apparently, it had been on for several years and I had never watched it. If you're like me and you're clueless about the show, in twenty minutes, I was able to deduce that there is some type of apocalypse, a bunch of zombies and people trying to stay alive.

The show got me thinking and I came to this conclusion: If the apocalypse came and I had to help choose a leader, what characteristics would that person have to possess, understanding that we're going to get eaten and die if we appoint the wrong leader.

Now let's address your business and employees. If the apocalypse was here and zombies stood outside of your gate, would your employees choose you as their leader?

Before you answer that question, let me take you back in time...

You've probably had a multitude of bosses and a multitude of mentors, but how many would you follow if the apocalypse was coming and you had to pick one person to guard you and your family for the rest of your lives or at least till the end of the world came?

Who would it be? Who would you think of? Who would you put in that spot? Who would you trust with the ultimate authority over you and your family's lives?

The apocalypse IS here. The zombies ARE at the gate.

Every day as a business owner or CEO, you face the apocalypse. Your company lives or dies based upon your daily decisions, good or bad. The zombies, your competition, are always at the gate waiting for that one error in judgment from you.

Your employees' have staked their lives on your leadership and judgment–their mortgages, food, clothing and necessities of life all depend on their pay check, which is based on your ability to grow and prosper the company.

So I ask you the question again, if your employees were allowed to choose their new leader tomorrow, would they still choose you?

I'm not just picking on you. How many leaders, CEOs, presidents and/or owners have the chutzpah to go to their staff and ask them that question?

If you don't have the stones to go ask them, you shouldn't be in charge anyway, because you're the wrong person for the job!

My "Walking Dead" experience inspired me to do some research. I started doing face-to-face interviews with employees of companies of differing sizes, industries and sales revenues. My one criterion for selecting interviewees was their position. I did not interview anyone above a Vice President level.

I wanted to know what the "rank and file" employee saw as important concerning leadership and the characteristics of leadership.

I asked them two questions.

1. Do you think your current CEO or owner is someone you would follow if the apocalypse happened tomorrow?

2. What are the characteristics that you look for in a leader that you would follow if the apocalypse came tomorrow?

Out of the approximately 400 people I interviewed, only thirty-four picked their current leader.

The thirty-four that picked their current leader were very vocal in their support of their leader and they way the leader was leading the company and inspiring the employees. These individuals were willing to do whatever it took to perform their job at the highest level on a daily basis. These people said that their CEO or owner was a leader inside of the job AND outside of the job and that the company was a direct reflection of their leader's values.

The other 300+ employee interviewees based their lack of support for their leader on the following:

- Unclear who owns or runs company

- Current treatment from company management

- Media portrayal of company

- Series of layoffs

- Lack of clear guidelines for pay raises or promotions

- Lack of fair adherence and enforcement of company policies

- Company allows customers to treat employees inappropriately

- Leader did not communicate a clear mission and vision for the company and the employee's role in the future of the company

- Constant turnover in management

The employees were willing to answer the questions because of guaranteed anonymity. The most interesting thing I discovered was that the majority of the employees didn't want to leave the company; they just wanted the leadership to change the management policy issues.

People don't have a problem being led; they just want to be led in the right direction.

When I was talking with "the thirty-four", their passion and fanaticism for their leader and their company reminded me of the enthusiasm and zeal I see every weekend in my home state of Georgia when fall rolls around and SEC college football begins. For fourteen weeks, I watch peoples' entire lives revolve around a school's football program and their wins and losses. Their fans wear their colors, sing their songs, fly their flags, decorate their cars, and spend enormous amounts of money around six tailgating opportunities every year.

The word "I" is removed and the word "we" is inserted into every single sentence. No longer does the fan talk about "the team" and "the school" as if it is its own entity. It's "we" did this, "we're" going to do this and "we've" got a big game coming up. The team, the school and the fan are one. The funny thing

I've noticed is that school attendance has nothing to do with loyalty. The fans adopt their school team and bleed the colors of the program. My wife attended the University of Georgia. When I go to football games with her, I would swear that every single person I hear talking before the game, went to dinner at the head coach's house and helped map out Saturday's game plan.

I'm from North Carolina, ACC country. I just didn't get "it" until I moved here and got indoctrinated into the "true" meaning of "Saturday afternoon."

An "outsider" would swear that this is some kind of cult.

Isn't this type of loyalty that you want for your company?

You inspire this type of loyalty by being a person and leader of character.

You can pick up any dictionary or business book and look up some version of what's included in "character." Instead of going through that process for my definition of character, I wanted to use the definition provided to me by the "rank and file" employee that was fanatical about their leader and the company. Since these individuals get to observe their leadership's behaviors on a daily basis, they have a very clear understanding of what it is they need and want in a leader.

Before I cover the sum total of characteristics that were expressed to me, I want to make one point very clear:

You are the owner or CEO of your company, which means that you have accepted that you live in a glass house. Every habit you have, every behavior you display, every word you speak, will be evaluated, scrutinized and interpreted by someone in your family, in your company or in public.

Your company and your private life are a reflection of your values.

Now that there's a clear understanding that private and professional are "one," let's get into the necessary components of a well-qualified, competent and inspirational leader.

## CHARACTERISTICS OF A LEADER

### *HONESTY*

I, like most people in the world, want someone to tell the truth. How many times have we seen this scenario in the media: people go to work and find that they're unemployed because there's a dead bolt on the company door or the parking lot fence? One of the most popular restaurants in my neighborhood just did this to their employees (and patrons). And this place was packed — every night. People in the neighborhood were shocked. No explanation, no apologies to the hard working employees or loyal patrons. Just, sorry Charlie, put a lock on the door and we're closed. They lied to the government, they lied to their employees and they lied to their patrons — and everyone paid the price.

I mean, really, come on man, be honest with people. If you're honest with your people, you don't have to keep track of all of the lies you've told and you don't have to cover them up. Secondly, if you're honest with people, at the end of the day, people can't come back and say you lied to them; you were straight up. You don't have to be in "defense mode." When you sit with someone who's a client, customer or employee, tell them the truth, and give them the facts. You allow them the opportunity to make a fair decision based on facts and honesty. If you say it or promise it, do it. That's a winning combo.

If you lie, it always comes back to you. Don't forget; out of the 100% of communication, verbal is only 7% of that equation. That means 93% of every other form of communication is STILL going to give you away.

A dishonest leader has constant turnover, money issues, tax issues, vendor difficulties, a fickle customer base, theft, higher workman's compensation issues, more employee sick days, a dissatisfied spouse and disgruntled kids and associates.

An honest leader has little or no turnover, money issues caused only by standard, expected market correction, zero tax issues, appreciative vendors, a loyal employee and customer base, minimal shrinkage, little or no workman's compensation filings, employees who are glad to be at work and work when they are sick, an appreciative spouse and grateful kids and associates.

## DISHONESTY=

- You lose your job
- Your company goes bankrupt
- You're on the street
- Your spouse divorces you
- Your kids won't speak to you
- You will have no one to turn to because no one will trust one word that comes out of your mouth

## HONESTY=

- A company based on integrity
- A steady income that's based on fulfilling your promises
- A more harmonious office and home life
- Better relationships with spouse, kids and employees
- More loyalty from the community and business associates

*This is a courtesy tip from a relationship expert: If your spouse asks if they look fat in any outfit….*

**LIE!**

We, as a society, will excuse your discerned dishonesty at this time.

## *FAIRNESS*

Sometime in life, we normally hear or have uttered the following phrase in some variation:

"That's not fair."

My standard response to my own children and to the average person is:

"The fair comes once a year. It costs eight dollars to get in and you need to take extra money for cotton candy, popcorn and funnel cake."

What am I really saying through my sarcastic tone and words?

Life isn't set up to be fair. Life is about opportunities. Fair is subjective (feelings based). Opportunity is objective (fact based).

Whether I am at work with my consulting and coaching clients or when I was a high school teacher and coach, I always sit down at the beginning of our relationship to cover the rules and expectations.

And yes, I absolutely have rules to guide my interactions with my adult clients! It's not on them; it's my responsibility to do this.

I used to sit down with my team and I clearly let them know what the "coach to player" rules were. I also expressed my expectations for their behavior, in and out of school. Each individual understood that rules would be followed and that consequences always follow behavior.

I do the same thing now with my consulting and behavior-coaching clients. We go over the rules, establish the consequences and they agree to follow the rules. It's that simple. I personally don't enjoy surprizes when it comes to business and I want to make sure every single thing that we outline in our "pre-business discussions" is clear and mutually agreed upon. Mutually agreed upon expectations are fair to both parties and both parties have a clear understanding of what will take place and how to measure what takes place.

I often wonder why more business leaders don't do this in their daily operations with their employees, customers and vendors?

I couldn't expect my players nor can I expect my clients to follow rules that weren't reviewed. If it wasn't on the "rule sheet" or a mutually agreed upon contract, I could not expect any party to understand or follow unexpressed guidelines. Clear, expressed and agreed upon. That's the definition of fair.

Let's think about your company now.

Did you cover rules and expectations of employment when you hired your employees? Have you stuck to those established rules and expectations with your employees?

How do you choose who gets promoted, who gets a better sales territory, a better compensation plan, increased perks or consideration for more responsibility within the company? Do you use an objective or subjective rating scale?

Fairness in a situation has to be objective. All eyes and ears in the company are on you.

Is the job promotion going to be based on results or is it going to be based on who you go drinking with or who you go fishing with, or you play pool with, because if it's not based on results, it's going to come back to haunt you. You've just proven to your employees that beyond a shadow of a doubt, you're not a person of character and you cannot be trusted.

If this is the way you run your company, you might as well just print out your employees' resumes and send them to your competitors, because that's where they're headed anyways. Their sole thought as they walk out the door is to bury you and your company!

If you've set the expectation with an employee, customer or vendors that you're going to do something, do it. If you've told the employees: this is the measurement for promotion, then live up to it. All of your rules need to be based on results, not how you feel about the person. Don't ever forget that fairness is based on objectivity and measurable results.

You hired them, and you've told them, "I have enough faith in your ability as an employee to keep you in my company," so live up to your promises. That's only fair.

I encourage business leader to make rules, policies and preferences based on results. Again, let me reiterate, if you're going to promote your drinking buddy over the producers in your company, what does that tell everyone inside and outside of your company? That they should find a new job, because: 1) you're a liar and; 2) you're not fair and; 3) you're not objective and; 4) you don't have any clarity on what you're doing.

Never forget: your company is a reflection of you. Do your want your image to be sparkling and clear or muddy and foggy because your decisions aren't based on fairness? It's your company and your rules, but understand this; all actions have consequences.

## MISSION/VISION/ROLE IN LIFE FOCUSED

Yes, we all know that every business class, business consultant and business speaker discuss the importance of a mission and vision for your company. My guess is, right now, you already have some version of a vision or mission printed in your employee manuals, you have a copy somewhere in the home office and at some time, your employees have read it.

However, my research has shown that even if the owner/CEO and employees have read the mission and vision statement for the company, very few have a personal or professional connection to the statement.

In an effort to keep from being redundant and covering a topic that's covered in many business books and classes, I will be covering mission and vision from a different perspective.

As we discussed in Chapter One, everything starts and relies on your personal mission and vision for your life.

Your behavior in your personal and professional life will mirror your values and who you are at your core.

For me, I like having things in a chart. The chart below is to demonstrate that your personal life and your professional life really do blend together and represent your personal values and how they affect every life that touches yours.

| Personal Life | Professional Life |
|---|---|
| **Role Model** – Spouse, kids, family, social group, community | **Role Model** – Employees, vendors, clients, professional associations, community AND spouse, kids, family, social group and community |
| **Visionary** – Guidance for family, social group and community | **Visionary** – Guidance for employees, vendors, clients, professional associations, community |
| **Communicator** – Vision, mission, direction for individuals and unit as a whole | **Communicator** – Vision, mission, direction for individuals and unit as a whole |
| **Provider** – Security, respect, understanding, financial resources, perspective | **Provider** – Security, respect, understanding, financial resources, perspective |
| **Listener** - Spouse, kids, family, social group, community | **Listener** - Employees, vendors, clients, professional associations, community |
| **Service** - Spouse, kids, family, social group, associations, church/synagogue, military, community | **Service** - Employees, vendors, clients, professional associations, church/synagogue, military, community |

*Role Model*

All of your actions and words will be evaluated and replicated on a daily basis, regardless of geographic location. All eyes and ears are on you and you are held to an extremely high standard.

*Visionary*

Your family and your employees need you to provide a clear direction for the future. All parties desire clarity, guidance and direction, not only for their personal lives, but for their professional lives.

*Communicator*

Now you're communicating how the pieces fit together. Each individual understands how their role impacts and benefits the team's role as a whole and why all the parts are dependent upon each other.

*Provider*

Your actions will determine whether or not your family and your company personnel personally feel a sense of security concerning their finances and their futures. They will look to you during lean or flush times and expect you to provide perspective on a daily basis.

*Listener*

As a leader, you HAVE to listen to your family, your employees, your associates and the community. The feedback that they provide will determine your professional and personal impact in the future. You owe it to them to listen, evaluate and provide information that can positively influence their lives.

*Service*

Your company can be a basis for providing jobs and vocational training, boosting local economies and providing funding for local charities. Your family and employees will model services you provide, which blesses not only charities and organizations, but every life that is touched.

As the chart demonstrates, your values and actions impact every life that touches yours in some way, shape or form. Life does not take place in a vacuum and all actions have consequences.

As a leader, your actions have even deeper consequences. Next time you sit down to make a decision, look back at the chart and analyze how many lives that one decision will impact immediately. Decisions take on a whole new meaning when consequences have faces.

## DECISIVE

In a leadership role, decisions have to be made. Many times, a decision must be made quickly and without all of the facts. A leader must have the ability to quickly evaluate circumstances and provide immediate feedback based on a set value system built on time-tested experience.

People will follow a leader who makes value-based decisions because they will have a proven track record of success that is based on results, not on the emotion of the moment.

After twenty-plus years in academia, the following story is an example of my personal frustration with "so-called" leaders and why people hunger for a person of action in a turbulent environment.

A unique situation arose one day while I was teaching at a high school. A construction worker fell off a four-story beam and was impaled on a ten-foot piece of rebar. To make matters worse, three PE classes were out on the football field watching, school was about to be dismissed in fifteen minutes and the construction worker was located in the direct view of parents picking up their kids.

We as teachers went to our principal for a decision. Instead of making a decision, he said he would need to summon his executive team and they would need to make a collective decision, all while the construction worker was still impaled and screaming in pain and 911 had yet to be called — all in the line of site of students who would be traumatized.

Of course, we did what any good staff would do. We took over, called 911 and alerted the office that school would adjourn after the situation had been handled.

In every situation, someone MUST act. Unfortunately, at that time, our leader was completely ineffective and incompetent. This seemed to be a pattern of my twenty-plus years of involvement with the academic world.

There is a happy ending to this story and it doesn't involve the principal. The young man who was impaled on the rebar walked away from the accident with minimal stitches and no major lasting injuries.

Don't place your family or your employees in the position of having to take the reins of leadership away from you. No decision is a decision and you will force those around you to also make a decision. Frustrated family members and employees will turn on their perceived leader if that leader is deemed incompetent and unworthy.

## RESPECTABLE

A real leader is respectable. Maybe this is an old-fashioned word, but boy, do we ever need to break this one back out of the mothballs and put it back into fashion.

There's a slogan that has been plastered all over peoples' offices, on calendars and on post it notes everywhere all over the world, but few seem to live it.

"Respect is earned."

What's that mean? To me it means, as a leader, you live in a glass house.

Because you're the CEO or the president or the company owner, every person that you encounter every single day, whether they work for you or not, is evaluating you, and most know what you do for a living. They're going to watch you from the time you get up until the time you go to bed.

So you go get coffee in the morning; every single person there is going to watch what you do and how you treat the person who gives you your coffee. Then, they're going to watch you get in your car, and they're going to watch you stop for gas, and they're going to watch how you treat the people you encounter. Then, they're going to look at the car, the clothing you wear, the way you walk, and your overall disposition. People will say to themselves, "Is this a respectable man/woman? Is this someone I'd like to date, marry, be friends with or work for?"

Then, when you get to work, how do you act when you walk in your office first thing in the morning? Do you greet your employees in a friendly manner? Do you care about your employees? Do you ask them how their personal lives in a genuine manner? Do you ask them what's going on in their departments in a non-threatening tone? Or do you just walk in, grumble, go straight to your office and shut the door?

Just a tip: the way a person greets their employees is usually the way they greet their family at the end of the day.

Now that you've greeted your employees in an uplifting and acceptable way, how do you conduct yourself in meetings? Are you a "screamer" who demands respect but doesn't give it, who threatens anyone who dares question your ideas or point of view? Are you someone who barks out orders and expects complete silence and pats people on the head? Do you preach "open door policy" which really equals unemployment for anyone who dares walk through the open door? Do you take credit for your employees' ideas in front of the whole staff? Do you cut sales commissions for no rhyme or reason other than the fact that it gives you a more robust bottom line? Do you betray your employees' confidential information or conversations? Do you set up sales goals that are completely unreasonable and unreachable? Do you expect people to adapt to your mood swings?

Or are you a respectable leader that displays a consistent, firm and positive tone and mood at each meeting? Do you welcome differing opinions, while making the focus what's best for the company? Are you fair? Are you objective? Are you clear? Do you set appropriate sales goals for the sales territory? Do you increase sales commissions instead of cutting them for producers? Do you give your employees credit for their ideas? Does your "open door policy" give your employees an opportunity to vocalize personal and professional concerns without fear of reprisal or betrayal?

If I went home with you tonight and met your spouse and your kids, would I see a respected leader in his/her home?

You know the answer to all of these questions. The key is: If these answers aren't positive and beneficial to all parties, are you willing to change?

Generally speaking, your employees have got you pegged for who you are as a person. They are going to look and say, "Is this person a leader and would I want them to lead me in battle against the zombies during the apocalypse?"

If they can't say that and you're not that person, you had better change, sell your company or find a new job somewhere else. Your employees deserve to have a real leader.

## DISCIPLINED

Most of us have worked for the boss who said one thing and did another—who worked one hundred-plus hours a week and expected us to do the same, who expected us to travel six days and week and still asked us why we couldn't travel seven, who spoke in abusive tones to staff and family members, lifted money out of the till, creatively used company resources for personal reasons, changed company policy based upon the weather outside, initiated inappropriate relationships with staff, conducted illegal activities on company property, didn't pay their taxes, and the list goes on and on...

Before I go any farther, do you fit any of these descriptions?

Is it possible for a family member or an employee to respect someone who has absolutely no self-discipline?

Before you burn up a whole lot of brainpower on this one, I'll help you answer this one.

The answer is NO!

A person without self-discipline cannot be trusted.

Your employees will only invest in you and your company if they have a reason and without you having self-discipline, they have no reason.

Because I want to be very clear on this issue, your employees do not want to work for or invest in someone who does the following:

- Takes liberties with expense reports and company assets

- Doesn't pay their company and/or employee taxes

- Changes company policy at the spur of the moment or

based upon a new relationship that has an influence on them

- Ignores their personal appearance by being grossly overweight, out of shape or misunderstands appropriate attire for their position

- Stays out all night drinking and doing drugs, acting like an overgrown adolescent

- Has uncontrollable emotional outbursts

- Plays favorites based on sexual activity

- Expects 24/7 work activity

- Constantly inappropriately berates an employee publicly

- Hires employees based upon personal relationships and not based on expertise and ability

- Fails to establish clear chain of command (especially in family businesses)

- Constantly "acts busy" and unavailable to staff (even though employees know the leader is playing solitaire or working on their fantasy football team or reviewing fashion trends on the internet or other inappropriate personal activities)

- Allows inappropriate behavior from certain individuals on staff without consequences

- Says they love their family, but never spends time with their spouse or children and expect you to do the same

However, people will gladly invest in a person who does the following:

- Has a clear direction for their own personal life and for the company

- Not only talks about a "healthy life", but lives it in the way they eat, exercise and relax

- Understands personal and professional boundaries and respects those boundaries

- Provides employees with the tools they need to do their jobs at an optimal level

- Understands that an employee is a asset and not a commodity

- Makes decisions based on facts, not feelings

- Controls emotions and handles delicate issues privately

- Handles financial responsibilities with transparency, prudence and due diligence

- Only hires employees who are qualified and can benefit the company in many ways

- Allows no in-fighting or drama and has a pre-determined and fair system of dealing with combative employees, vendors or partners

- Provides opportunities for productive employees to use their gifts and talents inside of the company – if the leader can no longer offer a productive employee advanced opportunities within the company, the leader will help the employee seek opportunities outside of the company.

- Understands that a 24/7 work ethic is an unacceptable expectation of any employee

- Encourages employees to spend time with their families and provides opportunities to do so

As I said earlier, everything starts with you. You must display discipline in your own life before you can expect ANYONE in your company to display discipline in the workplace.

Now is a good time to evaluate your own performance and give yourself an honest grade. I said honest grade. Nobody's watching. If you want your company to make an impact in addition to making money, the qualities I've outlined in this chapter are a MUST in your life.

In conclusion, leadership isn't a slogan, a motivational cliché, a double life, a title without merit, an over expanded ego, an inherited position, a name plate or name tag with a position listed, a degree with initials or a ladder-climbing tool with a brass ring and a corner office. Leadership is a value-driven life that reflects honesty, integrity, courage, decisiveness, toughness, strength and an ability to bring out the best in each individual in your organization, your family and the community.

# BONUS

As an added bonus to this section, I wanted to bring in two men that have mentored me, that I consult with, that I respect and that live the definition of leadership. This question and answer session will not only bless your business, but your life and the life of everyone that hears their message. They are Lt. Col Alan Tucker and Dr. Jeff Magee.

## *LT. COL. ALAN TUCKER*

Lt. Col. Alan Tucker was a senior level Air Force leader with over thirty years of experience leading diverse organizations to improve productivity heightened leadership and greater profitability. His success lies in the ability to analyze and identify problems and then conceptualize and provide leadership to implement solutions. Lt. Col. Tucker has successfully reengineered company infrastructure, articulated clear vision for the future, and provided energy, direction, and confidence necessary to excite company employees, vendors and customers.

He was selected as commander of the largest Munitions Squadron in the USAF with an inventory of $2.5 billion. Prior to assuming command, the squadron was rated as one of the poorest; however, because of his leadership, in 2 short years, the squadron was acknowledged the best munitions squadron in the United States Air Force. His unwavering leadership and devotion to his country and his duty cultivated in him being awarded the prestigious Bronze Star.

*Scot: In today's society, I hear people in the business and sports arena use the words "battle" or "war" as a motivational terms or slogans. You are someone who has seen "real" battle, defended our country and asked men and women to come with you in defense of our country and engage in the battle of their lives. Can you explain what is really means to "lead men into battle?"*

Lt. Col. Tucker: Leading men into battle is the hardest job I ever had to perform. The planning is so intense prior to the deployment; it is almost a relief to deploy. For me personally, I feel you have to show confidence to everyone going with you. If I am not confident, the troops will not be. I had to set the example that even though I was feeling the same anxiety every person was feeling, every thought has to be for the mission and the welfare of the troops. My major concern was I would lead the men to the best of my ability, let none of them down, and take all of them home safely.

*Scot: How do you motivate and lead soldiers to go into battle without the certainty of who will come home alive?*

Lt. Col. Tucker: When you are preparing to deploy, you have fill out your legal will. That is a very sobering experience for everyone, and as a leader, you have their undivided attention when this is done. I would tell them to depend on the training they have received, depend on the man next to you, ensure that the man next to you can depend on you, concentrate on your job and we will get through this. I always reminded them why we were there and yes, I always spoke in patriotic terms. I never minded waving the flag in front of the men. I was always honest with each person about the situation. We never spoke about not going home alive; just accomplishing the mission, getting through the deployment, then going home.

*Scot: You took over a very difficult situation in a unit that was drastically underperforming. How did you lead an underperforming unit from worst in the Air Force to the best?*

*Lt. Col Tucker:* I had to instill a positive environment in order to build a team of excellence. The unit I was assigned were good units, but lacking in leadership. Evaluating the unit personnel was the first order of business, which meant, in some cases, moving the negative person out and putting a positive person in their place. In order to build up the unit, our core team had to tackle each individual's low morale, in order to build increase the spirit of the entire unit.

I had to build them up, make them feel good about what they were doing and help them understand that their job mattered to the Air Force and to the national security of our country. One munitions unit I directed needed to be continuously assured and reminded that the bomber that was going up had a job to do; which meant that we had a job to do and every person, ground or air, was depending on us to get the job done.

A leader must instill discipline and define each person's responsibility; leaders cannot hold someone accountable if they haven't instructed their subordinates on exactly what their mission is. Leadership means setting the standards high, insisting everyone measure up, and understanding the importance of being the one who sets the example.

*Scot: I know you as someone who takes his leadership role very seriously. What role did your leadership play in the turnaround your unit experienced?*

*Lt. Col. Tucker:* I believe that leaders must get out from behind their desk and leave footprints. In my units, we worked three eight-hour shifts, so it was imperative for me to be seen by all three shifts; that meant that I was cheerleader sometimes, waving the flag, but always maintaining a positive environment. I wanted to know the individuals in my unit and I wanted them to know that I was observing their drive, their desire for excellence and their commitment, not only to our unit, but to our country.

As a leader, I saw it as my job to subtract negative individuals from our unit and promote individuals that understood excellence in duty and performance.

There is no instant way to turn a unit around. A successful turnaround is based on a formula of hard work, a desire for excellence and a belief that any job can be done.

One of my senior NCOs once asked my wife, "When does he sleep?" She told him, "Normally, between 10PM and 2AM." My philosophy is: A leader has to put in the time to get good results. Leadership isn't about talking a good game, but spending time with the individuals in the organization. In my case, it was the brave men and women of the Air Force.

*Scot: As an officer who has faced many challenges during the span of your professional career, what do you see as the three keys to leadership?*

*Lt. Col. Tucker:*

1. Hard work is a must in any organization or unit. I understood my role as a leader was to be the model of hard work and that my behavior would set the tone for the organization or unit to follow. The successful leader is the one who sets the trend, not the one who follows it.

2. Always be fair. Remember, every person in your organization or unit is an individual first and as individuals, each person is in a different place in life and needs different types of inspiration and motivation. That

may mean a kick in the butt for one and a pat on the back for another. The individuals in your unit need to know that when the chips are down, you are there for each one of them.

3. Always be honest. Never compromise with honesty, integrity and always be consistent with your actions.

*Scot: Throughout your career, is there one idea about leadership that has served you well?*

*Lt. Col. Tucker:* "Great leadership is hard work, but the benefits and rewards can be incredible and everlasting. Being a leader means you continuously live in a glass house. Everyone is watching so every word and deed must set the correct example. The price is high, but so are the rewards."

## DR. JEFF MAGEE

Dr. Jeff Magee has been called one of today's leading "Leadership & Marketing Strategists." Jeff is the Author of more than twenty books, two college textbooks, four best sellers, and is the Publisher of *PERFORMANCE/P360 Magazine*. Dr. Magee is the former Co-Host of the national business entrepreneur program on Catalyst Business Radio and Human Capital Developer for his private business clients for more than twenty years.

*Scot: What are three things that a leader can do on a daily or a weekly basis to make sure that they are being a great leader for their employees and their organization?*

*Dr. Magee:* I think the first thing that a leader can do, should do, needs to do, and is actually responsible for doing, is to make sure that their values are congruent with the organization they lead. A leader must make sure that the organization's values and their own are congruent.

And if they are, then the leader's values will drive their actions, behaviors, and decisions and how they engage people. So the old adage of "walk your talk" would be the number one thing for a leader to do. Again, "walk your talk" is not just an adage, it comes from your values; your values drive your behaviors, your values drive your vision, your vision drives your mission, and in "corporate speak", your Mission Statement.

The number two action for leaders to take is to make sure they are really operating through the lens of strategy. The leader is responsible for strategic decisions, thinking, guidance, implementation, and then, after strategy, operational execution. This may sometimes get "crossways", as I like to say, with people internal and external to the organization. Whether it's an internal or external constituent, stakeholders, shareholders, customers, vendors or employees, not all will be "on board" with a leader's strategy. Sometimes, the leader has to make the tough choices — tough decisions regarding changing operationally, how to do things to be profitable and efficient or changing people.

And then the third part of what a leader can do in addition to strategy and operations is the tactical component — the tactical things a leader does, which have to be performed as the right things to do at the right time.

So, the first thing is going to be about values, the second thing is going to be about strategically and operationally executing the proper direction, and tactically directing the movements of the company and the employees. That's what the leader is really all about.

And I think what's important for a leader to do every day, is to be mindful of why they are in the organization they are in and to remember why they are in the business they are in. Whether you are for profit or not for profit, whether you are a public servant in government or you are in military leadership, what's the reason for being there?

If the leader reminds themselves of those responses, that

allows them to always be going in the right direction, which sometimes will put them in favor with people, and they'll be Mr. or Mrs. Popularity, and at other times, it may not make them very popular at all.

But that's what a leader does, they make the popular and unpopular decisions and those are the three ways that the leader knows they are headed in the right direction.

*Scot: Which leads me to the next question, which is probably one of the questions in the "behavior world" that people disagree on the most. Are leaders born or are they made, and can you train someone to be a leader?*

*Dr. Magee:* That's no longer the $64,000 question; it's the zillion-dollar question. There is an entire industry, human resource development that is all about creating an environment conducive for the development of leaders.

I think the answer to your question is, yes, yes and yes.

Are leaders born? I think yes, some are.

Can leaders be framed, conditioned, groomed, cultivated? I would like to think that answer is yes, or a significant number of us don't have a reason to be on this planet!

And then do circumstances and situations create a leader? I think that is also a yes.

In regards to all three, some people are not born leaders, and some people do not have the internal mettle to ever be trained, conditioned, groomed, or cultivated into being a leader. Some circumstances will actually show that someone that was put into a position, and trusted in that position, or elected into a position to be a leader, do not have the capabilities of being a leader because a leader really has a unique set of DNA.

Anyone can be a manger, with all due respect, because managers are simply functional components of a business, knowing how to do this, how to do that, dotting the "I's", and crossing the "T's." But a leader knows when to do those things and why to do those things, and who can do those things.

*Scot: Let's say you are called and asked to come to a company that's about one month from shutting their doors; however, there is a bright light if you can provide three strategies immediately that will work. What would you do?*

*Dr. Magee:* That's a great question for me because I have actually been there. I have been there with billion dollar corporations, and I have been there with entrepreneurial medium-sized businesses. And the answer to what an organization can do is exactly the same, no matter the size of the company.

Number one: You have to announce that if people aren't in, they have to go. That includes you. You may not have the DNA to be the leader. So, that may sometimes mean a significant change in leadership, or a change in who's in power to be the leader.

It starts at the top. Sometimes you have to replace the leadership or the leaders have to get the right people at the table because with egos and arrogance at the top a good company can be taken from a good company to a dead company.

Leaders have to fully engage everyone's brain, spirit, heart, and mind, and the physical energy to come to the table to say and do what's relevant for the company.

I call it 20/20 vision.

You have to get every single person in the company to understand: how can we increase revenue given the target by 20%? And how do we save the revenue given the target of 20%?

I, as a leader, believe that my employees in the organization know how to generate income and know how to save income. And, if can get everyone to do the math by creating a 20% gain, and a 20% savings, that's a 40% generation of energy and revenue. That's where you get the profitability fast.

When merged my company a few years ago with a much larger firm, I recognized that the people I partnered with had grossly mislead me as to the financials of the company and other massive HR issues. I didn't realize you could actually cook the books and keep two sets of financials in the world of professionals!

I wasn't about to go under with this company, so I sent an email out to 144 employees-part time, full time, virtual, 1099, and on payroll. I invited them to what I called a mental DNA test.

I asked for anyone who could give us ideas that we could implement easily and quickly in the next thirty days or less; ideas that could help us to make money as an extension of a product or service we have, or a new product or service the market place would buy. I asked them to bring ideas to the table; like a virtual suggestion box on the wall. I would be the gatekeeper of it, so I could see what the mental DNA was in my employees. I gave the first person who submitted an idea I could use and implement a $100 bill.

What we found is that we that had twenty-two usable ideas. Each idea submitter was made the "idea chairman" of that idea. We had twenty-two proactive teams implementing ideas. One idea was a way to deliver online training on an iPad, and at the time no one in the United States was actually doing it, so this was a cutting edge idea.

This one idea generated hundreds of thousands of dollars of profit in ninety days. And I went to that one employee and said, not only, "Thank you," but also, "What's something you would personally like that would be my way of saying thank you? "And I don't mean for you to use your work or part of the department, but something you personally want." She said, "An iPad." I said, "How much do those cost?" She said, "About $800."

I gave her the company credit card and said, "Go buy one. It is yours."

So that's an example of walking into a crisis, putting in an action plan, coming up with solutions, generating a cash flow, and recognizing and rewarding the employee who did that. For all of the idea managers, we did different things, but with this one employee who wanted the iPad, she was very humble. She was not flaunting it (her reward), but a couple of people in the management team got a little bit sideways and pissed off because, oh wow, why did she get an iPad? And I looked at them and said, "You give me some ideas that can turn hundreds of thousands of dollars worth of profit and I'll give you all one."

They all shut up.

And it really won people back.

Those are three things that I went and changed, and I'm big

believer that you and I and people reading this book have come to us because we do have the ability to see business through a different lens. We have a chance to interact with people all over the globe, so we see best practices of what does and does not work.

But sometimes believers in our approach do get into trouble because sometimes you can have an executive team that is a cancer in the organization. But if the executive team, or the owner of the company, or the CEO, has the tendency to give someone a second chance for the fortieth time, the negative person in a team knows it, seizes it, and takes advantage of it. So you have to start at the top and make sure you engage everybody.

And yes, you can turn anything around. You can solve any problem. There's a saying that says basically "The mind of man that creates a problem cannot solve a problem with the same mind." You have to take your mind to another level. So if you look at things through different lens, you create it, you can fix it, but only if you look at the problem through a different lens.

*Scot: What are the most disturbing behaviors you see in business that affect employees, the profits, and the clients?*

*Dr. Magee:* I will go right back to where we started. I think it is an inconsistency in values and visions that drives actions to follow these procedures, endeavours, and activities. I think another thing that kills is arrogance and ego. If you and I screw something up, and we admit genuinely, sincerely and quickly, it takes all the fun out of anyone beating us up, or taking it out on us. So now you can move to okay how do we fix it, what do we learn from it, how to make sure we don't do the same thing twice? The problem in lots of business is we have such arrogance and egos that people are not willing to admit when they are in over their head.

I'll make up an example.

Let's says we elect somebody president of the United States whose entire life and resume and experience would fill up a thimble. That person could still be a great President, if they surround themselves with people, secretaries and cabinet members who have phenomenal resumes that do each of those things the President can't do. But if that President is clueless...

Ronald Reagan once made a statement, "If "A-level" people surround themselves with other "A-level" people, you are phenomenally successful. The problem is that sometimes we've got "B-level" people that are management or leadership in government, and so they surround themselves with "Cs" and "Ds", so that they always look good." And so again, back to my made-up story, we elect basically a B-, C+ president, they surround themselves with C-s/Ds, and so, they have no clue what they are doing, and they're proving it every single day.

And when you have that in management and/or leadership, we can all see it in politics the devastation it causes, within a business, it is the same thing. You are going to have great performers who are going to excel and then leave your business and go somewhere else. You are going to have average employees, and an average employee can be great if they are shown greatness, and an average employee can become pathetic if they are shown pathetic. But those average employees will typically stay, your great ones will leave, and everyone's performance will get scaled backwards because again why work hard with the leadership team if they are next to clueless or lost?

*Scot: You are one of the few people to have the opportunity to address all of the service academies. What did it feel like being asked to address those young men and women, and what did you say to them?*

*Dr. Magee:* When you interact with people in the military academy and the staff that supports them, the faculty that teaches them, it just goes back to the very first question and the answer I gave you. It's supposed to be driven based upon a value system, and that value system reinforces the purpose of why it's there. The academy is there to create career military leaders and officers. It is not about the politics. It's not about "I'm going to work for forty years and maybe get four or five years military, and I can leverage that into a major cooperate job and get paid hundreds of thousands of dollars."

These men and women have a civil servant mind set; it really is always about staying true and focused, not getting caught up in rhetoric and not getting caught up in commentary of the day. You have one core job and that is to be a leader, to build a strong military structure, to help to create, guide, and make the future military leaders, officers, and NCOs.

And so I would say to everyone: stay true to your cause, never forget your values, your integrity is all you have, and make sure that if you don't have the technical ability to do your job, then surround yourself with people that do, because again, a great leader does not have to have the answers.

A great leader does not have to know how to do everything. A great leader has to know how to ask questions and shut up. Great leaders don't always have the answers. They have the innate ability to ask the right questions at the right time to the right people. They'll get great answers. And then from those answers they could select a solution to be implemented.

*"The speed of the leader determines the speed of the pack."*
Sargeant Preston of the Yukon

# CHAPTER 3

# HIRING & FIRING

It was my original belief that this chapter was basically a "no duh" and that most, if not every company, followed a guideline and procedures when it comes hiring and firing of employees. However, after speaking with several retail establishment general managers and doing my own observations over a six-month period, it appears that my "no duh" moment was a bit premature. The retail general managers' interviews were valuable because, on a retail level, an observer sees what is actually happening and hears the sights and sounds of whether corporate policy is being followed or if a corporate policy is in place. If there is anywhere that the attitude of "it's not them, it's you," attitude shows up in glaring form, it's in the area of hiring and firing.

As a way of illustrating my point, I want to relay several experiences that my wife and I personally observed during our travels.

When we walk into an establishment, we look to see if we'll be greeted, if the host/hostess/employee is friendly or if someone is there to greet us at all.

During our time doing surveys for this book, we encountered two employees that greeted us in a friendly manner and sought to meet our needs immediately. Our survey pool included twenty different establishments and only two establishments had apparently trained their employees to greet their customers in a positive manner.

My assumption that their outstanding greeting had come from adequate training was quickly erased by asking the employees one question: "Were you trained to greet customers in this manner?"

Each employee politely said, "No, sir. I just enjoy talking to people."

"So you mean to tell me that you weren't trained to greet the customers this way; that this just came naturally to you?"

"Yes sir."

This helped bring my "no duh" moment full circle. I had taken it for granted that companies or management understand how to hire the so-called "right" people and place them in an optimal position to serve the customer.

Only two establishments out of twenty had hired the "right" people and it was my gut feeling that this was due to blind luck, not company policy.

In addition to what I assume was blind luck in the hiring process, I'm also seeing another puzzling trend of placing brand new employees directly in front of customers, after receiving little to no training.

I remember my first job; I was a fry cook. I was fifteen, turning sixteen, and my first job was to make biscuits and to fry chicken — that's all they let me do. And I sat and fried chicken for six hours straight. I breaded it, stuck it into the fryer, put it in the pan, and let someone else give it to the customer. You had to earn your right from the back to the front, which makes complete and total sense.

The other day, I went into a restaurant, a major hamburger chain, and I had to help the girl count my change back to me. She was manning the register. That was after I asked her to put her cell phone down to take my order. I was nice enough to offer to talk to her friend while she took my order. I didn't want to come off as demanding or anything...this sweet young lady in a serious tone looked at me and said, "Why in the world would I want you to talk to my friend?" Like, no duh...

And I would like to say this happens every once in a while, but unfortunately, this is becoming the norm for many places I go to, and it's a problem. I'm having to ask the grocery checkout staff to stop texting someone, or if they do speak, they're not talking to me, they're talking to another employee, telling them about what they did the night before, how drunk they got, where they were, what they were listening to, instead of actually saying, "Hello Mr. Patient and Paying Customer, how are you?"

On one occasion, after asking the two employees to take a break from their conversation, a young lady, after putting her hand in my face to shush me, informed me that she needed to finish her story first before she could proceed to checking me out.

This story does have a happy ending: after the young lady so condescendingly and graciously checked me out, I had a riveting conversation with the general manager at that store. After hearing the ending of the two employees' conversation and finding it quite interesting, I think the ending of my conversation with the store manager had a better twist and more excitement. She was happily pronounced unemployed and asked to carry on her conversation somewhere else.

After surveying several establishments, it appears that managers are taking the first person that walks through the door, instead of evaluating: Does this person meet our standard of hiring? Last time I looked, having a pulse was not a good enough reason to hire someone! I watch enough TV to know that even zombies can walk around and talk to people. That doesn't mean you want them working for you!

I have asked many general managers, "What is your company's standard for hiring?" And I have had several honest ones tell me, "We can't enough good people to fill the positions, so we are forced to hire whoever comes through the front door."

Is that true, are you seeing this type of situation? Or is this situation a reflection of what a company is forced to deal with when they lower their hiring standards?

From an observational standpoint, something that I have seen played out in the marketplace by many companies is a philosophy that if you treat people with respect, pay them a fair wage, create an atmosphere of encouragement and achievement, backed up with stern, fair and high expectations, the so-called "right" people will not only walk through the door, but will be more than happy to come and work for your company.

The business atmosphere is no different from the sports atmosphere I experienced for so many years as a high school coach. My players expected a definite direction, backed up by a fair evaluation process of their talent, playing time based on desire and hard work, results based effort rewarded by praise, negative consequences when needed and an opportunity to display their individual talents while building a team that was championship worthy.

People don't mind working for someone who sets the pace, gives a fair standard for what their performance is and pays them right — and paying right, that doesn't mean $100,000 a year; right is what is right for the position.

If an employer has a clear and simple set of expectations, provides an environment where hard work and performance are rewarded, evaluates performance using a standard set of objectives and rewards results with opportunity and financial compensation, there will never be a shortage of the "right" people employed in your company.

...and to think, I just thought this was a "no duh" and I didn't really need to cover it in this book!

Allow me to go back to my observations. If I were to grade establishments purely on an observational level, what I'm seeing right now is a void in leadership and an absence of a clear, objective standard for employee behavior as the behavior relates to the customer and to fellow employees.

As I discussed earlier, how is it that only two establishments had friendly people appropriately greeting their customers? Keep in mind, that the employees had stated that they had not received training in the area of customer service. After all of my experiences over the last several months, I have to ask this question: *Why would a company hire an untrained or unfit employee in a position to greeting their most important asset — their customers?*

Let's compare hiring to a scenario most of us remember: dating.

The night could have gone great, the date was great, and then those last few seconds, the kiss wasn't good, the hug was wrong, the wrong word was used, the wrong impression was put in this person's mind and instead of going from a sure second date, you go to no date, no return text, phone call or email.

That's how a first time customer will say goodbye to your company. No response, no return visit, no nothing. A customer will not call and inform you that you hired the wrong person.

They just quietly disappear into the night just like your date gone wrong.

Regardless of your industry, whether it's hamburgers and hot dogs, real estate or sportswear, customers are not going to spend money with you if you have hired unfit, unsocial, inept employees.

Chances are, within one to three blocks or miles, depending on your city, there is someone who can take your place, do it better, and is currently hiring the friendly staff that your company really needs.

When I think of best in hiring practices, I think of one place: it's QuickTrip convenience stores. I actually coordinate my entire East Coast and Midwest driving routes around the locations of these stores. Before I even get in the car, I will look on the Internet, state maps and map out where all the QuickTrips are. And I will only stop there, get gas, use the bathroom and restock on food. Why? The bathrooms are always clean, I get the same experience regardless of state from every QuickTrip, the employees are always courteous and very helpful, the gas is always cheaper, and the place is impeccably clean. To me, that matters. Yes, clean bathrooms do matter, and if I go to your store and you have a dirty bathroom, I will never come back.

What does a clean bathroom tell me about the employee that you hired and about you? If they are not cleaning the bathroom properly, they are cleaning the food service equipment correctly and there are germs in the store and I don't want any part of that. Because if the bathrooms are dirty, so is the whole store, and so are each one of the employee's hands that are handling my money, my food and everything else involving my life on that visit. That just won't work for me.

If it won't work for me, it is not going to work for your other clients. And what I have noticed with QT, they don't have a problem hiring the right people. They don't necessarily pay any more than the industry standard. It is the way they treat their employees, and it is the expectations of the employees who come to work for them.

I knew a middle aged gentleman who had lost his job and I said, "Why don't you go apply at QT? They seem to treat their employees right, and every single employee I've asked enjoys their job and loves working for the company." When he got there to apply for a job, he had to put his name on a waiting list. A waiting list! People are actually waiting to get an opportunity to work at a convenience store! Unheard of! How many mangers get up every single day at any fast food restaurant or any retail establishment and have to go through thousands of applications to get the right employee?

QT, in our area of the U.S., has a backlog of the right people waiting for positions. QT has been listed by many popular financial magazines as an excellent company to work for and is growing at a comfortable pace.

I once asked one of the QT regional mangers, "Why does your company go through such painstaking processes to hire employees?" He laughed and said, "It's very simple — it saves time and it saves money."

When I asked him about the hiring process, he told me it's a several-tiered hiring process for anyone, regardless of location of store or position. The people that have governance over and responsibility for those stores are reviewing who is going to be in those stores. In other words, the folks managing the stores have accountability and responsibility for who is in their stores and what is happening in them as well.

Because various factors come in to play when you are dealing with the public, you have to have employees who can greet the public, understand their positions, their reward structure, and who understand that the only thing that matters is the client walking in that door several times that week to spend money with your company.

There are other convenience stores around the block; several even located directly across the street from many QTs, so what would make someone spend money with QT instead of going across the street and spending money with that other guy? My local QT manager told me that people are loyal to QT directly because of their hiring process. He told me, "We only hire the best. We allow everyone else to hire the people we don't want. For us, we are going to do our best to get the top employees."

Can you see why I love this company so much and why I gladly drive out of my way to spend money with them on a weekly basis?

## HIRING & THE IMPACT ON YOUR COMPANY

The number one reason for personal and financial ruin referenced on many TV shows, financial magazines and websites is marriage. Normally, in order to get married, you have to date. If you date the wrong person, you're going to marry the wrong person. If you marry the wrong person, as many marriage experts explain, emotional despair and financial ruin follow.

Hiring the wrong employees is no different than marriage and dating. Hiring the wrong person or people can cause you endless hours of emotional stress and untold amounts of income in damaged and lost business.

Your average customer will try you out at least once. It's just like when you were a little kid. Your parents got you to try broccoli, the vegetables, and for me, it was Brussels sprouts. Once I got those things stuck in my mouth one time, I knew, without a shadow of a doubt, there was no way I was going to eat them again.

That's how people see your company or your business. A rude experience, a rude cashier, a rude employee who just happens to be walking by your customers, an employee that's walking out to go home for the night who still has on your company shirt, still has a company affiliation and will keep the average customer from ever coming back.

So let's do some simple math. Normally, I go to a convenience store at least five times a week, and to a certain restaurant that I love, four or five times a week. Let's say I spend twenty dollars a visit. That's one hundred dollars that the business is going to get out of me every single week, and at the end of the month, that's $400. At the end of the year, it is almost $5000. If you multiply my average amount by, let's say, 200 people like me who do the same thing I do, we are talking some serious cash.

What happens if one of your unfit hires makes the "average me" angry one day? Now you have those loyal 200 people, not only angry at your unfit employee, but they're also angry at you because that employee is an extension of you. Since there is a competitor a block away from your store with courteous and competent employees, that customer will now take their $5000 a year down the street. If you multiply the $5000 times the 200 formerly loyal customers, that is $1,000,000 that is no longer being transferred through your cash registers — all because you hired the wrong person and made them an extension of you.

As simple math shows and any third grader could draw you out in crayon, lost revenues are one of the reasons that you don't want to hire the wrong people.

As I continuously say throughout this chapter, this is a "no duh."

But if this is such a "no duh", why is it that I just left a convenience store an hour ago and I will never return because of an unfit, rude employee?

Lost customers go with the lost revenues, and now I'm not only talking about the actual people that walked in your door. We're also talking about lost opportunities to gain new clients and customers from your existing customers.

How often do people tell others about a great experience they had? In this day and age of technology, viral videos and social media, it's frightening to think about how fast your reputation can be damaged not only in your community, but around the world.

Not only have you lost the revenue of the 200 former loyal customers, but now you have to worry about each one of them telling ten to twenty people they know about their bad experience with your company. That's 4000 people in a matter of minutes being notified that your hiring practices are unacceptable and your employees are unfit and rude.

In addition to those 4000 people being notified, you are now a part of a vicious rumor mill that is being circulated verbally and through social media. Keep in mind: now it doesn't matter if the information is true or not! Due to one employee, you are now losing business from people that didn't even know you existed one hour ago.

Was it worth having a sub-standard hiring procedure?

As a way of illustrating my point, let me give you another example: Before I stay anywhere or take a trip, I always go to Trip Advisor and look at online reviews of hotels. My wife and I stay in a lot of hotels throughout the year and like most people, we have our favorites in certain cities throughout the United States.

But if we are trying out a new hotel we've never been to before, we won't stay anywhere without a Trip Advisor recommendation. That recommendation makes or breaks the decision on where we stay.

Guess where those reviews come from?

People that have actually stayed in the hotels.

They talk about rude employees, they talk about dirty rooms, they talk about bad food, they talk about noise, they talk about cleanliness in the parking lot, they talk about toilets not working, they talk about showers not working, they talk about no hot water, and the list goes on and on. These recommendations can make or break a hotel's business. One bad review can take down your occupancy rate in the click of a mouse.

I have picked hotels that may not have looked that great on the outside, but because every single person that rated the hotel gave them high marks and positive recommendations, we stayed there.

Guess what happened?

We usually have great experiences.

The one time we did have a bad experience, however, the general manger, and the regional manager made it right and that hotel is now back to one of our top tier hotels where we stay on a regular basis. The regional manager listened to our concerns and then all parties agreed on a satisfactory way to handle the situation.

The bad situation was not due to an employee; it was associated with a situation with another guest at the hotel.

Think of all of the opportunities that your customers have to "rate and rank" your company on the internet. Due to the ease of the Internet, many people will not spend money without consulting the web first.

In addition to sites like Trip Advisor and all the online reviewing services, there is also a little thing called social media. Yes, people do post their experiences of the day on all social media outlets. They do post what they have for lunch, who they talk to in parking lot, what they saw at the mall.

However, every time someone has a bad experience, chances are, they are going to go straight to social media and let every single person in their tribe know that you gave them bad service: the food was bad, the movie wasn't good, the furniture was uncomfortable, you name it, and it is out there — for infinity.

Not only are your customers going to write the review or the post, they are going to video tape how dirty their room is, how dirty your parking lot is, the fact that you didn't fix their air conditioner and anything conceivable that you can imagine is going to be on video tape and within five seconds, it's going to be on YouTube for the entire world to see.

You tell me, right now, is it worth scraping the bottom of the barrel, to fill a position for a short period of time, when you could have waited a little longer, worked a little harder and got the right person?

Not only do you get bashed in social media when, from the customer perspective, things go haywire, now let's look at what happens from a back-end standpoint of your profit and operations costs from hiring the wrong people.

It's amazing how that supply closet can get raided from time to time and things just start missing when you hire the wrong people. If you're in the restaurant business, it is amazing how fast your food costs can quadruple when stuff starts to go missing. Employees start stealing this or stealing that; you see it on the reality shows I was discussing earlier, all the time. One hundred pounds of hamburger meat came in, fifty pounds disappeared— some dude's feeding his family with it. Paper clips, tape, pads, pencils, you name it; little things just start to disappear.

That short-term, unfit hire you made to fill that position doesn't seem like a great idea, when you start doing inventory and half of your inventory is missing.

Maybe those unfit hires aren't walking out the back door with your inventory. Maybe they're damaging your stuff while they're on the job? If you hire the wrong people, do they really care if they damage your stuff? Let's say you own a hotel, do they care if the walls are damaged or if stuff in the rooms is damaged or if chairs on the outside where people sit are damaged? No they don't, why should they?

These "wrong hires" only see you as a source of revenue for themselves, not a continuous source of future employment or a long-term career. They have a very short-termed way of thinking and behaving. They don't take care of your property or facilities. If there is paper in the parking lot, they won't clean it up.

What's the first thing the customer sees when they walk into your building? They see the parking lot. What message are you sending your clients and customers? This message: Your company takes customers and clients for granted, and not only is your parking lot dirty, your company is dirty as well, and you are not going to take care of them if there is an issue. Your customers understand that little things matter and a dirty parking lot is the first signal that the little things don't matter to your company.

I realize this is the "no duh" territory again and maybe I'm the only who's taking crazy pills, but I don't think so considering that you can get in your car right now and ride through any retail or business center parking lots and see endless amounts of trash and paper. I am not the only person that understands curb appeal is a reflection of a company's internal business practices.

## VIBRATION MATTERS

As I stated in an earlier chapter, the vibration within an office environment is extremely important to the success of a company. If you remember, that vibration starts with you. What if your vibration is correct and you hire or one of your employees hires someone with the wrong vibration?

Think of it this way: You've got a twenty-five person staff and you've hired three "wrong" people. Because of the three "wrong" people, there is now a bad vibe in your office. So you've got twenty-two right and three wrong.

Now, the entire office has been weakened, the morale is tanking, nobody gets along, and what happens when nobody gets along? For one thing, people start laying out of work and calling in sick.

Two, people stop doing their jobs. Three, people start behaving irresponsibly with equipment, supplies and inventory starts to disappear. Four, your clients start to question the bad vibe in your office and start to question you as the business owner or CEO. Office drama always negatively affects your clients and they do know when things are out of whack in your company.

But really, who pays the price for that negative vibe?

You do. A bad vibe and a weak morale in the office also equals less revenue for you and less creative energy to find new ways to make money and sustain current income levels.

A negative vibe and low morale in your office also trickles down to your vendors who also understand that nobody in that office can stand each other, and then they wonder if they are going to get paid because your staff can't get along and get them paid on time. You vendor has to call and beg for their money; they want to know if they're going to be paid on a thirty, sixty, ninety-day cycle or if they are going to get paid at all. Let's say the person handling the check writing is angry with their coworkers and office mates. Their first objective in the day is not to handle the vendor and their needs, but to make the other people's lives a living nightmare, professionally speaking, taking the knife and sticking it in their backs on a daily basis.

Why would you do that to your company and yourself by hiring the wrong people and allowing them to establish a negative vibe in your company?

Now, half the people in your office are at war with each other, and because of this internal war, your vendors are pissed off at you. What happens when the vendor is mad at you? They stop selling to you and they go on to someone else.

So how do you stop the bad vibe, the back–stabbing and the full scale civil war?

You've got to periodically come through and weed these "wrong" people out.

Now is good time to ask yourself, "How in the world did the wrong people get hired to begin with? Who's doing the interviews? Who's looking through the applications, the resumes and making the judgment calls on who is going to work for you, represent you and your company's image?"

I mean, seriously, how did these wrong people get inside of your company?

Most sane business people understand that if you are the CEO or business owner and you've got over one hundred employees, you don't have time to hire everybody, so you're expecting your Senior Vice Presidents or C–level executives to make these decisions.

So, let me ask you: Who hires a Senior Vice President or C–level exec?

You did.

Even if you used a head-hunter, a temporary agency, your own company HR department, or an executive search firm, you're still responsible.

You're the one who gave them a job description and they filled it. Is just filling that position what you wanted? Because an executive search firm or a head-hunter all get paid when they help you hire someone. They don't get paid based upon what type of person they hire because they are simply operating on fulfilling their job description requirements you provided them.

You gave them seven lines of a job description, and they got people in front of you that fit the description you gave them. They can only do what you've asked and you asked them to fill a position based on a few sentences you supplied to them.

If the position is Senior VP or C-level executive, more than likely, you made the final decision to hire them. This is your fault.

That's right; everything is your fault and here is why: Regardless of who hired who, you hired the top person in the chain of command that hired all the other people who work under them. So at the end of the day, you are still responsible for the employee who can't count money at the register and who is rude to the customers.

Now let me reiterate.

At the end of the day, if you are the owner or the CEO, all of these hires are your fault. I don't care if you own 300 stores in three different countries, the person that you gave authority to do the hiring, hired the wrong person. And at the time they hired the wrong person, they became a reflection of a standard that was relaxed by you.

Let's look at it this way. We all know that the bottom line of all business is money. How do you get more money in the door? How do you get more profit in the door? How do you get all of these things to work together so you stay in business?

You hire the right people. I realize, again, this is another "no duh" moment, but is it really?

In reality, everything is based on the behavior of the people who comprise your company. The behavior of the people that work for you will regulate the behavior of people that shop with you or do business with you or your vendors.

If your employees' behavior lives up to the standard that you established, you don't ever have to worry about the outside world's behavior towards your company. The money will always be there, goodwill will always be there, and the right people will always be doing business with you and the best and brightest will be lined up to work at your company.

## THE RIGHT THING

A question many employers ask is, "How do you hire the right people?"

It's often heard in society and I heard the very same thing so many times as a child: Do the right thing; hire the right people; do what's right.

Really?

What does that even mean? How do you know what the "right thing is?"

How do you know when the "right person" is sitting in front of you?

As a child, I asked so many times, "Somebody please define "the right thing" or "the right person" for me." I would have taken a photograph or a picture as a definition if somebody would have just supplied me with one!

I've reached middle age now and I'm still waiting on my definition. This seems to fit into the "no duh" category. For some strange reason, society thinks we automatically understand the definition of "the right thing" or "the right person."

You've got to decide what your definition for these two things are before you can fully understand what that means for your company.

And "what's right" or the "right person" is different for different people and different generations. What happens if the person hiring is a Baby Boomer, a Generation X-er or a Millennial? The terms "right" or "right person" take on completely different meanings. Take the guesswork out of the definitions so that the generational gaps don't matter. It is up to you as the boss to define exactly what you mean in very clear terms, what the "right person" is for your company.

## HIRE PEOPLE OF CHARACTER, NOT PEOPLE WHO ARE CHARACTERS

So let me get back to distinguishing between the "right people" and the "wrong people" when it comes to hiring.

Of course, everyone is going to say that you have to hire "people of character." Again, it is another nebulous term, which is interpreted differently by different people.

What's that really mean, character? And how do I know if the person has got character within a thirty-minute/hour long interview?

The only way to measure someone's character is through observation of his or her behaviors or interview people that have known them or observed them for an extended period of time.

Part of that "no duh" sequence of hiring are standard character traits that each new hire needs to possess. Just so we're all on the same page now, and we all have the "right person" definition, let's review some of the character traits that are a necessity in your employees:

## HONESTY

Of course, one of the character traits you want to look for is honesty. Yes, I realize this is not news to you and this is not the first time you've heard this statement. However, this seems to be an issue that continuously comes up in the business environment, so I felt the need to cover it once more.

How do you know if a potential employee is honest or not? For the most part, you don't. Of course, you will do your due diligence to check their reference and do a background check, but all of that information could be a façade. Yes, honesty is extremely important when someone is dealing with your money, your assets, and your reputation, on top of your client's assets, time, reputation and money.

Remember all of the missing items and company property damage I discussed earlier? You will want to make sure you understand that hiring a dishonest employee to "fill a spot" is going to cost you more than money—that unfit hire will cost you relationships, workplace harmony and will distract those around them from moving forward toward the vision of your company that you need to meet your financial, professional and personal objectives.

## ABOVE & BEYOND

Roll with me on this one...on the surface, this seems like a "no duh" but as we discovered in Chapter One, a person's programming can play a major role in how they perform on the job for you.

Of course you want somebody with an "above and beyond" attitude. Yes, this is as nebulous as "the right person." What does "above and beyond" really mean? Here's what it doesn't mean:

- Someone putting forth minimal effort for a pay check

- Taking endless amounts of smoke breaks on your time

- Clock watchers

- Someone who understands that they get paid by the hour, not by the footstep

- Individuals who confuse activity with production

Above and beyond can mean the following:

- Exceeds the required effort for their current position

- Doesn't care how many footsteps it takes to get the job done

- Get irritated because break time interferes with their job performance

- Understand that results are the most important part of their job

- Are very clear that the company must turn a profit in order for them to advance

- They understand that extra responsibilities are opportunities for them to show their extraordinary talents

- They took the clock down off the wall and only worry about the task at hand

For some, this type of attitude or drive just comes with them. It's part of who they are. Why is that? Remember, when you are hiring a person (let's say you hired an eighteen year old), you are hiring the last eighteen years of what was developed and programmed into them by their moms, dads, aunts, uncles, grandparents, teachers, social situations, financial situations, environment and behavioral situations.

Never forget, just like I covered in Chapter One concerning you, that employees are going to come to you as a person with their own bundle of behaviors and habits. Do you want that bundle of behaviors and habits to be part of your team? Above and beyond is a programmed behavior that will be part of the employee you hire. Make sure you understand who you are hiring before a job offer is issued.

## *APPEARANCE*

The next "character trait" is not considered a part of character by a lot of people, but for me, it is. It involves appropriate appearance. I am not asking for somebody to show up in a suit and tie in every circumstance, I'm asking for the candidate to have enough sense to be appropriately dressed for the job that they have to do.

Let's say that your employee works in the IT department — shorts and a t-shirt are perfect for that job many times because the folks don't normally interact with customers. Let's say an employee works on a dock. Again, they've got to have "dock appropriate" clothes for safety and clothes that will be able to withstand the wear and tear of the job.

But if your employee is in front of customers, what is it that you want the face of your company to be to the public? This is what your employees represent. So, if they show up for the interview with dirty, wrinkled clothing, even if it is a suit and tie, they are probably going to show up in front of your customers in dirty, wrinkled clothing.

Remember, if your employee is dirty and wrinkled, your customer is going to assume that the rest of your company is a reflection of the individual they are currently observing.

## *POSITIVE DISPOSITION*

This next character trait can make or break and entire department or company. Your employees must have a positive disposition. This sounds like a no-brainer but I see management hiring negative people based on a resume, instead of how this person will integrate into their company environment and relate to fellow employees and clients. Again, this is a "no duh" category and I'm dumbfounded when I encounter "black cloud" people in business situations, especially situations relating to customers.

When you look at a candidate, ask yourself: Is this person just naturally positive, or naturally negative? Is the glass half full or half empty with them? If something happens in their life, do they start to bitch or do they find a way to move around it? Are they just generally kind people? Are they a genuinely nice person?

Genuine kindness and positivity goes a long way to make your workplace a more harmonious and productive environment with your employees, vendors, customers and clients. Don't overlook this very important character trait. Earlier in this chapter, I discussed the two employees that greeted me in a positive manner. They had received no training from their employers, but understood a gracious way to greet another human being. A smart competitor would offer these two individuals a job and probably will at a later date!

## INTELLECT/MATURITY

The special educator in me wants to clarify what I mean by intellect. For years, I took my intellectually disabled students on job sites for the sole purpose of them developing job skills which would allow them to be independent adults later in life. The IQ level of the majority of the students I took for community and job skills ranged between thrity-five and seventy. I speak for many special educators when I say: an IQ score is not a measure of ability or desire. When I speak of intellect, I speak of an individual's ability to use prior knowledge as a way of overcoming and adapting to a new situation. My students couldn't perform every job an employer needed; however, we did prepare them for a job and they would perform that job to the best of their ability. The desire to perform will always outweigh an IQ without desire at all.

With that being said, there isn't one benefit to hiring stupid people. What do I mean by stupid? I think Forest Gump summed it up best: "Stupid is as stupid does."

Stupid people know better and do it anyway. Stupid doesn't pertain to IQ, it pertains to an outward display of a pattern of behavior that makes the onlooking audience shake their head and say, "What the hell is wrong with them?"

You must hire those who can think and do the job appropriately. Basically, you must match intellectual ability, maturity and behavioral ability. Your employees must be able to retain and display the information that you spent hours training them to use. That information must be observable once they are standing in front of a customer, a client or a fellow employee.

I am simply stunned and amazed at how many people are willing to train their employees over and over and over on the same tasks on a daily basis, while these employees continue to make the same mistakes, ad nauseum. I don't get it. This is costing precious time, money and resources. Get rid of this type of employee if you have them and make sure you don't make it a standard practice of hiring people who don't have the smarts or maturity level that is needed for the position.

## TRACK RECORD

Again, maybe I should call this a "by product" of character. Hire employees who can show you their professional, proven results of employment success.

You must have proof of proven results when you are hiring candidates in the sales, operations financial, IT, HR and executive positions in your company. Why? To be blunt, you just don't want to hire somebody who doesn't know what they are doing.

What's the fastest way to verify proven results? Call former employers, all their references, re-verify who the references are and listen to what they're saying (and NOT saying) about the candidate. We all know that the résumés lie; we all know that you can make up sales goals, and you can make up sales results. I am happy to see the trend with sales personnel that companies are taking when they ask for the candidate's W2. That's a given practice for sales, but do we do it for other positions as well?

It's unfortunate, but you must be aware that candidates will lie when you ask them directly about their proven results.

Lie? Really? Do they? Every single day.

Do people lie when they are trying to get hired? Yes they do.

Are people of flawed character going to get through your process sometimes? Yes they are. But you want to minimize it to 10% or less of the people that are vetted through this your hiring practices. People do lie, they do make stuff up and some people are great actors. It is true that you can fool some of the people some of the time so be on guard and make sure the applicant's actions relate directly to all verbal communication. Actions truly speak louder than words.

## THE HIRER

Since you are ultimately responsible for everyone who's hired within your company, you want to make sure the person interviewing the hiring candidates is a person of character as well. Again, the responsibility for everyone who's hired comes back to you as CEO and/or owner — this also includes the individual hiring everyone. It goes all the way down the chain, directly from your desk.

Personally, I am not a big fan of just using a "checklist" when interviews are being done. Checklists get the basics out of the way, but have no way of measuring the desire of the applicant. My position is that once the applicant has gone through the vetting process and has arrived for the personal interview, the interviewer needs to have the freedom to make a judgment call on the applicant. Some people call this a "gut feeling" or "certain vibe." As we've discussed in previous chapters, vibration is a key component to environment and success.

A good practice for companies is to allow "hirers" to have the freedom to hire the person they feel is best for the job, not just refer to or respond to a checklist or form. Hiring personnel need to develop the ability to examine behavior and identify candidates of the highest quality who will contribute the most to the company. This is a win–win for everyone involved. Why? Because these "hirers" generally have to turn around and train someone else on how to interview and hire candidates for the company. That way, the hiring "programming" and processes are being taught from the top down, which will ensure that from the bottom to the top, companies will always have the best employees.

## CHARACTER/BEHAVIOR REVEALERS

So how do you teach someone how to identify behaviors that reveal character? The easiest way is to ask questions associated with the task that the soon to be employee will be performing on a daily basis or ask questions that are based on characteristics that the company feels are important to their brand.

For example, if I interview someone who is going to be working with the public, I'll look them dead in the eye, not giving them much opportunity to get comfortable, and I'll launch in to the questions. It goes something like this:

"Say hello to me. I just walked into your establishment; I'm a customer and I need greeting. Go!"

I usually shout the word "go." It unnerves people and makes me laugh.

In my opinion, potential candidates HAVE to be able to think on their feet during an interview because that's what's going to happen with them when they are dealing with the public on a daily basis.

What's the reaction I am going to get from the candidate? I am going to get the sum total of their training and programming to this point because I have startled them by yelling, "Go!" Because I have just asked them to do an exercise that requires thinking on their feet when they're rattled and understanding how to treat a customer, whether they've ever had a job or not, their reaction is going to reveal their character and their programming. It's a really cool process to watch.

Let's say the person has never had a job; what are they going to say to me? Even if they've never had a job and have decent programming, they are still probably going to smile and say hello to me. That's a great answer for someone who's never had any training; at least they spoke to me. Like I said earlier, when I walk into establishments now, I'm lucky if anyone even speaks to me, so this kid is already ahead of the curve and in my book, he's already in the top percentile for good hiring potential candidates!

What they do in those five to ten seconds will tell you whether you should hire them or not. Do you really want someone who doesn't know how to address someone in public? Why in the world would you want to waste your money and time training an individual who doesn't possess basic social skills?

Basically, during these types of questions, I'm looking for the gut reaction of the person answering the questions. Are they smiling, are they kind, are they friendly, do I feel welcomed by their response?

When they answer, I'll know exactly if I want to hire them in five to ten seconds. By then, I've usually already made my decisions on whether or not to go any farther with this candidate.

You may be saying, how in the world can you tell anything in five to ten seconds?

Remember, I'm looking for individuals who have a positive disposition and are naturally friendly. I'll know in a few seconds if they fit that description.

Yes, I realize that certain departments have certain personality traits and in many industries, those personality traits are tolerated and excused. I don't subscribe to that way of thinking. I understand quirkiness can be part of certain areas of business and the individuals in those areas.

However, friendly is friendly and a positive vibration vibrates through an entire company. There's always room for moody and quirky at someone else's company.

I understand quirky 'cause I are one!

But I also understand that my quirkiness is no excuse for unfriendly or unsocial behavior with a fellow employee or client.

I like to keep the questions obviously based on what the job the candidate is going to do for my company. If the company is a retail establishment, I ask "retail related, gut reaction" questions. If the company is a wholesale establishment, I ask questions related to communicating on the phone more than greeting people in person. If it is a sales position, I take them out and put them in situations that they would experience in a "real life" sales scenario.

Some of the next questions I ask deal with workplace harmony. Because harmony in a company is so important, I want to know how they are going to deal with their fellow employees on day-to-day basis. The vibe in your company matters and harmony is a big reason employees will stay with your company.

My next question is usually something like, "If you have a disagreement with a fellow employee, how do you handle it? Go!" Remember, I shout the word "go."

Again, I am forcing them into a situation where they are revealing their gut reaction, which forces them into a behavioral situation where their reaction is going to be based on who they are as person, not what they "think" they ought to say or do or what they have been trained to do in an interview situation.

How did they answer it? Naturally, each company is going to have certain ways they want employees disagreements handled. Some people want it referred to superiors, some people want it referred to the actual person, and some people want it referred to HR. But those aren't the answers that you're looking for right now. You want to know what the candidate's gut reaction is regarding how they're going to handle a disagreement; because one little disagreement can turn into an office-wide disagreement if it is not handled properly and immediately.

The answer I always love to receive is the candidate looking directly back at me and saying, "I would handle it according to company policy once I've been hired and instructed on the procedure for handling disagreements." This answer tells me that the candidate understands their role in the company and that this isn't about them personally, but the company as a whole and they also understand that their personal actions are a reflection on the company. Plus, it also shows me that they understand that if they mishandle this situation in real life, unemployment is not far behind.

Next character revealing question: "If a customer, a vendor or a client uses profanity with you in an abusive way, how do you handle that type of situation? Go!"

Again, we all have those manuals that tell employees how to handle this situation. But again, I don't care about that right now. I want to see if they've ever encountered this situation or had to deal with it in the past. I'm looking more for a gut reaction that displays their programming or to see if they have received behavioral training on handling individuals that display hostile or difficult behaviors.

The responses received during this process can be very entertaining. I once had an individual tell me that they would just scream profanity back in the client or employee's face and if the client or employee did not shut up, they would just smack 'em! I gave this person an "A" in entertainment value for me and recommended working with the public was probably a bad idea for them. I did tell them that I appreciated their honesty and wished them well for their future. In one question, I was able to decide yes or no based on a real life scenario that eventually, would take place in work environment.

If the candidate's programming tells them to scream back when someone is screaming profanity in their face, how do you think they're going to react in a real life situation? They are going to go with their gut reaction, scream back, and cost you money, customers, time, resources and a possible lawsuit in the process.

Let me reiterate why you are asking these questions the way I'm telling you to ask them. The questions and the reactions are all based on a person's programmed, subconscious behavior. That behavior is based on the programming that they've received throughout their lifetime. During a high-pressure situation, a person will fall back on a natural programmed way of handling a situation. You want to make sure you are not hiring someone who has flawed programming and who will display that flawed programming at your place of business.

When you are able to get someone to do something quickly, without the opportunity to think about the situation in an in-depth manner, the only reaction they have to fall back on is based on their previous programming and training prior to meeting you. Remember, the programming they have received is based on the three charts I included in Chapter One.

So let's say you ask a candidate to greet a customer and their response is "W'assup?" You know this candidate probably isn't going to work for your company if your public expects employees who can communicate in an effective manner. I actually had this response to my question one day. I busted out laughing and thanked the individual for stopping by. End of interview.

Any time a person is placed in a position of reaction and can no longer be proactive, and can only be reactive, they are going to react the way they always react—no matter the location. Programming is not going to lie.

Now you've revealed what his or her gut reaction is going to be with every single customer or client that walks into your establishment. Because employees do get caught off guard, have bad days, or go through tough times, we need to hire employees whose gut reactions are going to match the company's ideal profile of customer treatment.

That's the whole purpose of these character and programming, behavior—revealing interview questions. You want candidates to reveal who they and how they are going to handle a certain situation immediately. That way, you have magically erased the power of a puffed up resume, a great acting job or a string of pathological lies as long as your arm.

Okay, now imagine you've sat through an hour-long interview which provided a fairly good picture of who the person is and how he/she will act in any given situation.

You've just been able to gauge within a matter of seconds how this candidate is going to handle things in your company when the going gets tough. We all know that if you are working somewhere and you are dealing with the public, people are going to call in sick. There's always going to be a shortage of enough help and the workplace is going to turn into a pressure cooker. How are your people going to react to it? Are they going to react positively and just get the job done, or are they going to react negatively and take their frustrations and ill temperament out on your customers and fellow employees?

So let's say the potential employee gets through the "gut reaction" check. Your hiring staff approves them and says, "Yes I would like to have them on my team." Then hire them!

Again, let's go back over this: you put your hiring staff in the position to be your legs, your thoughts, your feelings, and to be a representative of your company. Let them be! Let them do their jobs! These folks are building their team as well as yours. The candidates generally have to work for people hiring them, not you. Let them govern their kingdom. You gave them the job, let them do it.

## BAD SEEDS

Let's discuss what happens when an occasional bad seed gets in. No matter how good the process or your people, it sometimes happens. Some people are good lairs, good actors, and good fakers. They can fake it for about a month and then you eventually weed them out. As long as you identify the bad seed, and get rid of them quickly before they affect the rest of the company morale, don't stress over it. But don't let the bad seeds hang around, either. Cut it off quickly and cleanly and move on to better candidates. Don't beat yourself up over it, but don't let it continue either.

If you've got a manger that has a track record of hiring the wrong person, you must deal with it. Don't stick your head in the sand and hope that they'll do better next time.

Here is a tip on how to handle this situation: First of all, remember that every single person in your company, whether it's two people or 20,000 people, is a reflection of you, you personally, and you professionally. Period.

Your employees are going to mimic everything that you do and the tone you set. You set your tone through the people you hire from senior management on down.

Let's say somebody has a string of bad hires, whose fault is it? For one it's yours, because you, either directly or indirectly, put whoever was in the position to hire this person in place. But let's take that off the table for a second.

Because accountability is important in every step that is taken, my position is that whomever hired the person who is doing a crappy job is in just as much trouble as the person who's had the string of bad hires. That's called accountability. It's used in sports and the military all the time. When things go wrong, the entire team is responsible. When things go right, the entire team is responsible.

Let's say you've got a retail establishment or a call center and you've got three or four bad seeds at your company. They're rude to customers, they steal, they don't do their jobs, they text instead of helping customers, and basically, they are doing anything and everything but what they were hired to do.

Whose fault is that? Well, for one it's the employee—they've got to go! Who else should be fired? In my opinion, anybody that even touched that hire. I would fire them on the spot. Because now, the hirer has proven they have flawed character, flawed judgement, and they are going to reflect badly not only on you, but also your company, your mission, and your vision as a leader in your company. They all have to go.

Here's the thing: If there is scrutiny during every single hiring interview, every single new employee should be scrutinized. Here is what I mean. There shouldn't be any weak links in the chain, except the occasional bad seed who might be a good actor who thinks well on their feet. But normally, when it comes to questions like greeting the public, dealing with internal infighting or handling inappropriate behaviors, you get a feel for who is going to be the right fit for your company.

If the hiring staff can't identify the right candidates correctly, why shouldn't they lose their job in addition to the bad seed employee? They hired the wrong people, they trained them, and they're the one that is spending forty hours a week with this new employee. This is not the first time this new employee's inappropriate behavior has been displayed.

And normally, if the new employee's offense is a fireable one, it is definitely not been displayed for the first time on the job — they've probably already displayed these behaviors on break, at lunch, at home, etc. Why didn't somebody see it? Why not? Because the person you had in charge is flawed and is not being held accountable for the bad hire.

*A flawed person with flawed character has no room in your*

*company because at <u>all times</u> they will reflect badly on you, your image, and affect your bottom line.*

Let me go over this point.

Many people may disagree with me, but this is a point I have watched replicate over and over and over again in the academic and business world concerning flawed character.

**You cannot train flawed character out of someone.** If they are a bad person and a bad seed, they are a bad person and a bad seed. You can't train it out of them. You can't change them.

Here's why:

They don't want to change!

Why would you want to take on this responsibility? You aren't running a community jobs program for misfits. You are running a for profit company that's a reflection of you as a person. Always be willing to let your competitors hire the misfits.

The dollars are too important, and your time and the company's time is way too important to continuously hire the wrong people, fire them and then recoup all the losses that have taken place due to stealing, customer dissatisfaction, property damage, and the list goes on and on. So keep in mind when you are hiring people, you cannot train flawed character out of flawed people. It won't work; it is never going to work. Don't waste your time on trying to hire these people.

No matter how low your "bad seed percentage" is, you still need to go through and weed these bad seeds out, probably every single month or every quarter just to make sure you are getting rid of the deadwood that is preventing your company from being everything you want it to be.

# THE TEST

Once I've hired and trained by your designated trainer, it's a good practice to test their knowledge.

A casual way to do this is to walk up to them and ask them questions. No, not the questions you asked them in the original interview, but questions based "company specific" issues and policies.

New hires could receive questions like, "What's our company policy for greeting people?" or "What's our company policy for customers who have a complaint?"

This is a quick way to see if they know the answers and to check proper training protocol. Sometimes, wrong actions or answers truly aren't the employee's fault; it is the trainer's fault. And if it is the trainer's fault, you can address that with the trainer in private.

A best practice is to establish some form of accountability in all areas of your company. One practice used is "mystery shopping" which allows the "company shopper" an unfiltered view of the actions and behaviors of the employees being observed. Many companies use this practice as a way to gauge hiring and training policies. This practice can be performed on the wholesale and retail level.

My oldest son is a restaurateur and a sommelier. For years, he has managed and invested in unusual and eclectic restaurants. I'm happy to say as a proud father, I've had an opportunity to watch my son do several grand openings and evaluate his performance on a personal and professional level. It is a pleasure to watch him work. Understand that me telling this story, I'm not cutting him any slack because he is my child. I am using this story as an illustration because after numerous observations, I watched what I would consider the best display of managerial skills I've ever seen pertaining to the operation of a restaurant. My son is a big believer in performance and customer satisfaction. During each grand opening, I watched him endlessly grill his staff on company policy and procedure and as one employee told me (out of earshot of my son), "Failure was not an option."

Of course, all of his questions were asked while the staff was doing their jobs, under pressure, when the restaurant was full. They were being forced to think on their feet, while in motion, which placed them in a position to provide only gut reactions. If the employees made it through the evening, they were retained on a full time basis. My son has no problem permanently excusing employees who do not meet his standards.

Sound familiar?

Now this may sound very harsh to many, but in reality, he has very little staff turnover because he hires the right people, he vets them during the heat of a shift and tests how they mesh with the other staff members. In one shift, he knows how each individual will gel with the restaurant staff and customer base. He expresses his expectations up front and if the individual doesn't meet the expectation, the individual is terminated immediately.

He is very clear, he is very fair, and he makes sure he hires qualified people and he provides very, very thorough training. This process has allowed my son to make his mark on the restaurant industry.

He uses the "Greet me" question. Let me express that I did not teach him how to do any of the things he does. He developed this entire process on his own.

I am very proud to say that my son is one of the top restaurateurs in the United States and he does it right. Many restaurateurs come to observe my son to learn how to make sure they always get it right when it comes to hiring. He makes me very proud.

## ARE THEY QUALIFIED?

Yes, we're back to a "no duh" section of this chapter. Since common sense seems to no longer be common, I've got to address hiring employees who are qualified for the positions. This is not ground shaking news or the first time you have ever heard this information. However, just because you heard it doesn't mean you've listened to any of the information provided to you.

I, like many, see this all the time in companies. Fraternity buddies are great, but only if they are hireable. Sorority sisters are great, but only if they are qualified. I understand brother and sisterhood, but really, let's all make sure that your brother or sister is a competent individual that brings skills remotely connected to the job they're expected to perform for adequate compensation.

An even stickier topic is family in business. Now, I know you are going to have a nephew, an uncle, or a cousin that wants a job or a family member that keeps asking you to hire them. I understand you can pick your friends, but unfortunately, you're stuck with your family and family normally doesn't care how much they bug you or infringe on your time or you financially.

Should a family member or close friend work for your company?

Should your own brother work for your company? Sometimes this is just not a good fit. Just like any other candidate, you've got to pull their resumes out. You may already know their references because they are your family, but would you hire them if you didn't know them? Would you want them working with your customers on a daily basis? Because the reputation at stake is now yours and your company's, not theirs. People are going to judge you based on their actions. Just because your brother could make fart noises or burp out the alphabet when he was a kid doesn't mean he's qualified to be a part of your professional team. You can love someone, but recommend someone else hire him or her.

So when it comes to family, make sure they are qualified. I know a lot of times business owners are asked to give family members a break. When you are asked to give a family member a break, what does that normally mean? They've screwed up something and they call you and say, "Hey man, just give him a chance, I know he has messed up in the past, but he is not going to screw up this time." Do you really want him screwing up on your dime, and on your reputation? No, let somebody else do that.

But if it is a great family member or friend and they are highly qualified, highly motivated, and reflect you and your company's mission, knock it out, hire them!

## MATCH STYLE WITH THE JOB

Your employees have to reflect and match the same psyche, tastes and preferences that your customers display.

I wouldn't want to go into a tattoo shop where no one had a tattoo! I've got piercings in my ears, and I look a little different than your normal behavior/business consultant. I make it a practice to always go to tattoo parlors when I get my piercings. Why? Those guys know what they are doing, that's their profession and I want my guy covered in tattoos from head to toe. He needs to look the part when I come in, which increases my comfort level, which provides me with a positive experience and gives me a reason to not only come back to that establishment but also be a referral source for that business owner.

An unusual place, but enjoyable one, is Dick's Last Resort. If you've never been there, it's a place where the waitstaff insults customers. Management doesn't normally look for congenial people to hire and work in this establishment. Nice people need not apply. The attraction of the place is dealing with a waitstaff that is hateful and spiteful, but witty and funny. Their job is to ridicule customers and create and energetic and unusual atmosphere. This company wants people with quirky personalities that match the expectations of the customers. If you dislike one of your siblings, make sure you take them for dinner. The wait staff will make sure you enjoy your evening.

A good friend of mine is a custom tailor and when he comes to see me, I expect to see a version of Cary Grant walking through the door. My expectation is for him to be the walking embodiment of the sharp dressed man. I can say he hasn't failed me yet.

One last example is the salon I go to get my hair done. I have very long hair, especially for someone my age. I am very particular about who touches my hair and of course, the girl who does my hair has long hair herself, colored with many colors of the rainbow. She fits my expectation of someone I would choose as my hairdresser. She matches her profession and her customer base.

Your employees and your customer/client expectations have to match.

Make sure that the employee's personality and skills match their assigned job. It's a plus if they enjoy the job.

Now I know that you are going to pay them a pay check at the end of the week, they are going to work for forty hours and they had better do their jobs — I get all that.

But wouldn't it be beneficial to your bottom line and your customer base to match your employees and their personalities with a job that fits who they are and allows them an opportunity of enjoyment during their time working for you?

If you've hired a bubbly person, where do you want that fun, bubbly person located? Greeting customers! Because he or she is fun, they make the customers feel comfortable and their personality provides a party like atmosphere. Who better to be the first smile to greet a returning or potential customer?

When life is a party, customers spend more money and tell all of their friends, family and coworkers why your company is the party that can't be missed. I say, "party on!"

Likewise, if you have hired a person who's a little withdrawn or shy, you may want to place them in a position that does not require initial customer contact but allows them more individual space and less direct contact with other people.

Yes, this takes some effort and consideration but matching someone's personality to their job task is an effective way to boost morale, increase employee longevity and provide opportunity for the individual employee to grow within your company.

# IT'S A NEVER – ENDING JOB BEING THE BOSS

Let's say everything is going right. You hired the right person, they are doing everything you've asked, you've matched their skill set to the job, and you can trust them with the customer.

Now what? Always re-remind your employees of these facts:

- What the company mission and vision is;

- The customers they serve pay their pay checks by purchasing goods and services from the company;

- If the company doesn't make money at the end of the day, neither will the employees;

- When sales decrease, available employment opportunities decrease;

- Every single person in your company is a reflection of you and you will be watching to make sure that that projection and reflection is accurate;

- People will judge you the CEO or owner personally based on the outcome of their experience with your employees

I realize that on the first day of hiring, you are going to cover the "do and don'ts" of the job and chances are, you've already got a employee manual for the employee to read, but review is a great reinforcer. You must continually review, train and drill your employees about your policies, your procedures and your mission and vision.

Issues will arise without clear understanding and clear expectations shared between management and employees. An issue I am seeing on the rise in each business I observe is cell phone usage. As I discussed earlier, I have literally had to ask employees to get off their phone to check me out or wait on me or handle something I needed as a customer. On two occasions, I have placed calls to a call center and could tell the person is doing social media or texting while they are supposed to be handling my issues. One even made a reference to his fantasy football team! The best was when I called into a center and the employee asked me to hang on while he finished his personal call. The problem is; he didn't put me on hold and I could hear the entire conversation. I really enjoy having to tap teenagers on the shoulder to get them to bag my groceries because they are in the middle of an engrossing conversation with someone on their cell phone.

I know all of the companies have existing policies in place regarding cell phone usage and employee expectations. So why am I constantly having to deal with this highly irritating and angering issue?

Because expectations are unclear, policies and procedures are not being reviewed and management isn't doing their job.

## WE WOULD APPRECIATE YOU WORKING FOR SOMEONE ELSE

I would be remiss if I didn't cover the reasons why an employer needs to let inept, unfit employees, bad seeds and wrong hires find the unemployment line in a swift and timely fashion. Yes, I realize this fits in the "no duh" category, or at least I thought it fit in that category until I began my observations for this book. Apparently, several business owners did not receive the "no duh" memo on hiring and firing. During this section, I will cover what I originally assumed to be "no duh" termination policies. Clear explanation and expectation are extremely important for your business, especially regarding termination of employment. Now if you will allow me, I will highlight a few simple guidelines:

1. Provide to the employee in written and verbal form, clear expectations of acceptable on the job behavior and the guidelines of your personal conduct policy.

2. Provide periodic reviews of those policies and provide answers to employee concerns and mis-understandings.

3. In the event an employee violates a very clear policy, take the needed steps to terminate the employee swiftly and immediately.

4. Terminate employees in private whenever possible.

## FIREABLE OFFENSES

### Stealing

Fireable offenses usually include stealing and this seems to be a no-brainer to me, but lately, I'm seeing a lot of companies give employees unlimited numbers of "do-overs" regarding theft. We'll give you another chance. Really? What the heck?

Let's say a burglar came into your house tonight and stole everything you had. Are you going to invite him back over for dinner the next week? Why in the world would you let somebody who just stole from you come back?

I see this in a lot of family owned companies. "Well, we just need to give him another chance," is what someone invariably says. Another chance to what? Get everything he didn't get the last time and have a U-Haul come over and clean us out?

No, thank you. Immediate termination.

**Sex**
Sex on the job? On company time?

Believe it or not, this is the one that seems to be an increasing on the job issue. Now, I remember when I was in high school, I wasn't always Mr. Goody Two Shoes, but as wild as I was, I didn't even do this on the premises or on company time. I mean, let's be real; if you want to have sex, that's great; that's your personal life, but really, just not on company time or premises. Please understand; I'm not a prude. I enjoy sex as much as the next person.

If I'm a company owner or CEO, I am not paying employees to have sex if I am not in the adult film industry, so therefore, I'm not writing a check for two employees to do this on company time or my premises. If I am in the adult film industry, I'm only going to pay employees for the time they are clocked in and filming a scene!

**Alcohol**
Drinking on the job?

I remember back in the day, when I was a teenager, I sat and drank with the owner on the job. Is that a good practice? Hell no! I was also underage at the time and the establishment wasn't a bar!

In no way, shape, or form should that be tolerated either by yourself or anybody on your staff. If you own a bar, alcohol is to be consumed by your customers, not your employees. If you don't own a bar, why would anybody be drinking on the job anyway? Again, you are not paying these people to get drunk; you are paying these employees to offer a service to your customers and carry out the duties of their employment. I have personally observed employees taking a couple of nips on the job while I was doing my observations for this book.

## Drugs

I feel almost crazy for having to mention this, but after observing several employees who had obviously puffed the magic dragon before clocking in, I feel I need to say it!

Drugs. Same deal as alcohol. You can't tolerate drug use at the workplace (not even in the parking lot). Even employees in legal marijuana distribution facilities are not allowed to spark it up while they're on the clock. Again, employees are there to work. No drug use in any form should EVER be tolerated.

## Porn

My father-in-law owns several banks and has been the CEO of a few and on the board of a few more and has consulted with them for years. He's had to fire countless numbers of CEOs and Bank Presidents from his banks for watching porn while on the job.

Wait a minute. What? You read it right, bucko—watching porn on company time on company computers—computers that the board of directors can examine at any time.

It blows my mind that an employee can even consider that this type of behavior would go unchecked or undiscovered. In this age where every single keystroke and click of the mouse can be checked and verified, why in the world would an employee take the chance? If an employee doesn't have enough sense to use their smart phone instead of your company computer to watch porn, then do you really want this idiot working for you?

100% termination, no questions asked.

## Threats/Abuse

Physical threats or abuse towards employees, vendors, customers or clients of the company unless it is self defense, is never to be tolerated in the workplace and should be treated as an immediate and swift fireable offense.

If the situation is truly self defense, let your employee defend themselves, but immediately involve law enforcement so that your company, vendors, other employees, customers and clients are protected. The "Ex Factor" — ex-husbands, ex-wives, ex-love, ex-boyfriends or girlfriends — for some reason, love to show up at the workplace to cause trouble for their interested parties. Make sure that you have policies and practices to protect your employees from this situation if it ever occurs.

Make sure that your employees understand that abusive behavior will not be tolerated. Make sure these policies are handled in a verbal and written fashion during time of employment. Issues of this nature need to be handled in a systematic way that has been previously outlined in the employee handbook or manual.

Bad seeds create bad vibes and bad vibes are your competitor's problem.

## No Shows

Not showing up for work without notifying management, in my opinion, is grounds for termination. In this day and age of technology where most everyone can send an email, text or make a phone call with someone else's cell phone, it's virtually impossible not to have access to some form of communication that will allow management to know that the employee is unavailable.

I live in a major metropolitan area. Sometimes, because of an accident, it could be six hours before your employee could get to their place of business. But, most people usually have their cell phones with them in their cars. They can always call.

Make sure that your employees are very clear regarding your expectation pertaining to no shows and late arrivals. When this type of behavior occurs over and over in the workplace, company productivity and morale are impacted immediately.

If this type of behavior is not addressed immediately, the individuals will continue the behavior until you are forced to address the issue. Save yourself time and frustration by dealing with the behavior swiftly, clearly and immediately.

## SUMMARY

As we close out this chapter, keep the following in mind: Hiring and firing isn't difficult if you have clearly defined rules of how to hire and fire and you follow them. The rules allow you, the employer, to make objective decisions based on a pre-determined criteria that benefits your company and your employees. Since each employee is an extension of you, the clearly defined rules will ensure that you are represented in the manner you desire. You are the zombie apocalypse leader! Remember, it's not them, it's you.

# CHAPTER 4

# BUILDING YOUR UNIT

As a former coach, regardless of level, I understood that it was my job to put together a team that would function as a unit. In order to build that unit and make that unit cohesive, I had to answer two questions for the members of the team:

1. What's in it for me?
2. Why should I?

If I could answer those two questions satisfactorily for each team member, I knew I would have a cohesive unit that functioned with one heartbeat and the opportunity for success was optimal. If I did not answer those two questions satisfactorily for each member, I knew the season would be filled with daily arguments, complaints about playing time, disgruntled parents, a lack of discipline, academic issues, more losses than wins and the season would feel like it lasted for years instead of months. Yes, I know you agree with me, answering the two questions satisfactorily is the only way to produce a desired outcome.

How did I do it?

## RIGHT PLAYERS/RIGHT EMPLOYEES

As we've discussed earlier in the book, hiring the right employee makes all the difference in your company's success or failure. The business of coaching is no different. Yes, you must have players on your team with incredible talent, but you can't choose talent over cohesion and teachability. Just because a kid possessed an amazing amount of talent doesn't mean that kid was given an opportunity to play on the team. Talent doesn't necessarily translate into an ability to communicate, endless effort, understanding, a desire to learn and grow, a general concern for teammates or a desire to make the others around him/her better. Self-absorbed people will not buy into a team concept and will eventually destroy team chemistry and weaken your company. Something important to keep in mind is the fact that self-absorbed people will never be happy with you or your company, regardless of how you answer the previously posed questions. If you hire them, they will continuously sew discontent and dissension throughout your company.

Remember the behavior revealing questions we discussed in the hiring chapter? Those questions serve as a "tryout" for potential employees and gave you a chance to not only see their talent, but to also evaluate their relationship skills. The answers they provided you during the interview allow you to decide whether this individual could not only produce results, but also be part of a cohesive team that functions as a unit on a daily basis.

## ANSWERING THE QUESTIONS

Since you've done your due diligence, provided a tryout period and picked your squad, you can answer the two important questions that will build your cohesive unit. There are certain things that you, as the employer, can provide that will answer the two questions "Why should I?" and "What's in it for me?" for your staff and team on a daily basis.

## PAY

Yes, people show up at work for a paycheck. If the amount's large enough, they will show up regardless of opportunity or treatment – for a while. A pay stub just isn't enough to keep talented people as part of your team. Eventually, someone will offer them equivalent pay and more intangibles than you are willing to provide. At that time, they will pack their stuff, wave goodbye to you and move on to a perceived better opportunity. A paycheck will never be enough to keep a team together.

## OPPORTUNITY

Every single kid that ever played in our program was looking for an opportunity for playing time. In the high school arena, playing time meant more popularity at school, potential newspaper clippings, TV interviews, county-wide recognition, a chance to be in the record books and, if the player was talented enough, an opportunity to play in college and receive a free education. Depending on how his/her college game progressed, playing pro ball could eventually be a possibility in this individual's life.

Your employees are looking for the same things. The employee wants to know if they will receive a chance to show their skills, be recognized for those skills, have an opportunity to win awards for those skills, be praised for those skills, be promoted for those skills and receive the big payday for those skills. If the employee feels that you provide opportunities within your company, they will understand why they should work extremely hard on a daily basis and the benefits they will receive for the hard work.

## CLEAR EXPECTATIONS AND CONSEQUENCES

As a coach, once I decided on the individuals that were to be a part of our team for the season, I outlined my expectations not only concerning basketball, but also concerning academics and personal actions. I was very clear when I explained those expectations and the players could quote the expectations verbatim. I never expected my players to read my mind or read between the lines. I knew that if I did not verbally express it in a clear, understandable way, I could not expect those kids to understand my meaning or understand what was expected.

All my players knew there were consequences for not meeting those expectations and those consequences would be immediate and fair. The reason I use the word fair is because no player was above the rules. Every single individual, including myself, was held responsible for an expected code of conduct. Once the expectations were explained during a team meeting, all team members understood the expectations and rules would be enforced immediately.

My players appreciated the fact that I was very clear on what I expected of them as players and people and the fact that they could depend on me to enforce the rules swiftly and without favoritism.

Your employees are no different than my ball players. Since your goal is to build a cohesive unit, your team members expect a clear and simply explained set of rules that govern daily operations. At no time should your employees be expected to read your mind or read between the lines or understand an implied rule. It is your job to communicate clearly and effectively all expected and enforced expectations.

Your employees/team members also expect equal treatment

under those rules and to receive consequences outlined by those rules. Your team members need to know that at all times they can depend on you to be clear and objective when it comes to dealing with their fellow team members.

Your employees/team members will never mind consequences that are attached to clear expectations and equally enforced throughout the team. Dissension takes place when those clear consequences are not enforced equally when dealing with certain team members. Subjective consequences destroy morale and dissolve any team unity.

When establishing your clear set of expectations and consequences, be sure you can also live under the weight of your own words. Your employees will respect you as a leader and as a boss if your expectations of them are clearly defined and clearly enforced. At no time, will they ever question, "What's in it for them" if you are fair and objective.

## UNIQUE ENVIRONMENT

### Trust

Most high school ball teams have a gym, locker rooms, uniforms, warm ups, sneakers, balls, nets and goals. From a physical perspective, there is very little that is unique about being part of a ball team. All the teams begin the season on the same date and the regular season ends on the same date. For many ball teams and schools, the only difference between the ball teams is uniform color. As a coach, I understood that I had thirteen completely different individuals. It was up to me to establish an environment that allowed those thirteen individuals to display their personalities, share their uniqueness, showcase their talents and provide an avenue for the things that made them special to shine. In allowing thirteen completely different people to share their uniqueness with the entire team, we grew strong and cohesive as a unit. In order to get those thirteen individuals on that same page, we had to build trust as a team first. The kids had to trust the fact that I had picked thirteen individuals that gave them an opportunity to compete and win. They also had to trust that I had their best interest at heart, that they could share their dreams with me and trust that I had the knowledge and the know how to get them to where they wanted to be as a ball team. As most athletes can tell you, a locker room is a unique environment where trust is a premium. I realized I wasn't just a coach; I was a father, a leader, a counselor, a teacher, a driver, an instructor, a sounding board, an encourager, a disciplinarian, a scheduler, a cheerleader and a swift kick in the pants when they needed it.

To further build trust, I would sit down with each player at the beginning of the season and outline what I saw as their role with the team, their current skill level, their academic performance level, their personality traits and temperament, their top three gifts and talents and areas of needed improvement. Once the conversation had taken place, I made sure that my players could count on me to remember what had been said and live up to the guidelines that had been established during our conversation. They understood that at no time would I lie to them, betray their confidence, "sugar coat" anything, mislead them or let them down when it came to fulfilling my end of the bargain. Yes, throughout the season, there are bumps in the road, needed attitude adjustments, "motivational" conversations, and consequences to be dealt. At no time did I ever give my players a reason to doubt their trust in me.

## Family Atmosphere

Trust is one way to build a unique atmosphere. Establishing a culture of "family" is another way to build a unique atmosphere within your corporate structure. No, I'm not talking about a traditional family. My traditional family when I was a kid was a disaster and my home life was awful! Also, when I say "family," I don't mean a continuous supply of hugs, singing songs around a campfire, excusing poor performance, group circles where we share our feelings or snacks provided by me. I mean an environment where grievances are handled methodically and differences of opinion are handled "in house," an understanding that thirteen people have your back at all times, respect had to be earned, that no individual is bigger than the team, an acceptance that if someone's having a "bad game," the other individuals have to step it up, and a clear expectation that no matter what happens, we face it as a team. As the "father figure" of our locker room family, the kids expected me to be the leader and the keeper of the code that existed within our family structure.

## Like-Mindedness

No family can survive without a central message or vision. Regardless of position or playing time, a team cannot be successful without possessing like-mindedness. If a player was ever unsure of whom he/she represented, I instructed them to read the name on the front of their jersey. Each time they suited up, the name on the front of the jersey always mattered more than the name on the back of the jersey. Our vision as a team revolved around our dedication to that jersey, the name on the front of that jersey and each individual that wore that jersey on a game-to-game basis. As a collective group, we understood that a successful season depended on us having a clearly defined vision, constant focus and a "do whatever it takes attitude." Everyone understood what we, as a team, had to gain.

**Time To Shine**

Once the game starts, a coach will tell you, "It's out of our hands." The next four quarters or two halves will show us how well we are doing our jobs. Part of doing our jobs is allowing our players to assume responsibility for their role on the team during the game.

During practice that week, we covered all the aspects of our opponent, each individual's role and how to handle specific situations. Once the whistle blows, the players take responsibility for executing the game plan. I allowed my players the freedom to read the game as it flowed and choose the best way to attack their defense and execute on offense.

My captains served as my voice on the floor and I allowed them to do their job. I could trust my players to display their skills when the team needed them the most and work as a unit for all four quarters to get the job done. Our system was in place; I had to be smart enough to get out of my players way and let them play.

The outcome of the game wasn't based on all of the fancy plays I drew up during the time outs—our winning or losing was based on our execution of fundamentals, our work ethic, our focus, our communication, trusting each other to do our jobs, and our overall desire to compete as a team. Our reward for our efforts would be displayed on the scoreboard at the final buzzer.

**Express Value**

Once the season concludes, most programs have some form of season ending celebration. This gives us as coaches an opportunity to express our gratitude to the school, the parents, our fans and our players.

Before the banquet, I normally met with players to review his/her performance during the season and let them know what needed to be worked on in the off-season. I gave them a clear picture of the coming season and their role on the team. At that time, they had an opportunity to vocalize any concerns and decide if they would accept their role for the upcoming season.

I wanted my players to understand their options, but also understand their value in my life and in the lives of their team members. During the banquet/celebration, I had an opportunity to express my gratitude to all thirteen players in front of everyone.

This night wasn't about discussing statistics and performance; it was about expressing to the world my personal feelings and thoughts on those thirteen individuals that chose to be part of a team and become a family. It was my time to speak boldly about their individual gifts and how our team was a starting point for the rest of their lives. Their value was clearly displayed throughout the season as being part of our team, but their real value still was yet to be uncovered and would be displayed throughout their lives for the rest of the world to see.

## BUILDING YOUR UNIT

I told you how I built my team and unit and now I will supply some guidelines that will allow you to build a cohesive unit within your company.

### *RIGHT PLAYERS/RIGHT EMPLOYEES*

- Make sure you do your due diligence on hiring candidates backgrounds

- Ensure that candidates' resumes aren't fiction

- Ask behavior revealing questions during the interview

- Hire intelligent, competent people

- Hire individuals with a positive disposition

- Secure people that display effective communication skills

- Hire individuals that are teachable

- Hire people smarter than you

- Be very clear on your expectations of their performance and behavior and be consistent with correction or instruction based on those expectations

## *PAY/COMPENSATION*

- Pay a fair wage for the position

- Expect production for the wage provided

- Reward exceptional performance by establishing realistic and measurable goals

- Do not change compensation plans to take money out of employees' pockets to put into yours

  - Once the compensation plan is established, stick to it. Remember, your employees base their monthly and yearly budgets on the established compensation plans that you agreed to honor.

  - If you are forced to change the compensation plan due to unforeseen events in the business cycle, explain the changes in detail to all parties that are affected by the changes. This just isn't about dollars;

it's about lives and the impact on individuals and their families.

- Compensate each department for meeting their goals

- Pay doesn't have to come in the form of a raise — ask your employees for ideas on ways to compensate them in more ways than just money!

## *OPPORTUNITY*

- Realize that the "right" employees desire opportunity within your company

- Recognize exceptional performance with job enhancements and additional job responsibilities that provide the opportunity for the employee to display their exceptional skills

- Promote the deserving!

- Don't play favorites

- Reward above and beyond performance

- Give employees opportunities to "try out" different departments within your company

- Ask your employees what opportunities they would like to be offered

## *CLEAR EXPECTATIONS AND CONSEQUENCES*

- Provide crystal clear job performance expectations

- Provide crystal clear behavior expectations

- Enforce job and performance expectations

- Be objective, not subjective

- Follow your company policies that are in writing

- Provide immediate consequences at all times

- "Fair" means following through with "pre-explained" expectations and consequences

- Remember that consequences are neither good nor bad; they are just outcomes of a behavior

- Employees appreciate clear expectations and outcomes

- Clear expectations combined with follow through build trust in a corporation

## UNIQUE ENVIRONMENT

- You must earn your employees' trust

- Trust is an essential part of a cohesive team

- Job competence builds trust

- Following through with consequences builds trust within your company

- Create a family atmosphere within your company

- Create and live out a unified vision for your company

  - Make sure every single employee understands the vision for the company and how that vision impacts their job

- Make sure your employees know you have their back

- Give your employees the freedom to make decisions

- Your employees were competent enough to hire, so leave them alone and let them do the job you hired them to do

- Openly praise hard work that produces results—all departments need "press clippings"

- Handle internal matters discretely within the confines of "the family"

- Express appreciation to your employees for doing their job

- Reward hard work, focus, dedication and results with generous compensation

- Allow employees to express their opinions on how to provide solutions to company problems

  - One smart solution could save your company millions of dollars

- Always praise in public

- Handle negative consequences privately

- If a rule or procedure needs to be changed, make sure the change is beneficial to the company

- Keep in mind that you establish the daily tone for the company by your actions—you establish "the vibe" in your company's environment

The difference between winning and losing can be fractions of a second. The difference between you and your competitors needs to be worlds apart. You have an opportunity to set an amazingly high standard that will have the world taking notice. If you follow the guidelines that I've described in this chapter, building a unit will never be an issue for your company. By following simple procedures and guidelines, you can build a company that not only impacts the world today, but will for generations to come. As I said earlier, it's not them, it's you.

# CHAPTER 5

# BEHAVIOR RULES FOR "THEM" AND "YOU"

What I want to do in this section is help you, as the leader of your company, establish rules or standards of operation that help your company work more efficiently and allows you to understand behavior for what it is: it's just behavior.

Behavior reacts to rules; rules give guidelines for how people need to interact at your facility or your company. Rules provide clarity, which helps maximize employee output, which maximizes profit for you.

The following list is not exhaustive. It's a tool or guideline that may help you re-examine your daily operations.

## #1 BE ON TIME

As a child, I remember many mornings of watching my Dad awake before the sun came up and leave for work. Finally, one morning, I asked him why he left for work so early. He told me that he was the boss, there was a job to do and he had to make sure that his employees saw him arrive on time, understand that he expected them to arrive on time and that the job had to be done correctly, efficiently and on time.

My Dad had served in the military during the Korean War and still lived his life as if he was part of the Army. That meant if he lived his life as part of the Army, my brother and I had to do the same. From an early age, the concept of time was drilled into me on a daily basis. My father's philosophy in life was: Being on time just wasn't good enough. Someone who is dedicated is **always** early. My father modeled this concept until he died.

I have carried on this tradition my entire life and my adherence to time has served me well. As an executive, as I've expressed in earlier chapters, you are the model that your employees will mold their daily schedules after and they will mirror your actions and behaviors. Being on time for meetings and appointments is a sign of respect that is expected from all parties. Since respect is an earned commodity, your employees will automatically respect you, knowing that you will be where you say you will be, on time, ready to accomplish the given task. Your being on time gives your employees a form of security and comfort, knowing that you do have a plan and a system in place that provides order for your life and theirs and that the company is managed in an orderly fashion. This also allows your employees to understand that you have a solid work ethic and that principles govern your daily activities, which provides more security and incentive for them.

As far as employees are concerned, an expectation that employees arrive on time for meeting and appointments is standard operation. As a coach, my players understood that tardiness was never tolerated and would receive immediate consequences. I expressed to my players that being on time was part of a life success formula and that much bigger things were coming in life and they needed to develop those life skills now in order to be successful as adults. Same holds true for employees.

If an employee is late for a meeting or appointment with a client, that is a reflection on you personally and professionally and expresses to the client that their time and their business is unimportant.

Tardy employees also cause multiple layers of stress within the office by forcing other staff members to delay deadlines, important phone calls and delivery dates on products to clients. A lack of time management skills gives the impression of a life and office in chaos and sends a red flag to potential clients that doing business with your company may have adverse side effects, financially and professionally.

## #2 SWIFT & IMMEDIATE CONSEQUENCES

In speaking of consequences, I want to make something very clear: Consequences are neither good nor bad and do not have feelings attached to them. A consequence, positive or negative, is a response to a displayed behavior. Swift and immediate consequences provide employees and clients with:

- Security

- Order

- A reliable system of checks and balances

- A clear understanding of expectations

- An incentive to perform and excel

- A reason to work above and beyond

- Respect for you as a business person

- A visible demonstration that your business is run in a systematic and orderly fashion

- A sense of fairness and objectivity

- A harmonious work environment—the "right vibe"

- Trust

- Cohesion

- Inspiration

- Longevity of employment

- The ability to build team unity

- An understanding that objectivity is a premium

- An environment that does not lend itself to "drama"

- A sense of pride in knowing issues are handled in a systematic, orderly fashion

- A clear vision of financial opportunity

If an objective and fair approach is taken towards your staff and clients, the rewards are endless. Individuals only ask for clear expectations and clear consequences. By handling this one area of your business, you can subtract most of your daily headaches off the balance sheet.

## #3 PERSONAL ACCOUNTABILITY

Personal accountability is probably one of the most discussed topics at personal improvement and business leadership conferences.

Have you ever wondered why a topic can be discussed this much and so few really act upon the words that are spoken?

My previous question was asked because from an observational standpoint, I haven't seen a great deal of people take this topic very seriously. Every day, some form of media is reporting on a lack of personal accountability and the issues that surround a personal or business life spinning out of control. This kind of reminds me of when I was a kid and my parents used to tell me that I was never allowed to drink or smoke. You guessed it— they had a cigarette in one hand and a drink in the other while we were discussing this policy on accountability. After my enlightening discussion with my parents, I grew to understand that personal accountability works much better in someone else's life than our own!

If only we lived in an invisible world, that would be a true statement. However, since all public behavior is visible, and all private behavior will eventually become visible, personal accountability is a must for success in life.

Success in business is based on relationships and relationships are based on effective communication and trust. If your employees and clients know you are a person of character and expectation for yourself first, then the trust in the relationship will be there. The buck should stop at your desk, which means personal accountability starts at your desk.

"Do as I say, not as I do" didn't work when I was a kid when discussing issues with my parents and that philosophy will not work with your employees or clients.

## #4 REWARD ALL PRODUCERS

As a coach, I made one promise to my players; that if they produced in practice, they would play in the game. Sounds like a very simple formula and it was. Is this same formula part of your business culture and compensation plan?

For amusement, I ask non-sales personnel about their compensation packages for production and the answers vary from long strings of profanity to screaming and shouting or a complete refusal to speak to me. All of this is followed up by, "...only the sales team receives any form of commission or bonus for production."

I realize this is not true in all companies, but it is true in many.

Should sales people be rewarded? Of course!

Should everyone else connected to the execution of the product sold be rewarded? Of course!

So, where has the disconnect taken place? Why are some companies only rewarded sales people for production? That would be the equivalent of a thirteen-member basketball team winning a state championship, but only three kids get a championship ring! The other ten members are reminded that they were only support staff and really didn't contribute that much to the championship. No, of course, that wouldn't work. Every member of that team participated in summer camp, conditioning, practice and games so every member of thatteam deserves a ring, even if they're bench-warmers.

The same can be said for the staff of your company. I'm not talking all expense paid trips to Hawaii for your whole staff, but I am talking about an equitable reward system for a job well done. In some companies, staff members would collapse if a C-level executive patted them on the back and said, "Thank you."

If "Thank You" is a pulse-stopping action in your company, imagine what a real reward would do for your staff. Of course I want you to say thank you to your staff for producing results, but why stop there? Now that you've got the party started, let's have some fun! Rewards can come in many forms and staff members will appreciate recognition for being part of a results-oriented team. The fastest way to develop an equitable and fair compensation plan that's not based solely on money is to take suggestions from your staff. They will tell you how they want to be rewarded for getting the job done and helping to make your company profitable.

## #5 DISCIPLINE IN PRIVATE

It's a cliché, "Praise in public, discipline in private," but it does make for a much more harmonious business environment.

Anytime you're going to discipline an employee, do it in private. Period. There's nothing worse than having a huge explosion in front of the company staff. Your staff, vendors or clients will not forget inappropriate public behavior and when you behave in this manner, you have the possibility of losing their respect. If you lose their respect, you have lost them as employees, customers and service providers.

When you follow the rules of disciplining in private, you show respect in a difficult situation which provides all associated parties with an understanding that you're a person of substance and outcomes are not based on emotion. This method will allow you to be viewed as an objective, systematic executive that only wants continuity and productivity within their company.

## #6 GREET EMPLOYEES WITH A SMILE

I used to have a boss that came by every single day and thanked me for being at work on time and ready to perform my duties. I appreciated the fact that he noticed I was there and I appreciated the fact that he took the time to walk down from his office and personally shake my hand. He would normally say, "Thank you so much for being part of our team. Thank you for doing your job and thank you for being an inspiration to others." Many of us on staff looked forward to speaking with him every morning and he provided a lift for the entire day. One handshake, combined with a smile, provided an energy that permeated through our entire staff on a daily basis. This one gentleman set a standard, and we as a staff, appreciated the standard and went above and beyond the call of duty for this individual.

One smile, combined with a thank you can be the key difference in producing results at your company. You set the vibe and if that vibe is positive, appreciative and respectful, your employees will mirror your actions inside and outside of your company.

## #7 GIVE YOUR EMPLOYEES FREEDOM & AUTHORITY

Give your employees the freedom and authority to fix problems. Nothing is more irritating to customers than to sit and wait for an authority figure to fix and issue that an employee could fix very easily. I remember, one time, I went through a drive through and I was missing an order of fries. So, I got out of line, parked my car and went inside. I had to wait on three different managers to get my fries when all the employee had to do was reach over and hand me an order of fries. Instead, I had to wait fifteen minutes for three managers to come to a consensus that I was missing my French fries.

Give your employees the freedom to solve an issue. I am not talking about a multimillion-dollar issue of course. In order for you to feel comfortable with this type of situation, put a dollar amount on what they can fix. But if you have taken the time to hire the right staff, you don't have to worry about that because they are going to handle the issue the proper way. They are just waiting for you to give them the opportunity to handle it and do the job you hired them to do.

## #8 TRAIN YOUR EMPLOYEES

This is going to fall into the "no duh" category again. Please make sure your employees are properly trained. There is nothing more irritating than having to deal with employees who don't know what they are doing.

I've noticed a disturbing trend lately. Many establishments are placing untrained and unskilled employees as their first line of contact with customers. That is the equivalent of showing up for a first date without taking a shower for three weeks, no wallet, wearing your high school letter jacket at the age of forty and explaining to your date that you still live in your parents' basement because you are the anchor of the family and they just couldn't make it without you. Yes, I see we agree; there would be no second date. Same thing with your customers. There will be no second date. Not only that; they're going to tell all of their friends not to date you either.

When you're asking people to spend their hard-earned dollars with you, why in the world would you want them to feel frustration and irritation during the first two minutes of an encounter with your company? I beg you, on behalf of the buying public, please place a well-trained and well-spoken individual as your first contact with the public. Not only will it make the entire buying public swell with joy, it will also make them more than happy to throw many dollar bills your way.

In addition to making sure your employees are trained, make sure your trainers know what they are doing. I have watched trainers in retail establishments train employees incorrectly. My first assumption is these employees are not a true reflection of the CEO of this company, however, somewhere along the way, there is a huge communication breakdown. To this day, I have never met a CEO who wants inefficient, untrained employees working with fellow employees or working with customers. This comes back to having a chain of accountability and making sure the correct people are in place that will allow customers an opportunity to experience a true representation of the CEO's values and experience the true sense of what it means to be a valued customer.

I have observed that people are forgiving and many times, they will give your establishment a second chance. From my viewpoint, optimizing the "first chance" is the best course of action and the best way to acquire and retain a customer. When training employees, the focus needs to be on making sure the customer has been treated so well, it would be insanity on their part to even think of going somewhere else.

## #9 LISTEN TO YOUR CUSTOMERS

In our house, oatmeal is a touchy subject. You may ask, "How in the world could oatmeal conjure up such feelings of anger and frustration?"

I'm glad you asked. I'll be happy to tell the story.

Not long ago, in a far away land, I ventured into a breakfast kingdom that was known to have excellent oatmeal. Much to my dismay, the evil CEO had changed the magic formula for the oatmeal. I asked, "Why, pray tell, didst thy evil CEO changeth thou tasty formula?"

The fair maiden serving me informed me that an evil twenty-something marketer had come down from the castle and decreed it. "Fair maiden," I asked, "doth other members of the kingdom enjoy this new magical formula?"

"No, sire, the members of the kingdom are most displeased."

I asked, "Would it be too much to ask for the marketer's head to be placed on a platter?"

She said, "No, sire, we would all gladly help."

You may think that my Shakespearian form is making much ado about nothing. However, I protest.

Okay, enough about Shakespeare...all I wanted was a freakin' bowl of plain oatmeal. I was informed by the general manager that there was absolutely no way I could get a plain bowl of oatmeal any longer at this establishment. The marketing department for this company decided to make a change, *without asking their customers what they wanted!*

All was not well in the kingdom and the kingdom was experiencing a period of unrest, ill-fated decrees and the rumblings of an uprising.

I was so irritated; I just couldn't let it go. I proceeded to go to four more of the same establishments in four different states — only to hear the exact same story. Each general manager told me that they themselves were very unhappy with this decision and the home office did not care for their opinion or mine.

Normally, I chalk this up to disgruntled employees and slough this off. This time, I knew they were telling the truth. How could, from the same restaurant chain, five general managers from five different restaurants, located in five different states, all have the exact same story? In addition, each general manager told me that the majority of their regular "oatmeal eating" customers all had the same complaint.

Again, normally, this would not be a big deal, but each general manager I spoke with was seeking employment with other establishments and each spoke with me under the condition of anonymity.

Doest thou seest the damage that one small bowl of oatmeal can cause a kingdom?

I'm sure you probably have an online survey that you have your customers fill out. Convenient, isn't it? To date, do you want to know how many I've filled out?

Zero. Nada. Nothing.

And now, marketing research is indicating that these surveys are actually turning customers away because they are so tired of being nagged about doing yet one more task after leaving an establishment.

Between the store and my home and filling out the survey, life seems to always step in. I would assume I am not the only individual that has life collide with filling out a survey.

Which leads me to ask this question: How useful is a survey that only represents 5% of your customer base? I'm using 5% as my example because that's the percentage the five general managers quoted me on survey response from all customers. That's responses from satisfied and unsatisfied customers for this company. Your customer response rate on online surveys could be higher or lower than 5%. However, doesn't it make sense to get a wider response in order to meet the needs of your customer base?

This is not rocket science! If you ask your customers what they want, they will tell you.

For the love of God and the kingdom, give your general managers the freedom to make your customers happy!

My pilgrimage across the kingdom for one bowl of plain oatmeal has turned into a full crusade against the king, his minions and the throne. I appeared as a happy customer, dreaming of oatmeal in springtime…I left as William Wallace, painting my face and crying, "Freedom from the tyranny of eating flavored oatmeal! They may take my oatmeal, but they will not take my freedom!"

Dost thou thinketh that the banishment of plain oatmeal was a good idea for the kingdom?

## #10 PROFIT MATTERS

I realize that you know that profit matters because you are directly connected to the profit and loss statements, the stock reports and the tax returns. However, I wonder, after much observation, how many employees realize that their jobs actually rely on the profits of the company? It appears that many employees think that the company is there to serve them, instead of the other way around. How did I formulate this opinion? By dealing with customer service, the average retail employee, the average restaurant employee, by watching the news, reading the paper, reading online blogs and by casually sitting in establishments, watching and listening as employees go about their jobs.

When I was sixteen, I went to work at a grocery store and I will never forget what the owner told me when he hired me. "Scot, if I don't make a profit, I'm firing you first." And sure enough, about two months later, as he was a man of his word, he fired me, and a few months later, closed the doors forever. This even taught me a very good lesson:

Unless a business makes money, I will receive no paycheck. Plus, I learned that an old guy, who says he will fire you, normally follows through. I appreciated his honesty.

If I may borrow a quote from the movie "Ben Hur":

*"We keep you alive to serve this ship. So row well…and live."*

So what did I learn at the age of sixteen and from Ben Hur?

All are expendable unless the coffers overflow.

As a favor to yourself and to your customers, make sure your employees understand that companies must make money and that the employees' jobs only last as long as the company makes money. Profits aren't evil. Profits provide jobs.

## #11 STAY FOCUSED & SELF DISCIPLINED

I grew up in North Carolina and one of my favorite places to go is the Outer Banks. As a child, I was fascinated with life on the sea. I dreamed of being Jacques Cousteau and traveling the world, searching for new adventures by sea. My fascination also extended to lighthouses. In my home state, around the Outer Banks, there are five unique lighthouses. Each lighthouse has its own unique characteristics, but each has the same function — be a guide to keep ships and sailors safe. As the captain of a ship, focus and discipline are a premium or you end up on the rocks with cargo and crew as casualties.

No, I did not become the next Jacques Cousteau, but I still

have my love for lighthouses and the lessons those lighthouses taught me as a child.

Without keen focus and a proper navigational system, ships and individuals will become lost and many times, end up on the rocks.

The same can be said for business. You are the captain of your ship and your cargo and crew are depending on you. Your self-discipline and focus will determine the direction and longevity of your company. As with many family owned companies, the internal drive and focus doesn't always make it to the second, third and fourth generations. Many times, the business must be sold because a lack of desire has extinguished profits.

Lighthouses can only be a guide. They can't steer the boat or handle crew or cargo. Only the captain can decide a steady course that provides safe passage for all. The lighthouse is a tool, not a destination. Captains have to be smart enough to use all available tools, and combine those tools with experience and a clear course in order to make it to port safely. Jacques Cousteau probably shut off the cameras if problems at sea occurred.

You can't.

If you map out your course, stay focused and commit to the journey, you will have an optimal chance of survival.

## #12 NEVER FORGET THE MISSION

I know I have reiterated this, and I have gone over this, and I have said this, but why would I be saying something over and over and over if it wasn't important and a big deal?

Why?

Because when I go around companies and ask employees to either state the mission or the vision for their company, very few can.

What does that tell me?

- The mission or vision was deleted out of the training manual

- Nah, that can't be it...

- The company sprang up out of nowhere and there was no time to write a mission or a vision

- Nah, that can't be it...

Maybe during training, nobody focused on the mission or the vision of the company.

What does that also tell me? Your employees don't understand how their job is connected to profits, what the company does and how it performs in the market place.

If your employees do not understand where your company fits into the market place, how their job contributes (or deletes from) profits, and how it all works together to complete the mission and vision of your company, then you've got an issue.

If employees aren't going to do what's right for themselves, they are not going to do what's right for the company, and they are not going to do what's right for the customer.

You never saw John Wayne stop in the middle of a movie and ask, "Why are we here? Who are the bad guys?" Of course not. The scriptwriters did a better job than that! John Wayne had to fight the battle and win the war. Nobody wanted to watch a movie where John Wayne didn't know what he was doing.

He's the epitome of tough and cool. John Wayne always knew the direction and the outcome needed for any situation.

Do you?

An unclear mission and vision will destroy a company.

# #13 THE CUSTOMER ISN'T ALWAYS RIGHT

I realize that a few pages over, I was going all William Wallace on you (vivé la révolution), but I had a good reason. If you haven't figured it out by now, oatmeal is not the reason I was upset. I was upset that a company had no use for loyal customers' desires or opinions. My irritation came from the fact that I'd been a customer of this chain for over twenty years and for over twenty years, I had happily eaten the same oatmeal. Then, one day, I go in and they have changed the formula and when I vocalized my disapproval, they basically told me to "stick it." In this case, the customer <u>was</u> right.

However, I've never been one to subscribe to the notion that the customer is <u>always</u> right. Sometimes, you need to let a client or potential client walk out the door. Your competition needs customers — why not give them all of the ones you don't want?

If you "do business right", you get to choose who shops with you. This is just like dating. You only go on dates with people that fit in to your long-term plans and relationship goals.

Same thing with customers. Why continue a relationship with an abusive customer who berates your staff, refuses to be made happy, tears up your property, doesn't pay their bills and constantly badmouths you to the community?

Like I said. Your competitors need customers. Show some love and let 'em have 'em!

## #14 BE CONSISTENT

By now, you're starting to realize that I've said this before. Hopefully, it borderlines on a bad dream and the concept of "consistent behavior" is starting to haunt you like a never-ending nightmare.

To that, I say: Good!

Your employees will thank me.

If you say it, mean it.

If it's a rule, follow it.

Always be clear, fair, objective and consistent.

People will follow you if you consistently display care for their needs and maintain and objective perspective when handling company matters. Consistency breeds harmony.

## #15 IT'S NOT PERSONAL; IT'S JUST BUSINESS

Okay, I just couldn't help it. "The Godfather" is one of my favorite movies.

What do I mean by "It's not personal; it's just business?"

Employers who think their employees don't bring their emotional lives to the office are stupid.

I can't tell you how many workshops I've been to where the all-knowing speaker told the entire crowd to make sure that when it comes to business, that they leave their personal lives at the door. I really have to put this one under "stupid clichés" that have no meaning whatsoever.

Human beings have feelings and feelings don't change just because somebody went through a doorway. An upset employee in the parking lot is an upset employee sitting at their desk inside your place of business. I realize that you are not paying them to suffer through a divorce/take care of a sick kid/end a relationship/mourn a family member or pet/endure a personal illness or deal with life's daily issues.

I'm on your side. You are paying them to do the job that you have assigned to them and to do it well.

However, every employee, including yourself, is going to have "one of those days" or weeks. Make your expectations clear, but give your employees the freedom to handle the situation in private, with grace and dignity, in a timely manner. Bad days aren't going anywhere. Neither is death, heartbreak, disappointment or tragedy. If you are clear on your expectations and temper those expectations with understanding, your employees will be more appreciative and loyal than you ever anticipated or expected.

It's not personal; it's just business, but a personal touch goes a long way in your business.

# BONUS

Rules regarding behavior only have meaning if the individuals associated with those rules see clear and beneficial results. The gentlemen I interviewed for this section are true leaders — living testaments to success, self-discipline and how the systematic application of clearly defined rules can not only build a successful life, but pass on a never-ending positive legacy.

## *COL. STEVEN SEROKA*

Col. Steven Seroka is a thirty-year US Air Force fighter pilot, strategist and leader and recently became the Chief of Staff for the Las Vegas Metro Chamber of Commerce, one of the largest of its kind in the nation.

In his final military assignment he served as the Chief of Staff for the 11,000 person U.S. Air Force Warfare Center, headquartered in Las Vegas Nevada with thirty-three operating locations in twenty-two states across the nation. As part of his duties, he deployed to the Middle East where he led the real-time execution of over 30,000 air combat missions and was responsible for billions of dollars of aircraft and equipment and actions that impacted over 100,000 military members.

As the Chief of Strategy NORAD, he authored the strategic plan to defend North America from an air attack, which was subsequently put to the test during 9/11. He has served around the world gaining cultural competency for developing, fostering and furthering military and diplomatic relationships between nations.

Active in the Las Vegas community, he was selected to join executive business and community leaders for the prestigious Leadership Las Vegas class of 2012 sponsored by the Las Vegas

Metro Chamber of Commerce. He volunteers and supports many community organizations such as the American Red Cross, the USO and the Las Vegas Scleroderma Foundation. As a senior military officer, he has been a keynote speaker on topics ranging from leadership and strategy to patriotism, attitude and personal development.

He has a BS in Operations Research from the Unites States Air Force Academy, an MA in Strategy from Air University and a MBA from Webster University.

*Scot: What really drew you to become a part of the US military? What draws other people to the military?*

*Col. Seroka:* When I spoke to my troops, I discussed that question with them, saying, "We join the military for a variety of reasons, but for those of us that "rejoined", why do we stay?" That's where the real story is.

A lot of it has to do with the challenge that comes with military service, but, for me, I believed that the challenges and the success of overcoming the obstacles put in my way, including the demands of military training, would set me up for whatever I was going to do with my life, especially after my military service was over. I believed that the military would push me to where I thought I could go, before I joined, and would also make me ready for many challenges that I never expected in my life.

Some people join the military because a court judge sent them — literally. Some join for the benefits, some join for the college education and some join because they had nothing better to do.

But at decision time, when it's time to decide whether a person is going to stay in the military or not, the decision is usually made for the same reason, for everyone: I stayed in the military because I felt good about what I was doing everyday. I felt that I was defending the ideals of my country and the physical safety of my neighbors, friends, and family. I felt good about that. Others do too.

The next reason I stayed is because I believe in our country. I believe that our country is not perfect, but at least we try to do the right things. If you compare our country to other nations in the world, especially if you've ever lived in some of those other countries, you'll realize that truly, there is no other nation like ours. There are some that come close and some of them are our allies, but they do not really have the ideals and the set of values that we do. We actually try to hold ourselves accountable to those ideals.

And the last reason many of us join and stay in the military is because you have the privilege to work with an amazing group of Americans. Probably the most amazing thing about the people that I got to serve with is that they are motivated purely by their heart—in what they believe in. It has nothing to do with how much money they make. It's not about how much money you can pay somebody that would make them willing to lay down their life for another person—that comes from within, you can't pay for that.

I've been truly blessed to be part of the greatest military force in the history of the world—maybe the best organization in the world—and I was blessed to be part of that.

*Scot: You are now the ever first person that has ever touched me with an answer like that. You began by being a fighter pilot; decisiveness is part of the daily business of that job. Decisiveness is part of the military life, but especially important as a successful pilot. How important is decisiveness in staying alive?*

*Col. Seroka:* It's true; decisiveness is a part of staying alive in the military. When you break down decisiveness, it's really important for you to know what you need to do and when to do it. And that's really what decisiveness is: You are doing what you need to do at the right time.

So, what happens in combat is; the bad guys are trying to get you to do what they want you to do because that will give them the advantage. You have to be decisive in that environment. You have to be thinking ahead responsibly to understand the conflict that is going on. You do what is best for you and not what the enemy wants you to do, which is their goal — to anticipate and lure a man into a position of disadvantage.

By being decisive, you're constantly making decisions and split second decisions that keep you in the position of advantage — and usually, you have to make those decisions very quickly. As a pilot, you are constantly adjusting to the situation you're currently in.

Decisiveness starts from the ground up — you have to examine the decisions you have to make before you ever commit to what you are going to do that day.

Being decisive is all about understanding and committing to what, why and where are the best actions for you and your teammates.

*Scot: Which leads me to my next question: There are rules for behavior, especially in military engagement, for everything that you do, especially when you are in your flight suit and in that plane. What are the important behavior rules you use to be useful in fighting and also in life?*

*Col. Seroka:* When we are fighting in the air, we are fighting a war. We know that the fight will only last for a period of time because somebody will eventually agree with our position or they won't. Our goal is that they (our opponents) stop doing what they want to do unless what they want to do is work with us (the military).

How you fight is huge. How you work with the opponent after the fight is over is important also, especially if you win. When the war is over and nobody wants to work with you, how does that make things get better? If you are fighting in a way that is respectful, people will still work with you, even when it's over.

So, in relationships, especially in the workplace, when you are at "the fight," which happens because there is conflict in working, it's important for people to voice their opinion in a respectful way. In conflict, one side is trying to "get" their opponent by pushing their will onto them. When you do that, you diminish the other person by imposing your will onto them.

If you are thinking ahead, you don't do that. You think about how to "fight fair" with somebody. You want to fight in a way that, when it's over, you have won over your opponent's hearts and minds.

When you are fighting as a team against an opponent, you have to have certain agreements so that you understand how and what your team members are thinking.

As a pilot, our number one rule is "shoot down the bad guy and not each other."

In warfare, as technology has increased and the fight is farther and farther away from our literal vision, we are shooting people we can't even see. We have to have rules because we all agree that our number one rule is not to shoot at our own team members.

We put restrictions and rules on ourselves that sometimes make it harder to do our jobs, because we know, at the end, the results end up being better. We, as pilots, accept those rules because we are accepting that rule number one is to take care of each other first.

For example, from a pilot's perspective, when you see a blip on your radarscope, you want to shoot it. You don't want that blip to get any closer to you because if it gets any closer, and that blip is a bad guy, then that bad guy may shoot you. But, as a pilot, if you have to go through a series of checks and balances before you shoot an unknown target (who might actually be one of your team), the bad guy may get a position advantage over you.

So, it's a little scary, that agreement that we made with each other and the rules that accompany that agreement. In order to prevent us from shooting each other, we have to install these extra series of checks and balances, but it sometimes takes away our ability to take out the bad guy. So, we accept the consequences of these rules, what could happen because of these rules, and we help each other in that process.

*Scot: In the military, you have a standard code of military conduct among pilots, officers and enlisted men. Why is it so important to enforce that code of conduct?*

*Col. Seroka:* A code of conduct allows us to understand exactly where people are coming from and allows us to count on each other to follow the rules. At the same time, we all make mistakes. None of us are perfect. However, we understand that if we mess up, there are rules and consequences for our mistakes when we violate those rules.

This code of conduct and rules help us uphold our military

standards. The life experience, expectation and standards in the military are much higher than anywhere else in our society. These high standards are very difficult to achieve. If you fall short in the military, it doesn't mean you, personally, are a failure. You may be asked to leave the military because you fell short of those standards. That process doesn't mean you are a failure; it just means that in the high intense, high standard environment of the military, you didn't measure up to military standards.

If we know what the standards are, we can count on each other. If we don't hold people accountable, the standards are very easy to lose and then, people don't make the effort to achieve that high level of conduct. When we achieve those high levels of standards and conduct, everything is better for the family, school, state and nation.

*Scot: You've been an officer, a pilot, you're a dad, and you're a husband. Do you have a favorite quote or saying or something that you read or listen to every single day that reinforces exactly what you've said about a code of conduct - a code for life, a code for being a husband, a code for being a father. Do you have a code or something that you keep with you and give to others to help inspire them, to carry on with that code of conduct?*

*Col. Seroka:* It is very important to gain the trust of the people around you and have them count on you. You need to do the right thing. Even if nobody is watching, what we need to do is to do the right thing, for the right reasons.

You could make a decision that appears, on the surface, to be the right thing; you think you can sell it to your friends, your family, your subordinates or boss—and, on the surface, it appears you're doing this for the right reasons, but really, you're doing it because there is a personal gain in it. And you hope that everybody won't see through that. So, while it looks good to the "outside world", it's not a good decision at its core.

So if you do the right thing, at the right time, every time, make sure you're doing it for the right reasons. Then you'll feel good, even though the right thing may be really hard to do. As I tell my people, the number one thing to do is: Do the right thing when nobody is watching. But, most importantly, do it for the right reasons, for the right motivations, for the right goal and for the right results.

## *AARON YOUNG*

For over twenty years, Aaron Young has been empowering business owners to build strong companies and proactively protect their dreams. An entrepreneur with several multi-million-dollar companies under his own belt, Aaron has made it his life's work to arm other business owners with success formulas that immediately provide exponential growth and protection. Below are some of his career highlights:

As CEO of Laughlin Associates, Aaron has served as a strategic-thinking partner for more than 80,000 business owners across a wide range of industries. Having witnessed both their common mistakes and common successes, he knows what works and what does not. Clients call on Aaron for his opinion and help brainstorming every aspect of business operations, including corporate structuring, asset management and protection, growth strategies, partnership issues, leadership, and corporate compliance.

An engaging teacher who speaks directly to the hearts and minds of entrepreneurs as only another business owner can,

Aaron is regularly invited to contribute articles, blogs, or his expert opinion for media outlets nationwide. As a celebrated keynote and breakout speaker, Aaron has addressed entrepreneurial and business audiences for major players in global trading and finance. He is in high demand for his expertise on asset-protection tax planning and is noted for his signature speech, "Building Your Corporate Fortress." Over the years, he has spoken to more than 100,000 people on four continents. Aaron has served as a board or advisory board member for several organizations — including CEO Space International, California Women's Conference, SMART Women International, International Crowd Funding Association, Portland Center Stage, and Integrative Medical Arts Center.

*Scot: Aaron, tell me a little bit about you and your company.*

*Aaron Young:* Basically, we are a company that helps businesses grow business. I am the CEO of and one of the owners of the company. We've been in business for over forty years. We take care of thousands of clients. I'm an entrepreneur and that's the right career for me.

*Scot: Why is it so important for a business to establish behavior rules and put them in place, from a legal standpoint and from an operational standpoint?*

*Aaron Young:* The simple answer to that is; when you know what the rules are, it's easier to stay out of trouble. As the owner or the CEO, you have to clearly define what is supposed to happen in the work place. Whether it is the factory, whether it's an office, or if it's working virtually, you must be very, very specific about what is acceptable and what is not acceptable.

You're not taking this from a "right/wrong" or a "punishment" perspective if you break the rules, but simply from a perspective of helping somebody understand why we do the things that we do and why we have the expectations that we do and why it's important that they stay within a certain guideline. It's a way to be efficient. It's a way to be safe. It's a way to keep from going into the quicksand, which you can do in business, especially in today's world that's so litigious. If you don't have rules, then you have anarchy. You have nobody doing anything in an organized, constructive, intentional way.

*Scot: I will back it up with this question. What are some basic business behavior rules that you could recommend to every business owner you work with addressing conduct in the work place and how you handle it?*

*Aaron Young:* In our company, one of the things I tell everybody is that it's clear to me that while this may be my dream, my goal and my big project, I've enlisted them into my dream and I understand that, at the end of the day, their goal is to live their life and their dream, not mine. So when they come in to work, for the most part, I know this isn't the most exciting thing that they are going to do in their life.

What I want to have happen when they're at my office is that I want them to feel happy. Even if bad things are happening elsewhere, I want them to come in and feel like this is a good, supportive and a safe place to work—there's not going to be a lot of politics and backbiting. They still walk through the halls and their co-workers work in a way that everybody feels safe, even if they are not best friends. Then it's a safe place to work.

From a conduct standpoint, one of the things that must happen is clear and immediate consequence. In our company, we had an executive who was violating company policy towards some of the other employees. When I took over as CEO of the company, these employees contacted me to complain about this executive's behavior. It was the first time these employees had ever felt safe enough to address these policy violations, as the executive's inappropriate behavior had been going on for some time.

I listened to their stories individually and I asked them some questions. I knew both the women very well already, as I did the man. So I listened to the employees, hung up the phone, bought me a plane ticket, and was in the office the next morning and let him go. With no ceremony, I just said, "Hey we're cutting you loose today, here's your check, have a nice life".

His behavior was absolutely unacceptable. Now, if I thought that these two employees were playing an angle, I would have had a sense of that. I had a sense that I was right in my assessment of the situation. So, from a behavioral standpoint, people need to be safe in the workplace and everybody needs to play by the rules, even the executives.

Everybody needs to understand and they need to be reminded regularly of the mission of the company, what's working or not working and understand that while they're there, they're expected to be putting in eight hours and that there's not lots of going out on smoke breaks when you are having a bad day. It's ok to do it once in a while, but it's not ok when you're leaving your work to other people and everybody gets bogged down because you can't do your job.

In my company, we have very high retention rate from our employees. I have about thirty employees and the average tenure in my office is twelve years. So people stay working for me, but it didn't used to be that way. When I bought the company, it had been a revolving door when it came to employee retention.

When we first went into the company, we cut about fifty people. We eventually added some more people back and then, from time to time, if we find that somebody is becoming a negative influence, even if they're doing a good job, we let them go.

There just has to be a good sense of harmony in the office in order for the whole thing to work. The only way employees can do that is if they know what to expect and they know the culture. A big part of creating the culture is up to the owners and the management team. Once that's established and if it's generally working, you sometimes still have to make "surgical moves" to remove problems when they don't show any tendency to want to change their behavior.

It's amazing when somebody is in an executive or senior position and the "rank and file" employees understand that they are breaking the rules—everybody feels unsafe. This type of "unsafe behavior" makes everybody guarded and uncomfortable and there's a lot of gossip. Then, when the employees talk to the owners and the owners are prepared to remove a senior or executive employee because of rules violation and the owners believe the employees over the senior employee, morale improves immediately. The employees see the owners keeping the standard of rules and consequences.

Rules are important so there's very, very clear understanding of the overall mission and what the company's objectives are. The employees just know what they are supposed to do and why.

As a rule, we give our employees license to make decisions and the freedom to make mistakes. If they make a lot of mistakes, the first thing you do is re-train them and then, if they can't learn from the training, then you have to remove them.

But in our place, you have to let employees make mistakes that are not fatal issues. I'd rather have an employee do something to help fix a client situation, help solve or find an answer to a mistake they made. I'd rather them make a decision and help that client feel heard and understood, even if it might not be the same decision I would have made. Employees need to be able to do that and act in "real time" and not feel like they have to always go to somebody up the chain to get permission to solve a problem.

My final recommendation on basic rules in addition to clear objectives and employee freedom to make (and resolve) mistakes is to create and use simple reporting that gives a very good idea of kind of all the critical elements of the company so that you can see if you are bogging down some place or you should be able to say, "if this, then that, if this, then that." And if all of a sudden that is not working, it's easier to look at the report to figure out why.

Ronald Reagan once said, "Trust to verify". I think it's really critical that you can see if things are working, if people are doing what they are supposed to do or if they are behaving in the way they are supposed to behave on the job. If you tell them exactly why they're there and what their job is, you let them act without being terrified of making a mistake. Then, if you regularly inspect your expectations and tweak and train as necessary, you end up with a very happy work force. You end up with people who grow your business much faster because, if everybody is doing the right things and making decisions, they're not sitting around waiting for two or three key people who have to initial every little decisions made.

So those are different ways of looking at conduct but they are also, for me they are from the CEO perspective. Those are my rules of how I run my business.

*Scot: Why are rules important to overall success of the Company for operation now and years to come?*

*Aaron Young:* If people know what they're doing and they have the freedom to act, they're going to be happy in their job and if they're happy in their job, they are going to stay in their job. If they stay in their job, then they become better at it than you are. They become much more of an asset to the company and pretty soon, everything you want to do as an owner is just magnified by this high quality experienced labor force that's right there, working towards clear objectives.

If these same people feel safe, they feel like they have the right to act and they have some ownership of how their job gets done, they feel successful because they know what to do and they're helping people and they're solving problems. They're not getting yelled at, they're not getting belittled and over the long haul, you are going to make a ton more money in your sales efforts in keeping or earning and retaining clients, but you're also going to save untold amounts of money in going through the hiring and training, firing and replacing of employees.

It's a sad event when someone leaves our office because it's almost always it's because some significant life change for them and they realize that they are leaving a great place to work. I've gotten many letters saying, "This is the best place I've ever worked," and I have a lot of people that write to me on a regular basis, especially when the economy is bad, and they say to me, "Thanks for keeping me on. I know business is dim, I know money is tight and how they hope to be secure," and they stay and they work their buts off for you and it's just great for everybody.

When my employees go home at the end of the day, I want them to just forget about work and enjoy their life. That's how I think you get success over the long haul.

*Scot: What are the three business behavior standards or rules that you recommend, from a legal perspective, that should be in place in every single business? Because you do help entrepreneurs, you can also make recommendations for start – ups. What do you recommend to the existing and start – up businesses for some basic rules they need to have in place?*

*Aaron Young:* They have to have a clear sure vision of what they're trying to achieve. They have to know what the destination looks like. I tell people: on no more than two pieces of legal sized paper, in free hand, write down what your business looks like, if it was running perfectly. Since this was exactly your dream, what would it look like? Don't worry about how you get there. Just get a crystal clear vision of what you want it to be, so you begin with the end in mind. That's the first thing.

Once you have a clear vision of what you are trying to achieve and, as one of my wisest friends told me once, it's less important to be right, than to be sure. Let me repeat that...

In doing almost anything, it's more important to be sure than it is to be right.

A lot of us get stuck in trying to make the right decision. What we need to do is to make the best decision we can make right now and go after it, and then as we go down the road, and if it looks like our ideas aren't working out so well, then we can change directions. Most people wait around to be right and what's really more important is just to be sure and say, "That's my vision and I'm going for it."

So once you have the vision in place, then you can choose the right business entity. You number one rule regarding entity selection should be: Always protect your assets by using the correct business entity. Then, whatever the rules are for that business entity, follow them.

We know that almost no closely held companies are following corporate formalities. If you don't follow those formalities, if you're not having regular meetings, keeping minutes of the meetings, passing resolutions, issuing ownership either in the form of stocks or in the form of every step agreement by membership ownership, then all you're doing is wasting money paying state to be a corporation state because without the formalities in place, the business entity is completely worthless.

So know where you're going, get into the right entity, follow the rules and then keep track of things. Ignorance of the law is no excuse, so you need to keep abreast of what's going on in your industry. You need be listening to webinars and going to events when they're talking about your specific industry. It's appropriate to be involved in industry associations so you know what's going on from a legal and accounting perspective. That way, when you are working on your company and you are making decisions for the future, you know that your future itself is one you're going to be happy with.

I tell my kids the same thing; that the decisions you are making today are going to make your future self happy. You have to be responsible for yourself.

And so it's just absolutely critical that people take ownership and take stewardship of their business. I know people say well I've got an accountant, they're supposed to do that. The accountant's job isn't to manage with your financial health. The accountant's job is to organize what you've given them and then submit a report to the state and to the IRS. They are not your financial baby sitter.

Don't be lazy and think, "Somebody else is going to do that for me," or, "I don't have time to do that right now," because if you don't take care of the super structure of that entity, the entity will not protect you if you ever get into any trouble. So there you go. Those are of some rules from a legal perspective to be aware of.

*Scot: What is your favorite quote about rules or standards? Maybe that you read every single day?*

*Aaron Young:* I have a favorite quote; my favorite for many years. There's a saying that I read every single day. I keep it sitting right here next to my desk. It is from Henry David Thoreau, and it's from the last chapter of the book, "Walden." This is my rule - this is my standard that has served me well for thirty years so far.

I'll give you the business quote, which is my very favorite one. So here it is:

*"If one advances confidently in the direction of his dreams, and endeavors to live the life which he has imagined, he will meet with a success unexpected in common hours. He will put some things behind. Will pass an invisible boundary. New Universal and more Liberal laws will begin to establish themselves around and within him. Where the old laws will be expanded and interpreted in his favorite in a more liberal sense and he will live with the license of a higher order of beings."*

That quote colors everything I do in my life. Every single thing I do. It's not critical but you know how you are going to achieve your goals, but it is critical that you know what your goal is. Because if one advances confidently in the direction of his dreams, endeavors to live the life which he's imagined, he will meet with the success unexpected in calmed hours.

I can tell you over and over again of experiences in my career where things have happened that I could not have made happen, but they happened exactly the way that I needed. There's no way I could have scripted it. It just came. I met with success unexpected in my common eight-hour workdays and forty-hour work weeks.

It is very, very important to know what you are working towards and go towards it in baby steps every day. And as you do that, and as you can clearly articulate that vision, you have to be able to write it down. Not as a business plan, but as your dream and your vision, so you can clearly articulate what you're working on.

Others will hear what you're working on, the right people will appear, their ears will perk up when they hear it and things just start coming your way. You start attracting the right people and even though you don't know the path, the path opens up before you. It happens every single time without exception, without exception, it always works.

But it only works if you have a clear vision and you actively work towards your vision every day diligently, not just sitting there and dreaming, but moving every day. The path always opens up and every time I get bogged down, I realize it's because I've quit following that rule.

Now, let me give you my business quote. This is one of my very favorite quotes. It says, "When we deal in generalities, we will rarely have success. When we deal in specifics, we will rarely have failures. When performance is measured, performance improves and when performance is measured, and reported back, the rate of improvement accelerates." That quote is from Thomas Manson.

# CHAPTER 6

# ENVIRONMENT

The environment of your business or company will set the tone for every single thing that takes place within your company pertaining to employees and customers. Since your company is in business to provide a service and collect revenue based on that service and you are responsible for that, an optimal environment makes sense. If employee and customer alike enjoy a positive experience connected to your business, you will receive not only higher profits, but respect, appreciation, loyalty and an enthusiasm for your brand that is unmatched.

In an effort to be very clear, I am dividing the categories into two areas: Employee and Customer. The Employee area will be covered first since employees will be the deciding factor of the Customer environment.

## EMPLOYEE ENVIRONMENT

### *ATMOSPHERE/TONE*

What greets your employees as soon as they enter the door of your place of business? Does the greeting they receive help shield that employee from the traffic they just experienced, the argument they had with their spouse, a sick child, coffee spilled on their brand new suit, car trouble or life's general irritations that crop up first thing in the morning? For many companies, that answer is "No."

Many companies provide no greeting and if there is a greeting, the conversation starts with bitching, moaning and complaining about what hasn't been done and what needs to be improved. Are we having fun now or what? Most employees can get bitching, moaning and complaining at night when they go home.

This type of atmosphere destroys morale, disrupts continuity and is carried over to the customers. Why not switch it up a bit and give your employees a reason to walk through the door first thing in the morning? Even though the only thing you can control is what happens under your roof, make the decision to provide a positive experience on a daily basis for your employees.

**Greet Them With a Smile**
Smiles are free and priceless to the bottom line. How much effort does it really take to thank your employees for coming to work, doing their jobs and providing an exceptional experience for your clients? Keep in mind; you set the tone for your entire company. Like yourself, your employees also have a minimum of 12,000 thoughts a day. Those thoughts can focus on negative things, such as you being an asshole and this being an awful place to work, or you being a fair person with clear expectations who provides an environment of opportunity.

Your employees will appreciate someone providing a smile and a thank you first thing in the morning. One smile will set the vibration for the entire day. That positive vibration will permeate throughout the entire office and to every customer.

Now, instead of an employee's day beginning with, "What's wrong with my morning," and that spreading through the office, a positive vibe has been established allowing the employee's mindset to change and now an "attitude of gratitude" is projected out to each employee. The normal "bitch" session at the coffee pot or water cooler begins to evaporate. How many times, yourself included, have you or co-workers stood around the coffee pot just to discuss how wonderful life is and how great your day is? Normally, you don't! You bitch about last night's game, your spouse, your kids, your employer, your customers, your health, the amount of money you make, traffic and anything you can think of between your desk and the coffee pot.

How much better would your company function if the daily bitch session disappears? Ahhh, what's that sound I hear?

Harmony.

Not only does that smile help provide an atmosphere of harmony, it gives employees a reason to come to work when they don't feel that good, when the lake and the sunshine is calling, when the bedcovers are a little too warm or when their hearts are breaking. Without speaking one word, you create a desired atmosphere filled with appreciation and value.

## PROVIDE SECURITY

Employees want to know that some form of security is in place that provides them economic and professional opportunity. Now that you or someone in your company has welcomed the employee to the work place, what else do they need? Security can come in many forms:

**Belief in the CEO/Owner**
- Employees need the perception that the leadership is making the correct decisions connected to the company and the operations. The employee wants to know that their paycheck will be provided on the expected dates and that management is following steps that will allow that paycheck to continue.

- If an environment of clear and fair expectations is established, individuals within the company structure expect the rules to be enforced in an equitable manner. An employee needs the security of knowing that all rules will be enforced 100% of the time without exception. This practice allows individuals a freedom in knowing a job well done will be noticed and rewarded.

## *BUILD TRUST*

Now that an atmosphere of opportunity is provided, coupled with employees' understanding that management is making the correct decisions, an attitude of trust within the company can be built.

**Employee Behavior**
Since your company has hired the right people, rules are clear and follow through is immediate, employee behavior will mirror what the company and the customers need. Day to day issues of drama and office politics will no longer exist and productivity will be maximized. All individuals will understand opportunity is based on results and results are immediately rewarded. Trust is a two-way street and if your employees know that they can trust you, you will be able to trust them.

## Cohesion

Bonding will take place in an environment of trust, cooperation and competence. This works the same at home and work. A team can only function if each member knows that they can count on their team members. This trust is built through competence, meeting expectations, and effective communication.

Just like a basketball team, your unit is composed of individuals. Each of these individuals must do their jobs and must interact with each other to get the team goal accomplished. If your individuals have confidence in each other, they have the security of knowing that each individual will competently perform their individual responsibilities and do what it takes to execute the team goal. This is the magic ingredient of cohesion — trust.

Sometimes companies try to artificially simulate team cohesion through off campus activities such as ropes courses, leadership retreats or executive weekends. All of these activities can be extremely fun if addressed in a casual and fun manner. However, the only way to build true team cohesion is by knowing that each team member is competent in their area, will do the job to specifications, complete the job on time and will do so in a respectful manner, acknowledging the gifts of each team member.

## Longevity

In discussing the fact that acquiring employees can be an expensive undertaking, I'm not saying anything you don't already know. With this being said, when I'm in the marketplace, I'm observing several short-term solutions being hired. Why, as an employer, would you intentionally hire an unqualified, "short term solution" as a full time employee? Eventually, this individual, because of their lack of qualifications and social graces, will be fired at your expense. I don't know about you, but to me, this type of hiring practice does not sound like a winning formula for success and an optimal way to maximize profits.

I realize that this seems like a "no duh" once more, but if you went out into the marketplace with me for one day, and we sat and did nothing but observe employee behavior in various situations, you would be asking the same questions I'm asking.

Common sense would dictate that, as an employer, only hire

qualified people that bring a unique and desired skill set to your company. In addition to qualifications, the employee would possess a future-focused, dynamic and positive attitude that builds a positive atmosphere in your company and builds the confidence of their teammates.

By retaining great employees for the long haul, outstanding customer relationships are built that endure price wars, fancy remodeling, gimmicky sales pitches and fresh-faced college graduates. In addition to maximizing your profits, you will maximize good will by building a legacy that is built on a family atmosphere, hard work and opportunity for those who desire a career.

## CUSTOMER SATISFACTION

Employees that feel upbeat, valued, secure, and rewarded will share that feeling with your customers. All you, as the employer, have to do is to provide a supportive, rewarding environment and your employee will handle the rest.

Sounds easy, doesn't it?

Captain Obvious stopped by a little while ago and he agrees. If you treat your employees as valued members of a team that is rewarded for results, your employees will treat your customers with value, respect and with the utmost care, knowing full-well that their compensation is tied to the customers feeling of value and satisfaction.

Since myself, Captain Obvious and every other business guru believe this to be true, why am I having an incredibly difficult time observing this type of behavior in the marketplace?

Oh yeah, I know why. You or your executives are not hiring the right people, communicating expectations, expressing appreciation, rewarding results and being clear on all aspects of your company's mission, vision and desires for the employee and the customer.

It all starts with you. You are in charge of the atmosphere of your company and that atmosphere will determine your company's level of customer satisfaction.

## *OPPORTUNITY*

Longevity can have two layers. The first one is an employee for an extended period of time. The second is an employee that transitions from being an employee to being a customer or a referral source for a lifetime.

As a CEO or business owner, you understand that your entire staff does not have your dream and doesn't necessarily want the same things from your company that you do. One of the reasons you hired your employees was their possession of unique gifts and talents. When people have a unique skill set, sometimes they need to spread their wings and that could be a change within your company or a change from your company.

## Change Within Your Company

Sometimes uniquely skilled employees need an opportunity to express their skills within different areas of your company. Change breaks up the monotony of the day-to-day routine and helps develop new revenue streams for your company. A fresh opportunity allows an individual to grow educationally, professionally and emotionally. That growth will be reflected on your bottom line. Allow your employees to try out positions within your company on a temporary basis. If the employee fits into the new position, that position will offer more income opportunities for your company because the employee is being allowed to fuel a desire, increase their skill set and flourish in a creative environment. As the employee grows professionally, their good will towards you and your company also grows. As their good will towards you grows, the customer satisfaction level grows, which increases profits.

## Change From Your Company

Uniquely skilled individuals sometimes must change employment in order for them to realize their dreams and progress professionally. As their employer and since this person has been an outstanding employee for you, help them make the change with ease. Remember, they don't have your exact dream in life and they're going to make the change regardless. Why not keep them as a team member for the rest of their lives? This is not a personal attack on you as an employer. If you help them transition and fulfill their dreams, they will continue to help you fulfill yours by being a ready referral source that serves as a funnel for your company. Keep in mind you set the vibration for the atmosphere and that vibration impacts more than just the four walls of your company.

# CUSTOMER ENVIRONMENT

## *ATMOSPHERE/TONE*

Now that you've provided a rewarding atmosphere for your employees, your employees can transfer their feelings of good will to your customers. In setting the tone for a customer, many things impact that tone or feeling the customer will experience once on your property or connected to you by phone or keyboard. Each time a customer has an experience with your company, your company will generate some sort of reaction connected to your customers' five senses. Make sure that experience is one the customer wants to relive daily, weekly, monthly and yearly.

The process begins as they enter your parking lot, dial your number or pull up your website...

### External Appearance

As your customer pulls into your parking lot, bumpin' their favorite tunes, what are they observing as they look out the windows of their car?

- Signage

    - Does your sign have all the correct letters and is the name of your company spelled correctly?

    - Is your sign fully intact or would the customer swear a natural disaster hit last week?

    - Do the bulbs that light your sign work?

    - Have young pranksters used your sign as target practice?

- Has your landlord put the sign over the right business?

- Structure

  - Is the paint peeling off the walls of your office building?

  - Are the stairs leading into your office fully intact or falling apart?

  - Are the windows clean?

  - Is the sidewalk clean and welcoming?

  - Does the outside of your building resemble a storage closet with endless amounts of crates, boxes and storage devices stacked against the wall?

- Parking Lot

  - Does your parking lot resemble a landfill with trash strewn everywhere?

    - As a customer, if I see a trashed parking lot, I will assume that the inside of your business will also be unkempt and unclean. That assumption also extends to your business practices and your promises.

    - A trash-filled parking lot is also a signal to me, as a customer, that I may not be able to trust your employees, your brand and your merchandise.

    - Why would you want your customer to start their experience with you already having one strike against you?

- Are your parking spots clearly marked with adequate space for cars to maneuver safely?

- Do panhandlers continuously accost your customers as they enter and leave your building?

  - I will not allow my wife or son to return a business that has panhandlers anywhere near their parking lot. That means that business has lost my dollars forever, in addition to me telling every friend that I have not to go to this business.

- Do civic groups accost your customers as they enter and leave your building?

  - I philosophically support many of the civic groups that accost customers when they enter or leave a business. However, I do not support this constant barrage of financial solicitation when I am trying to quickly enter and exit a business for a specific purpose (shopping, groceries, gas, movies, etc.). Let me reiterate — philosophically, I support these groups and financially, I will write a check to them sometime during the calendar year; however, I'm just trying to get in a business, purchase needed items and get to my destination.

  - Many groups don't just stop at asking for money. They verbally assault you when you inform them that you are not interested in supporting their cause. When I entered the parking lot of this business, I didn't enter this parking lot to give to a charity. I entered to purchase a specific item as quickly as possible and to get home to my family. My irritation at the situation extends not only to the group soliciting, but also to the business that has given them permission to ask for money from customers. Two problems with this: I get hit up so much now, this solicitation has had the opposite effect on me and I refuse to give money to any group soliciting donations or selling items; also, now I'm irritated and I walk into the place of business irritated and I spend less money and then I have to leave the business only to get accosted again by the same people who don't remember me saying "No" the first time and then, I'm irritated all over again and I've "gotten attitude" from these groups twice because I refused to purchase or donate. Guess whom I am going to hold responsible? Your business.

- This practice is starting to keep me from shopping at certain businesses and I've started take my business to other companies where I do not have to endure this type of solicitation and verbal assaults each time I enter and exit.

- Your business has now allowed a civic group that isn't connected to your company, to affect your bottom line. If this practice irritates me this much, is there a possibility that I am not alone and you are losing customers on a daily basis? Now that this civic group has irritated me, I no longer care about your mission or vision or what your company has to offer until my irritation level has dropped. From a pure behavior standpoint, I will not be in your place of business long enough for an attitude change to take place that will allow me to receive and appreciate your excellent customer service practices, therefore convincing me to stay longer and spend more money.

- Aren't you in business to make money? If that is the case, make sure your customers can get from your parking lot through your front door without being accosted and being given a reason to be irritated, angry or anxious concerning their experience with your business.

If your customer visits you online, they're still bumpin' their favorite tunes, it's just from the comfort of a chair, not a car.

- Website
  - Is your website visually appealing?
    - Are there typos and grammatical errors?
    - Is your logo correct?
    - Is your company name spelled correctly?
    - Are the images appropriate for your business?
    - Is the website easy to navigate?
      - A difficult website goes unused! An unused website means no sales!
    - Can customers access information easily and is the information useful pertaining to contacting your company?
    - Is your company information updated and fresh?
    - Do you have a loud song that bursts forth from the speakers upon the launching of the site and can your visitors find the button to turn the song off? Remember; people do use websites during the day when they are at work. Yes, even your

employees. They don't want a loud noise coming out of the speakers that gives them away!

○   Do important links work or take customers to a frustrating dead end?

General rule of thumb: If an elementary school child can use your website, so can your average customer.

**Internal Experience**
Now that the customer has entered your business, unaccosted and relaxed, they want to feel welcomed and appreciated.

- Be nice.

  ▪ Customers appreciate a welcoming, relaxed atmosphere. Make sure your customer enters your business with the right vibe. A smile and a genuine welcome help create the right vibe. Customers want to know that they are valued and appreciated. Just like a family member, a customer needs to feel that "they're home."

    ○   Recently, while I was traveling, I needed to pick up a few items at a popular retail store that is known for their greeters. Upon entering the business, I noticed an older lady, with a cane, sitting on a bench just inside the entrance of the business and I asked if I could help her. As soon as the words exited my mouth, I noticed her nametag and realized she was the greeter. Due to a health issue, she experienced difficulty standing and speaking. Okay, now, I'm not trying to be a jerk, but really? Turns out she was a wonderful lady, but not my first choice for the role of "greeter."

○ When selecting a greeter, remember that this person is projecting your company's image and this will be your customer's first impression of their "family experience" during their time at your place of business.

▪ During your customers' time inside of your business, make sure you check back in with them periodically. Always greet them with a smile and an attitude of service. Be accessible but not "over their shoulder."

▪ As they leave your place of business, give them a reason to come back. Thank them for coming, let them know you'll see them again and express to them your gratitude for being able to serve them. Remember; make sure they feel like a valued and loved family member.

• What does the customer see when they walk in the front door?

▪ The first thing your customers need to see is your employees with extremely large smiles welcoming them to your business. The customer also needs to see a consistency in the way each customer is treated in regards to greeting, helpfulness, appreciation and value.

▪ Is your business clean?

○ Is the floor clean? Especially the floor the customer is walking on? Why in the world would I make such a big deal about this? Funny story time! Recently, my family vacationed in Florida and decided to take a break from the beach and get frozen drinks to cool us down. After surveying the area, we chose a nationally known chain, known for their frozen drinks. So, we go in and start filling up our cups. Our son starts complaining about his mom standing on his flip-flops. He keeps telling his mom to stop standing on his flops and she keeps telling him that she's not standing on them. Finally, after about thirty seconds, the three of us look down and realized that his mom wasn't standing on his flip-flops. The floor was so sticky; his feet were cemented to the floor! We actually had to bend over and pry his flip-flops loose from the floor! To make matters worse, the fountain that was supposed to provide the frozen goodness died while we were filling up. To make matters even worse, and to top it all off, we had to move two vagrants out of the doorway, just to get out of the store. Another pleasurable experience provided by top-notch management and employees!

- Can the customer see any visual signs of trash, lint, dirt, water, dead insects, or stains on the floor? If your customer is thinking about getting tetanus shots instead of buying your products, you have an issue.

- Are the windows or areas containing clear plastic or glass clean?

- Is the lighting in your place of business conducive to relaxation and pleasure for your customers?

- Is dust visible on shelving or for sale items?

- Are items stacked neatly on shelves?

- Is the store laid out in a simple and easy to navigate manner?

- Is store décor visually stimulating or overwhelming?

  ○ I recently left a popular retail store because the décor was making me physically sick due to the signage and the displays being so visually overwhelming. I can say that I will never shop with this business chain again.

- Are workstations neat, clean and orderly?

- Is furniture provided for the customer clean, well maintained and comfortable?

- Are employees neat and clean in appearance? Remember; an unkempt, unclean employee tells your customer your business is unkempt and unclean. Therefore, any items that you serve the customer are unclean.

  ○ If a uniform is provided, is the employee wearing it properly and neatly?

  ○ If a uniform is not provided, is the employee appropriately dressed for your place of business?

- Do customers see employees actively carrying out responsibilities or do they see them standing around, talking and texting?

  ○ I recently observed an employee at a retail store attempting to sweep the floor, while actively texting. From my observation, the texting was getting done way better than the sweeping. The employee stopped sweeping halfway through so she could finish the text. A person has to have their priorities, right?

- ○ One time, I offered to help a teenager finish her text, if it would get my items rung up any faster. She became offended and huffed and puffed and informed me that her texting was none of my business. She was correct. Her texting information was none of my business. However, her job performance was my business and I quickly informed management of her actions.

- ○ During another fun and informative outing, I asked a customer service rep for some help. After a series of "F- bombs" and "MF-bombs" dropped on a fellow employee, I abandoned my search for the needed items and instead began my search for the general manager.

- What does your customer hear when they walk in the front door?

  - Of course, you're correct! They hear a huge "Welcome to....!"

  - I would rather be annoyed by having too many people welcoming me to your business than be annoyed by the fact that nobody noticing that I had arrived.

  - The sound a customer hears upon entering your place of business will affect their experience and their spending.

  - Make sure the music being played in your business matches your clientele. You worked so hard to get your customer from their car into the door in a relaxed manner, you welcomed them with a great big smile and overwhelmed them with gratitude for choosing your place of business, DON'T BLOW IT BY PLAYING LOUD, OBNOXIOUS TUNES THAT WILL ANNOY YOUR CUSTOMERS AND ENCOURAGE THEM TO LEAVE YOUR BUSINESS AS QUICKLY AS POSSIBLE!

○ Unless you are a business that features music, be sure and keep the volume level of the music at a "background level." Background level means that your customers can carry on a low volume conversation without impediment or interruption. During the time I was writing this book, I visited several different establishments that didn't understand this concept and, of course, I vocalized my concerns to management. One manager basically told me to "stick it", one manager argued with me about the volume and since he was the one who chose the volume level, he wasn't going to change it, three managers told me that the music and volume were appropriate and I was just "straight out" wrong, and five told me that they had no authority to change the music or the volume level that had been set by corporate policy. What you didn't hear was the managers seeking to serve me in any way. They informed me that the type of music just didn't matter and that volume had nothing to do with the customer experience. They also expressed that they were used to the volume of the music and "they just didn't hear it anymore." For some reason, I thought I was the customer and that somehow, my needs (and my dollars) mattered. As you may have guessed by now, I have contacted the appropriate management and informed them that I will no longer be a customer of their business.

- Just so we are all on the same page, let me clear up a few things concerning music in a place of business:

  ○ Yes, volume matters. Your customers should not be overwhelmed by pre-selected music that they had no input into or have a desire to listen to. If a business meeting cannot be held due to the volume of your music, the volume is too loud. I have grown weary of entering businesses and being unable of carrying on a conversation with my clients and my family.

  ○ Music is not being played at your establishment to make your employees happy. The music type and lyric must match your clientele. Your clientele will become agitated and irritated by music that does not match their personal and age desires. An agitated customer spends less money and goes somewhere else. Make sure the person choosing the music for your place of business understands the needs of the customer outweigh the desires of the employees, regardless of age. The intent of music in an establishment is to create ambience, relaxation and an effortless experience. If I'm thinking how much "I hate the damned music in this place" more than thinking about what I'm there to purchase, I'm not coming back and I will tell every person I know about my experience.

○ The genre of music needs to match the establishment. If I go into a store that caters to teenagers, I expect to hear the latest in pop music. Now this music irritates the ever–living crap out of me personally, but I have an expectation of this music being played in this establishment. If I enter an urban establishment, I expect them to be bumpin' Biggie (by the way, I like Biggie and my reference to Biggie may establish my age). The main disconnect I'm seeing with business is a lack of understanding when it comes to who is spending dollars in their business. Provide a soothing environment and the people will come and spend money. I've noticed lately that some major retailers are disconnected from who is shopping and spending money in their stores. For some reason, many retailers are playing music for the "under twenty crowd" while expecting the "over forty crowd" to spend money with them. What makes no sense to me is the fact that these retailers have done the market research, but for some reason, feel that the music they play in their business is unimportant. As a kid, I used to make fun of "elevator music," but as an adult, I'm in favor of bringing it back! Light, orchestral music does not agitate, aggravate or irritate customers. Make sure the music in your establishment enhances your customers' experience and provides a relaxing environment that encourages return shopping.

• You've greeted your customers with an award-winning smile, seduced them with your suave welcome, enticed them with eye-catching cleanliness, and romanced them with intoxicating sounds — now, enchant them with the fragrance of pleasure...a pleasurable fragrance helps to provide a pleasurable experience.

- Many places of business for the most part, have no fragrance at all. There is nothing wrong with a fragrance-free office space. Fragrance-free means one less thing that can irritate your customers.

- I personally love going into grocery stores that bake bread or pastries. The smell of fresh pastries and donuts is intoxicating to me. The smell also activates a pleasurable memory from my childhood of spending time with my father and grandfather. This pleasurable memory will cause me to spend more time in the store and scan for more items to purchase.

- Just like with music, any smell or fragrance that is manufactured within your business environment needs to match your clientele.

- A word of caution: make sure your smell doesn't trickle out into the mall or your sales people don't spray the innocents casually walking through the mall. Nowadays, many people have adverse reactions to certain fragrances. Many types of potpourri can cause migraines, nausea and other ill effects. Give fragrances a "sniff" test before making them part of a business environment.

- The area of fragrance also extends to one of the most visited rooms in your business — the restroom. At no time should your restroom reek of urine or vomit. I bring this up because in doing research for this book,

I had the unfortunate pleasure of smelling both in several businesses I surveyed. A stinky and smelly restroom tells the customer you slack off on details, which means you'll slack off in providing service and care that meets their needs. A stinky restroom is a violation of trust between you and the customer and they will take their business elsewhere.

## PROVIDE SECURITY AND TRUST IN YOUR BRAND

Now that the customer understands that you mean business by providing an optimal environment that pleases their senses, back up that sensual overload with reasons to believe in and trust your brand.

*Train Your Employees*
As I have stated earlier in this book, a knowledgeable employee is a must for a company to stay profitable and continue into the future. In addition, stupid employees just irritate the hell out of people, as I'm going to illustrate in my following example: The day after my son's flip flop was glued to the floor of the frozen beverage store, I decided to tempt fate and give frozen beverages one more try. I had no idea that this adventure would lead me into five long, arduous days of combat with several individuals that showed up to a battle of wits unarmed. In an effort to tell the story of my gut wrenching experience, I will lay out each day in chronological order so you can relive the experience with me:

Day #1 After a carefully planned reconnaissance mission, a target was chosen based on a high probability of iced coffee being served. I entered the establishment, surveyed the menu and placed my order with a very bubbly, yet untrained, staff member. Five minutes later, I knew this mission was going south fast. Not only was there no iced coffee in my hand, but the bubbly, untrained staff member was asking me how to operate the register. I explained to the staff member that I was only part of the recon unit and that engineering must be called in. A rather robust engineer showed up and was also unable to operate said cash register. After ten minutes had passed, I disengaged from the target and retreated with a free, large, hot, black coffee. Since engineering was unable to operate the equipment, the undesired black coffee was free. The score? Me=0, untrained and inept staff members=1. Abort mission.

Day #2 After gathering more intel, I decided to change up my strategy and launch an early morning surprise attack. Goal of the mission: one iced coffee. The intel gathered provided information that informed me that only one size of iced coffee for $2.49 was offered. Objective appeared to be simple and extraction easy. Ten minutes later, a retreat appeared necessary, establishment evacuated, one small hot coffee with cream and sugar in hand. Me=0, untrained and inept staff members=2.

Day #3 After reviewing more intel with associated family members, a new strategy was determined with a launch time of 09:00. At exactly 09:00, the establishment was entered and all subjects were surveyed. A target was selected, and the target was assigned a task of supplying one iced coffee. After the target supplied me with a large, hot coffee with cream and sugar, an immediate reassessment of the plan was necessary. I immediately put my plan in action by handing the hot beverage back to the target and requesting an iced coffee. It was established that support would be needed and he called in ground support. Two members of his ground support team arrived and asked for an assessment. I inquired about the manner of training the target had received and asked if the target spoke English and was currently deaf or hard of hearing. Ground support assured me that the target spoke English and was neither deaf nor hard of hearing. Ground support took control of the mission and supplied me with a medium, hot, black coffee. With hot, black coffee in hand, I decided to regroup back at base camp. Me=0, untrained and inept staff members=3.

Day #4 After regrouping at base camp and reviewing the previous three days of intel, our team determined that some form of visual aid would be needed to complete the mission. Dawn broke early that day and in an effort to use the element of surprise as my weapon, I entered as the sun started to crest the horizon. My focus was sharp and my determination was unwavering. Today would be the day of victory. I would get my iced coffee. With my plan and my will, I entered the establishment. I surveyed the area, and picked a new target. The new target informed me that it was her first day on the job and that I needed to exercise patience and understanding when dealing with her skill level. After processing the new intel, I put my visual aid plan into action. I took her by the hand, placed her hand on the menu and pointed to the desired item —iced coffee, one size, $2.49. The target assured me that my intel was correct and that the plan had a high success rate. Ten minutes later, I entered the home base with a large, hot coffee with cream. Me=0, untrained and inept staff=4.

Day #5 After court-martialing the recon team for inadequate intel, the target was abandoned and a new target was selected. Aw, hell, who am I kidding? I said screw it and went to Starbucks. I'm not sure if I'm still welcome at this particular Starbucks, however. After experiencing the exhilaration of getting the EXACT iced coffee that I ordered, I hugged and kissed a surprised and anxious manager. It would have been cool, but I don't think I was his type!

Now that we have shared my personal pain of book research and the depths of my sacrifice for knowledge, let's move on...

Yes, most people have funny stories just like the one I just shared, but how do these funny stories begin? Poor or non-existent training, combined with placing the wrong individual in a position that he/she is currently unqualified to perform.

I understand there will be times where putting an inexperienced person in a temporary uncomfortable position will be necessary. I had to put a student manager into a ball game one night. I had suspended three players and six players fouled out. The look of terror on the student manager's face said it all when I tapped him on the shoulder and told him to go check in. He realized he was not trained for this position. His teammates realized he wasn't trained for this position. I also realized that he was not trained for this, but the official told me I had to have five players on the court. As you may have already guessed, the game did not go our way. We got pummeled, but the student manager was able to gain much-needed "street cred" and say he played high school basketball, even if it was for only a few minutes. Even though this young man had been at every practice and participated in every drill, it didn't mean he had the skill level to be a star player. I kept him as part of the team because he was a wonderful person and it meant a lot to him even though he knew he would probably never play.

I went with my last resort to fit a requirement for a very short period of time. A student manager never played in another game I coached. As the coach, I took necessary steps to make sure that that never happened again for the rest of my career.

How are you approaching training and talent in conjunction with your team and your business? Are you placing your star players "out front" as your first line of introduction and communication with your customer base? As a way of illustrating my point, the following are things I observed while doing research for this book:

- Employees manning registers were unable to count money

- "First day" employees who had been on the job for five minutes with no training greeting and ringing up customers

- Employees completely devoid of social skills being asked to greet customers

- Employees that were unable to answer basic questions concerning inventory or business policy in regards to their company

- Employees improperly dressed concerning company uniform

- Profanity used in front of customers—this happened many times

- Employees with extremely poor hygiene and body odor

- Employees complaining to customers about hours and work conditions in order to gain sympathy from the customer. For some reason, employees think this is a conversation starter. This is a conversation starter if you want your customers to shop elsewhere.

- Employees displaying a general lack of desire to help the customer

- A display of employee belief that they are "doing me a favor" by helping me

- An atmosphere of apathy and total disregard for the job itself

So what, pray tell, is the solution for all of the behaviors I observed?

Training, combined with expectations and immediate consequences.

Make sure all new employees meet the following criteria before being allowed to deal with customers:

- The right person is hired to begin with — hiring the wrong people cannot be fixed by training! Hire the right people!

- Develop a training protocol that each new employee MUST receive and makes sure your training staff is top notch and qualified

- Quiz your employees on policy and information continuously — if the wrong answers are supplied, re-train or fire them

- Be very clear on personal hygiene and uniform/ professional attire policies — quiz employees on these requirements. Review requirements periodically to make sure all parties are on the same page. If requirements cannot be achieved by employees, let the employee seek employment elsewhere.

- Make sure all employees dealing with customers are well-versed in being able to answer frequently asked questions from your customer base

- Put your best and brightest in front of the customer and keep them there! Customers need confidence in your brand immediately and the best and brightest can provide confidence. Customers will excuse slower service if greeted by a caring, friendly and knowledgeable employee. Make sure the employee is well-versed in basic social graces and understands how to execute those social graces.

The buck stops with you. A wrongly hired, untrained inept employee that helps destroy your brand is your fault. It's not them, it's you! I recommend you mull that thought over while you sip on a nice iced coffee!

**Provide Value**
Impeccable customer service and detailed product knowledge cannot make up for an inferior product. Customers expect value for their dollars. Your product(s) must meet the specifications that you display to your customers. A crappy product served with a smile is still a crappy product. Customers need to be able to trust that your product will last, do the job and meet all criteria specified by your company. In the event a problem is encountered, the customer needs the confidence that your company will do everything within its power to correct the situation that provides a "win-win" for both parties.

**Keep The Focus**
Customers are coming to you for a specific service or item. They have researched your company and decided you fit the criteria of their needs. Make sure you provide them with the expected service or item. As you are sitting here reading this, you may be thinking to yourself, "No duh, wise ass." But, as I have stressed throughout this book, there is a reason why I'm bringing this up. Many places of business are beginning to try to appease

too many groups at one time while losing focus of why their business has been established.

As a way of being crystal clear with what I mean, here are observations that all of your customers and I are making each time we do business with your company:

*Endless Amounts of Fund-Raising*
I'm not some unfeeling bastard completely devoid of empathy or sympathy. I personally have sat on the boards of several non-profit organizations and have been the Executive Director of one. However, enough is enough. Customers are coming to you to purchase a service or product—NOT to be constantly badgered for donations for an unrelated non-profit organization that has NOTHING to do with the original product or service connected to your company.

I began polling customers concerning this topic and I found out that this is becoming an issue of friction and irritation. Hitting your customers up for money by using guilt and pressure is not a way to capitalize on all of the positive customer service steps that your employees have displayed since the customer entered your business. Even though you've done everything right connected to customer service up to this point, your customer is now leaving your business frustrated and irritated because the focus is no longer on your product or service, but on something completely disconnected from your business.

The goodwill that your business is attempting to generate is being lost due to over aggressive employees soliciting donations and the sheer volume of donation requests. Customers do not want to be browbeaten into donating to a cause they do not support just to keep an over aggressive employee from badgering them. Your customers don't frequent your business for a large serving of guilt. They come to you for a specific product or service. Many individuals are choosing to take their business to companies that do not aggressively solicit donations to non-profits. I am one of those customers.

## The Tip Jar

More and more retail establishments are placing tip requests at the point of purchase. It has always been my understanding that a tip is for above and beyond service. Why do I know that? Because I bartended and waited tables for many years. Notice I didn't say, I got tips for doing my job that I was being paid an hourly wage to perform. Recently, I was asked by a coffee barista if I wanted to give her a tip for my $1.89 coffee. I expressed to my friendly barista that I would be more than happy to provide her with a tip. I told her if she wanted to make tips, to get a job that allowed her to provide "above and beyond" service to the customer and to stop asking for tips for doing her damned job. She asked for a tip—not for money. So, I provided her with a friendly tip.

As a courtesy to your customers, please get rid of this nuisance — the tip jar. I, as a customer, refuse to reward an employee for doing a job that they are already being paid to do. As a bartender and waiter, I was never paid the same hourly wage as other "non-tippable" staff members. The understanding was that I would make up the difference by providing a service to the customer, which would be rewarded with a tip. Since when is doing your job a "tippable" offense?

I will NOT frequent an establishment that expects something for nothing. Businesses expect me to pay for a service and don't hand out free products. As a customer, I expect the same respect from them.

## The TV

I'm beginning to see a disturbing trend of companies installing TVs in "non-customary" places. When I go into a place of business that is not a sports bar or entertainment venue, I am going there for a specific product or service. In addition to needing a specific product or service, I'm also seeking refuge from the "outside world" and its influences. I recently went into a restaurant for dinner and relaxation. I ended up getting a very tasty meal and a huge dose of stress. The stress I felt was provided by an extremely loud TV broadcasting the daily news. I don't watch the news in my own home. Why would I want to go to a restaurant to watch TV unless it was a sports bar? I asked management if I was going to be charged for the side order of stress that I did not see listed on the menu. I don't know what disturbed me most; the fact that they didn't laugh at my joke or the fact that they didn't care for my point of view on why I had entered their restaurant to begin with. I went there for a meal, not to be bombarded with the negativity of the media or a TV program that I have no interest in watching. As a business owner, why add to your customers' stress level? You want to be a refuge from the world and allow your customer to feel relaxed and at home. I left that restaurant irritated and determined to spend not one more dime with their business — even though the meal was one of the best of my life. There is the proof that an exceptional product must be backed up with excellent customer service and a relaxing environment.

## Business Within A Business

When a customer enters your place of business, that customer is there to shop with you, not to be hounded and badgered by separate businesses that happen to be located within your four walls.

Do not allow one more external source to irritate your customer and project a negative vibe into your environment. How many times do I have to say this? Irritated customers will choose to spend their dollars in an environment that does not irritate them!!!

If you stay focused on your products and services, so will your customer. Do not allow an external force to come into your business and destroy all of you and your employees' hard work. If your customer gets out of their car and is already working on a strategy on how to avoid: donations, unwanted tip jars, and aggressive solicitors that have nothing to do with your company, you have lost your focus and chances are, you will lose that customer. It is a choice that you will make and a choice your customer will make.

## IT'S ALL ABOUT THE CHILDREN...

As I begin this section, I want to clarify that I am a father and that I devoted over twenty years of my life to serving special needs children. That being said, I MUST cover this issue.

I am noticing a disturbing trend of a lack of parenting and an increasing supply of out of control, disruptive children in places of business. I acknowledge that you, as a CEO or business owner, in no way, shape or form can control the parenting style of any customer or what goes on in that customer's home environment.

However, you do have **total control** over what takes place in **your** establishment.

As I stated earlier, why work extremely hard to provide the ultimate in customer service and provide a quality product while allowing an external source to destroy all of your hard work and disrupt your relaxing customer experience?

Why are business owners allowing unruly children to destroy property, disrupt business flow and destroy the customer experience?

Let me put it this way: If an adult started tearing up company property, screaming at employees and customers and throwing company property, would this type of behavior be tolerated?

I'll answer this for you.

The answer is NO!

Not only would you ask this customer to leave, you would probably also notify the police.

Why do you allow a behavior that you would not tolerate out of an adult, out of a child?

As I was writing this book, I did an informal poll of fifty adults and I asked one question: What is the number one thing that interrupts your pleasant experience in restaurants, retail stores, sporting events and public venues these days?

Fifty out of fifty, without encouragement from me, said, "Unruly children."

I was shocked. I realized that this type of behavior got on my nerves, but I had never received 100% of the same response, especially if I did not provide any coaching towards the response I desired. This informal survey spurred me on to discuss my findings with various general managers in my area. I wanted to know if the general managers felt the same way as their customers.

All agreed.

The general managers said that their companies had instructed them to ignore unruly children and that their companies provided them with no universal way to handle the children or their parents.

Let me get this straight: Fifty out of fifty adults provided me with an identical, uncoached answer that matched the identical answer of the twelve general managers that agreed to be interviewed. If everything these individuals told me was true, then unruly children have become an issue that must be dealt with immediately. I would say before this gets out of control, but apparently, this IS an issue that is already out of control.

Customers do not come to your place of business for anything other than for a service or product that you provide. They do not come to be solicited, irritated, agitated, frustrated, or have an external source destroy their experience. Customers expect your business to provide them with a relaxing experience built on trust, value and attention to detail. They expect you, the place of business, to deal with unruly, belligerent customers — REGARDLESS OF AGE!

If you would not allow an adult to display this type of behavior, you cannot tolerate it out of a child. That child will grow up to become an adult that continues to display that behavior in your establishment. The adults I surveyed said that they would rally around any business that would take a stand to handle disruptive children and parents.

Random statistics do not lie.

I went out of my way to make sure I did not taint the results of my survey. I wanted an honest assessment and I feel like I got it.

The question is: Do you believe my results and are you willing to handle an issue that your customers have stated is extremely important to them?

You can no longer avoid this problem.

If your competitors decide to handle this issue, your customers will take notice and take their dollars to your competitors' establishments.

The environment within your home office and your entire company is dependent upon you.

What is the experience that you desire for your employees and for your customers? The entire future of your company is dependent upon the environment that is established.

Remember again, it's not them, it's you.

# Chapter 7

# Health

When you address a health chapter in a book, what you are really addressing is something near and dear and personal to your employees' hearts. Now I've been in Corporations and we all do the dance of Corporate Wellness and Wellness Programs. We talk around it and we talk to each other about it. We talk and talk and talk without any action ever occurring.

Do people take these programs seriously? Do people get back in shape? Do people start to get in shape? Do people even talk about being in shape? I want to ask you this question:

Did you? It's your company. You had HR come in and do the program.

Did you follow the program?

So many times I go in and talk to the CEO or business owners and they ask me, "How do you put this into effect?"

You want your employees from a service standpoint to be healthier, but are you following any of the directions that were outlined for your company? Over 50% of the owners and CEOs that I spoke with did not.

I look at them and I wonder, "Why didn't you?"

Your employees are going to follow your lead if you get lean, mean, and cut, they are going to as well.

But this actually goes into a bigger issue.

People don't like to be told what to do once they walk out the doors of your company. That's their life, their decision and you are not going to have any "say so" in it.

It's like parenting. It's hard being a parent. I can teach my child what to do all day long and I can enforce the bounds of the environment of our home. However, I've got to have him trained well enough to make decisions on his own, so when he goes out on his own, he can make the right decisions for his life.

It's the same way with your employees. You can only control your environment throughout the day. You can't control what they do as soon as they leave your office.

However, you can encourage them to make better decisions. It comes back to the "WSI and the WIIFM" – "Why should I? What's in it for me?"

It's easier to answer by listing the benefits to your company. People don't stay out of work if they feel great. I know there are sunny days, there's fishing and other activities to do on those sunny days when your employees want to lay out of work, but if you've already done everything else I've asked you to do throughout this book, they're not going to stay out of work. You'll get more production and better quality of work if your employees feel good, they've got some energy and they've got some spirit and they are already motivated by the excellent environment you've. On top of feeling good, they're going to get more done in a shorter time and the quality of what they do during that time is going to greatly improve.

When your employees are healthy, you've got fewer injuries on the job. I think the dumbest thing I ever did at work was to drive a staple all the way through my finger because I was tired. I stuck the piece of paper under it, moved the paper and I left my finger and did one of those karate chop staples. I went "WOOOOWWWW!!!!" in my best karate chop shouts. The staple went right through my hand — that was incredibly painful. I actually had to go find a pair of pliers and pull the staple out of my finger and then go to the hospital. That's a stupid injury caused by lack of sleep.

Think about all the injuries that can take place at your job and at your company. If your employees are focused, if they've had sleep, if they feel good when they get to work, and they are encouraged by your example, fewer injuries will happen.

There will be an increase in sales. It can't help but happen!

What happens if you take a non-trained person who's got a great disposition and is just friendly to people? You think they can sell something just on being nice to people? Sure they could. Now, take a seasoned veteran who's had plenty of sleep, who's eating right, whose body is functioning at the highest level that it's ever functioned. Do you think they can sell something? Yes!

In addition to the more sales, you have more customer satisfaction. You've got a joy-filled, "feeling good" person on the end of that phone or standing in front of that customer addressing whatever the issue is. They are doing it with a smile, they are doing it with a little "pep" in their step and they're doing it with the main goal of making the customer happy. And they're not having to think about how bad they feel, how bad their family feels or how bad their kids feel or, "Oh my gosh, I didn't get any sleep last night!"

See the difference?

Now you add to that a better home life for your employees. They leave you — they're feeling good. They get home - they're feeling good. They spend time with their spouse and their kids and the pets and they go out, enjoy each other and spend more time together. They are more active in the "talking" situations. They solve more problems together.

Then, they get up the next day and where do they come back to? That joy filled place that you provided for them. It's a very nice circle. It improves your sales, it improves their lives and if you improve their lives, you've improved the Company's visibility in the community.

People see your employees out in the community, whether it's the grocery store, the movies, the roller rink, at the lake, church or at community activities, and they say "Man, whatever it is in your company that is going on, I want to be part of that." Whether they want to work for your company or they just want to be a customer of yours. They're going to refer customers to your company. Their attitude will be, "If I can't personally be a customer of the company, I'm going to refer people to them because I see the positive impact it's made on my friends and their families."

In addition to that, now you've got lower turnover in staff and customers. If you provide a harmonious environment and then you provide a vehicle for people just to feel good about their job and physically improved their health, you've improved their energy and you've improved their family lives. They aren't leaving because their spouse won't let them leave. Your customers aren't leaving because they don't want to leave the energy that your employees have provided to them as customers.

Now let me reiterate this: I have never left a company, as their client, a place where I got that kind of energy from their employees...ever. I've had two people cut my hair in twenty years. I've had had three cleaners in twenty years. I've had two insurance agents in twenty-five years. I don't leave when I feel that energy and vibe from employees who feel good and who experience good health. I've gone to the same restaurants for 30 years because I know the owner; I know the experience I'm going to have as soon as I walk through the door. If CEOs, owners and employees feel good, I feel good. I automatically feel better as a person regardless of how my day is going because that certain energetic, "positive vibed" staff member is there. It's that simple.

Those are the benefits of having healthy employees in your company.

What are the benefits of having a workplace that encourages healthy living to the employee?

One of the things I hear about Wellness Programs and incentives is that people don't trust them. Many people don't trust the company and certainly don't trust information that they feel might be funneled to the government. Now we all know a corporation is really a piece of paper, but some employees see that as something lording over them and they don't want their privacy invaded.

Do they have a point?

Sure they do because we see that in the news every day.

So let's switch this around; imagine that you're not the owner any longer. Someone hands you a form and you've got to have your body mass index on there and you've got to put all your blood stuff on that form and you're giving someone permission to look at your health records.

Would you sign up for that?

I never have, but I was always fanatical about my health anyway.

I've always exercised, I've always eaten well, but I've never signed up for a Corporate Wellness Program because I don't want anybody looking over my shoulder, checking my life, telling me how to live my life. I'm already way ahead of the curve on that one.

Remember you didn't want anybody telling you what to do on the off hours. Neither do your employees, so you are going to have to re-position not only your thinking, but your employees' attitude as well.

Now, in an effort to make presenting "healthy alternatives" palatable to your employees, I have taken the time to interview three of the top experts in their field to help you position the information you need to provide to you and your employees.

Between the three of them, they have probably worked with half of the sports teams in the United States, some Olympic athletes, and have presented reliable and "common sense" health programs for HR departments all over the country. They've been on radio and TV and are listed as national experts and consultants in their respective fields.

I want to give you their opinions and their expertise to give you the maximum benefit of this chapter. As I said earlier, I'm not a medical doctor, I'm not a natural doctor, I'm not a counselor and I'm not a Psychiatrist or therapist. The medical and nutritional professionals that I have in this chapter are the only types of experts that can offer these health suggestions.

If you will listen to what they have to say, take it to heart and apply it first to your life and then help your employees apply it to their lives, you will see such a substantial change not only in your life and your family's life, but your employees' lives as well.

You will see a huge change in your company's environment and bottom line.

As a standard rule, when I interviewed these three individuals and experts, I had one goal in mind. That goal was for them to discuss the issues that employees have brought to them on a daily basis whenever they speak, or patients visit them in their offices and how these employee issues are going to affect the company's bottom line.

Remember: If you positively increase your employees' health, you positively increase your bottom line and how the employees view you, as the CEO or owner, in the company. You also positively increase the community's opinion of you and the company.

Before I introduce each one of these experts, I just want to clarify one thing.

It's the definition of health.

People always talk about health. What in the world is health? For the purpose of this chapter, I'm only going to address physical health.

Here's how I'm going to talk about it and they're going to talk about it: Do you say you feel good? If so, and you had to get your blood, saliva and urine tested, would your lab report back up how you say you feel? That's it. I don't want this to be complicated. I just want to make sure that you receive maximum benefit from the experts' advice and that your employees are able to take what they say and apply to their lives and positively increase you and your employees' health and the company's bottom line.

# FRANK TORTORICI

Frank was born and raised on Long Island, NY in an environment of a loving extended family. Yet with all the love surrounding him as a youngster, there lay a pain and darkness he shared with no one. It was the constant nagging symptoms that his family would come to learn as Tourette's Syndrome.

As a child he felt helpless, constantly being prescribed various medications to subdue the symptoms. No medication seemed to work and even then, Frank Tortorici often thought there had to be a better way. At the age of fifteen, Frank Tortorici had entered an all-natural bodybuilding contest. He quickly discovered that working out had an incredible calming effect on his body. The impact immediately triggered an understanding and belief in him that healing can be brought to the human body. He began to exercise regularly and it had its benefits. However, the "bad tic" days began to bring about obsessive thoughts. His body physically and mind mentally felt like they had simultaneously run for hours.

Frank was later introduced to a gluten-free way of living as an alternative to medications. He began to see results quickly, as his gluten-free diet helped to eliminate yeast growth in the intestines. He began researching and learned how to treat Tourette's holistically. He also learned that Candida (a yeast-like fungal organism) is caused by such foods as sugar, antibiotics and alcohol, which were contributing to his symptoms. For the next few years, Frank began to eat as a vegetarian, a raw/vegan and then, a conscious carnivore.

Frank is a certified personal trainer through the American

Council of Exercise and Crossfit Kettlebell and is a Functional Diagnostic Nutritionist.

## SETTING UP SUCCESS

*Scot:   What are some of your tips for setting up healthy office environments, not only for employees but also management and owners?*

*Frank Tortorici:*   The best tips for setting up a healthy office environment I think is to simply get rid of the soda and chip machines and start having fresh fruit and vegetables lying around the office. Having those chips and sodas in there appears to be harmless to the naked eye, but they create and wreak a lot of havoc on the employees when they get that sugar rush.

Those foods wreak havoc on employee focus, concentration and their productivity level. It benefits the employees and the business owner to have fresh fruits and vegetables available to substitute for all of the "processed crap" from vending machines. When employees eat healthy fruits and vegetables, the work product and productivity and energy levels will just sky rocket.

Another thing I find to be very effective when dealing with corporate entities is setting up weekly nutrition challenges. It works really well, it keeps the employees motivated, and I think human beings are, by nature, competitive. I have seen this competition work wonders when the employees are holding each other accountable, you can set up teams where you can do weight loss challenges. Overall, it's a win-win for everyone in the office and the business owner to take those types of actions.

*Scot:   If you opened a business tomorrow, what would you stock the break room with to allow your employees to get the most out of their day?*

*Frank Tortorici:*   What would I start with? Well I think we are seeing such a boom, even in Los Angeles, and as I travel back and forth to the East Coast, I see this; we are seeing a major boom of whole pressed juice shops popping up everywhere. Now that's one thing that I would have as a niche in any office that I would open up. And the reason being is that whole pressed juices are not pasteurized and they retain the microfiber nutrients, minerals and enzymes because they are not heat-treated. And these juices have a shelf life of anywhere from three to six days as long as they are not opened. Once they are opened, you have up to twenty-four to forty-eight hours to consume them without the juice spoiling.

So, juice to me is liquid sunshine. You are getting everything in there that most people would have a difficult time eating throughout the day. I do believe that juicing everyday for every individual is so important because it helps to get the blood alkaline. When the blood is alkaline, it is functioning better and it is not under as much stress. And let's face it, in our workstations, we are crunching numbers and we have certain goals we have to meet. Our thoughts produce acid in our body and blood when we are in stress related situations. In the workspace, you are going to be dealing with stress amongst employees and CEOs, so being able to get their bodies as alkaline as possible from juicing is crucial.

Instead of fast-food machines containing chips and things like that, I would just replace these foods with dehydrated snacks, fresh fruits and vegetables, and again, the juicing compounds. There are companies that are providing raw types of vegan meals, burgers and foods like that, that can be prepared and packaged and the will last up to ten days in a refrigerator. You just need to diversify the offerings and get people interested in these types of food. And the more alkaline the individual's body becomes, the greater the chances of them craving higher alkaline food is going to be. Little by little, as the boss of a company, I would then start trying to implement these small amounts of alkaline type forming foods, little by little, into my employees' work environment. And as they start craving more of the alkaline foods, it is pretty much guaranteed that we are going to see a spike in the productivity levels, and employees' overall well being within the company.

## THE BIG NUTRITIONAL MISTAKES
## EVERYONE MAKES

*Scot: What nutritional mistakes do you see people making on a daily basis which impacts their health, productivity and general overall quality of life?*

*Frank Tortorici:* When I do corporate speaking and wellness work with companies, this ingestion of processed sugars and starches seems to be the mistake I see owners and employees make the most. These foods wreak havoc on the gut and they perpetuate constant cravings of non-nutritional foods. There is a great documentary I point people to called *Fed Up*. In the documentary, they highlight studies on brain patterns when an individual ingests sugar. In addition, these scientists did a study on thirty laboratory mice, feeding them all cocaine and sugar. After a certain amount of days, all of the laboratory mice kept consuming the sugar and not the cocaine. Scientists found that when they study the brain patterns, they discovered that sugar triggers the same response within the human brain as cocaine does.

When you are dealing with the processed sugars, they create yeast growth in the gut, which then leads to Candida, which throws off the balance in the gut, and all of the healthy bacteria balance gets all thrown off. Processed starches convert to sugars and perpetuate fungus and yeast growth, which overall wreaks havoc on the body.

We see how processed sugar affects an individual the same way cocaine does. It's no wonder you start getting those non-nutritional cravings. If a person has one meal with sugar, it seems like it will do no harm, but the cravings leads to another craving and another one and then it just puts you on that hamster wheel of sugar cravings, and it is a vicious cycle that is hard for a person to get off.

## THE "2 O'CLOCK CRASH"

*Scot: How can people get rid of that "2 o'clock crash"? What causes it and what can we do to prevent it?*

*Frank Tortorici:* To prevent that "two o'clock crash", one needs to cut out all processed sugars and starches so they don't hit that sugar crash in later part of the day. Think about it; most people are having some form of pastries for breakfast or sugary cereals and then sandwiches and pizza and bagels for lunch and then by two o'clock, when the caffeine has run out, they completely crash. Popping the healthy omega-three fats from food such as avocados, raw nuts, seeds and coconuts will help keep the glycemic levels regulated and you won't crash.

I'm going to bring you back to the idea of cutting out the processed sugars and starches. Think of the average American. In America, a healthy breakfast is a very heavily starch based meal—cereal, bagels, doughnuts, croissant, waffles, pancakes - all those are starches and sugars. Those starches and sugars shoot up the glycemic levels, so there is no way you are going to prevent that crash form happening. Same thing happens when you are driving to work. Take a look at a Starbucks drive through line. The line is wrapped around the building; everybody needing that caffeine rush because the night before, they probably had a heavily starched dinner and a dessert loaded with sugar. So they wake up, and they are basically in a glycemic coma because their glycemic levels are so low they need that caffeine to jolt them up in the morning. But unfortunately, whether they are dealing with the sugars, the starches or the caffeine, when two o'clock comes, they crash.

So that's what I see as far as preventing that crash - cut out the caffeine, sugars, the starches and really up the healthy fats like avocados, raw nuts and seeds, coconuts, and olives. Whenever we are talking about weight loss, or an imbalance of energy, we need to balance the sugar levels. It is a very simple factor.

## LOW MAINTENANCE TIPS TO PREPARE FOR THE WORK DAY

*Scot: What are some "low maintenance" things people can do in the morning to get ready for the day to maximize their morning hours at work? (What should they eat, what should they not eat, etc.)*

*Frank Tortorici:* Start your day with a cup of hot water with lemon. It will alkalize your body and get it ready to digest food. Cut the caffeine out so you will not have a caffeine crash in the hours to come. Then, have a super food smoothie that can contain ingredients including things like hemp seeds, Goji berries, coconut milk, cinnamon, raw honey, chia seeds or any fresh local berries.

When you wake up in the morning, we are breaking a fast. If you break the word "breakfast" in half, it literally means to break the fast you've had during your sleep hours. It's bananas to me that we break a fast by eating processed foods, sugars, genetically engineered ingredients, coffee and all kinds of things that are bad for our body.

When we are breaking a fast, we have to wake our gut up; we have to wake our body up. The way to do that it's starting the day with hot cup of water with lemon, or a room temperature cup of water with lemon. If you are a person with low or normal blood pressure, you can even add half a teaspoon to a teaspoon of Himalayan pink sea salt. That will naturally drive the blood pressure up a little bit and in doing that, it will get your body revved up, without having to stress out your adrenal glands. The minerals in the salt will help to slightly elevate your blood pressure with a healthy result. However, when a majority of most Americans wake up, they are putting that caffeine and sugar in their bodies, and they are taxing the hell out of their adrenal glands, which leads to a lot of other problems, such as hormone deficiency, and a lot of other health problems.

You want to start your day with a hot cup of water with lemon and once we get that in our stomach, I like to recommend getting a good Kefir product in your body. Kefir is basically a raw organic yogurt. You can go to a store and find a vegan yogurt (not soy), coconut yogurt, or just plain yogurt, with no sugar added. The key is to go with low sugar, because, again, we want maintain balance with our glycemic levels. Then you can add natural sugars such as bananas, raspberries, blueberries, strawberries or any fruit to your liking. Yes, fruit has sugar, but you are also getting the fiber of the fruit, which kind of helps balance the glycemic levels. With this type of food, you're getting vital nutrients, vital chemicals, antioxidants and minerals, electrolytes, so it's a win-win situation when you start your day with this type of mixture. A more "vegan/raw" type of breakfast is very beneficial to your body, and is very easy for your routine because you can find these types of foods almost anywhere you live and they're quick and easy to prepare in the mornings.

## ENERGY BOOSTING

*Scot: When your energy does get low, how can you boost it? What things should people snack on, at the office or at home, to bring their energy levels up?*

*Frank Tortorici:* There are a lot of great supplements that give you the energy boost of caffeine without the jitters. One of them is licorice root. Licorice root will help support the adrenal glands to pump the cortisol through the body to help get your body going, and get your engines revved up.

Another supplement to boost energy is called maca root. It's a "super food" that's grown in Peru. You can get it in sublingual liquid form or powder. You can just add the maca root powder to a smoothie for convenience. Maca root gives your smoothie a butterscotch flavor which many people like. Bee pollen is another easy solution for a midday energy boost.

Any types of sugars that your body can process and use instantly, like sweet potatoes, bananas, fresh berries or apples, is a good way to give you a little pick-me-up boost. Another suggestion is to consume anything with dark leafy greens, like green juice or wheat grass shots. You can eat or drink these types of energy boosting items at the office without much inconvenience to you or your schedule.

One of my suggestions to my clients are to whip up a quick smoothie using some of these ingredients in it, prepare it the night before or bring in a cooler to work with your ingredients.

Most offices have refrigerators and you can have some healthy stuff stocked in there to keep your day fueled and going strong. All across the United States, there's a lot of these cold pressed juiced shops opening up. I see it a lot in Los Angeles, I see it in New York—I'm seeing them everywhere now, so people are catching on to these health ideas. If you want more information about some convenient, tasty and healthy ideas, simply consult my website at www.FrankTortorici.com or check out my Facebook page for daily updates, articles and recipes.

## HEALTHY ALTERNATIVES THAT EMPLOYEES WILL EAT!

*Scot: What are some realistic alternative foods that can be offered at company meetings instead of bagels, donuts, sweets, pizza, etc. that people will actually embrace and accept?*

*Frank Totorici:* I think it's real easy to help your company make this transition. Again, going back to what we've been discussing, you're going to want to cut out all of those processed sugars and starches—the bagels, donuts, sweets and pizza. We simply want to start introducing fresh fruits and vegetables into the mix. You need to purchase clean, organic fruits, vegetables and meats. You can have a lot of different types of foods that your employees don't normally expect at company functions—steak tartar, sushi, turkey, or chicken. But whatever you offer, make sure it is really high quality and offer a lot fresh fruits and vegetables with the meat. Keep a lot of raw nuts, trail mixes, avocadoes, and "healthy fats" in the office because you want to have those healthy starches available to your staff because that's what is going to keep your employees' blood sugar levels sustained throughout the day.

But the main thing for you, as a business owner, is to get rid of "the gunk" in your office that your employees are eating.

If your employees have a sweet tooth, every sweet product that they're used to eating can be replicated by using fruit. If they are making a smoothie, instead of adding sugar to it, you can just simply add two or three dates or figs or raisins or you can add raw, organic honey, which has a lot of health benefits for your body. There are numerous "sweet products" now on the market which can be easily purchased at natural or health food stores and groceries that your employees will love, including natural cakes and cookies made with the healthy ingredients that won't spike blood sugar levels, decrease productivity and negatively affect your bottom line. Whenever I get sweet tooth craving, I will always eat a raw vegan dessert, because everything can be duplicated with Mother Nature. You can get smoothies, carrot cake or apple pie — all made with raw fresh ingredients and that's the key to providing healthy choices for your employees — transitioning them into healthier alternatives.

These fruits and vegetables provide cleansing mechanisms to the body and they assist with the healing and building of muscle and brain functions that are going on in the body and the immune system. As a business owner, you can truly have those healthy food alternatives in the office. It might cost you a little more out of pocket, but you will see the productivity level of the employees skyrocket. It is a win-win situation for every single person involved in this process.

## NUTRITIONAL HABITS FOR EVERYONE

*Scot: What are your suggestions for habits that will point business owners, employees' and their families in the right direction, nutritionally speaking?*

*Frank Tortorici:* I encourage business owners and employees to simply go to Google and research "acid and alkaline charts." These charts will help you to understand what you are eating and how it affects your body. If you print the charts, you can put it on your refrigerator, your cupboards, in your office, and the office kitchen. You will have the charts hanging there to remind you of my simple rule of eating. I call it the eighty/twenty rule. As a rule of thumb, you want to consume 80% of your diet in alkaline forming foods and limit your acid forming foods to 20% of the food you consume.

That rule is going to create a lot of balance in your body. Science has shown us that diseases breed in an acidic body. So if you have an 80% alkaline/20% acidic balance, your body is more in a state of balance where you can function more effectively, as nature intended.

The best way to help people understand that is to take the example of a pool or a fish tank. You are always checking the PH level of the water. If the water becomes too acidic, a lot of things tend to die and fungus grows.

So here is the best way to describe the alkaline/acidic scale: You have a chart from the number one to the number fourteen. The scale runs from acidic to alkaline as you increase the numbers. Number one represents pure acid, with lesser levels of acidity to number six. Number seven is neutral. From number seven up till number fourteen, the alkaline level goes up to pure alkalinity. So we want our blood to be in an alkaline state. When our blood is in that nine to nine-point-five range, we are at an optimal stage where cancer and other diseases are going to have a very difficult time thriving in that alkaline state.

When we are talking alkalinity, we are talking blood alkalinity. That's the oxygen pumped into the blood, which creates the alkalinity. What we are <u>not</u> talking about is the need for acids in our stomach to help us break down foods, fats, and proteins. One of the most amazing foods that embody both of the acid/ alkaline principles is raw fermented apple cider vinegar. I recommend that people put it in their food, drinking it, putting it in your tea or lacing it in ice water.

Why is that? Apple cider vinegar is the only food on the planet that is still acidic in the sense that when it enters your gut, it helps promote the acid levels in the intestines but also makes the blood alkaline, whereas all other vinegars will make your blood acidic. So that's going to help with your digestion and getting the blood alkaline. When the blood is alkaline, you are going to have more energy and less disease.

This even stretches into the whole topic of grass feed beef and why we want to eat grass fed beef over grain fed beef. Same principles: If the cows are grazing on grains and corn, which are all genetically engineered crops, and they are not eating pasture grass, their blood becomes more acidic and they become more prone to Mad Cow disease, different types of cancer and environmental infections. When a cow is grass fed, they have a very high content of Omega 3 fats in the meat and then we consume that when we eat it, which in return, helps us to lower blood pressure, lubricate the skin and joints, and optimize the brain function.

So, not only is it important for our bodies to be alkaline, but it is important for us to look for animals that have been fed a much higher alkaline diet because we are what we eat. If we are consuming animals or food that are more acidic, that becomes a problem for us. With any animal that we consume, that food has an acidic effect on our body. However, the grass fed animals are going to be much lower in the acidity levels, but much higher in the Omega 3 fatty acids which are important for us, as I had mentioned.

When your body is in an alkaline state, you are minimizing the risk of diseases, ailments or illnesses forming. And aesthetically, an alkaline system helps to keep you leaner and keeps the body in homeostasis (regulating your metabolism correctly). You will find that the "yoyo effect" of weight is minimized because when the body is an alkaline state, it's in a place of homeostasis. This alkaline state gives our bodies complete balance.

One shopping suggestion to help keep and maintain your body's alkaline state: avoid all pesticides and try to find certified organic fruits, vegetables and meats if possible. If you can't find that in your "big box" grocery stores, you can generally find it in your local markets whether the produce and meat is locally sourced. Why is that? Usually, when produce and meats are locally sourced, they are coming from smaller farms. When these products come from smaller farms, they are not using pesticides or genetically engineered seeds. Even though these smaller farms usually don't have the budget to get certified as "organic", they're usually producing the type of product you want to purchase — organic.

So it is very important to know where your food comes from. A genetically engineered vegetable is the same as an organic vegetable when you compare them and consider the chemicals and pesticides used in the growing process. You simply cannot compare them — they are two different things! The vegetable with the chemicals will whack out the complete balance of your body. It taxes your adrenal glands and if you are taxing your adrenal glands, your hormones will suffer. When your hormones suffer, your mental health suffers, your body fat goes up, you get lack of muscle tone, lack of sex drive, depression and many other negative health effects—it is a domino effect. So getting the cleanest food sources possible is crucial to an alkaline body; I can't stress that enough.

## *ORGANIC VERSUS NON-ORGANIC*

*Scot: To maximize your health, and your energy level at work, why is it so important to have organic foods versus the foods that are not organic?*

*Frank Totortici:* To really keep it as simple as possible, eating organic is essential for everyone from a health standpoint and from a productivity standpoint. The reason is quite simple. When you are minimizing the amount of toxicity within your food, you are giving your body optimum fuel for it to produce results, to have mental clarity, and to have overall healthy qualities. So when you are eating organic, you are minimizing those types of chemicals that can wreak havoc on one's brain, and nervous system. So when you are able to fuel the nutrition, the minerals, nutrients, and the bioflavonoids, it allows all systems to function at optimum levels. And when functioning at optimum levels and success is right there for you to attain and to grab, you can do that without having to jump too many hoops, because everything is flowing and functioning as properly as possible.

## SUGGESTED DAILY EATING PLAN

*Scot: What is a daily eating plan that you would recommend for the average executive to get the most out of his/her day?*

*Frank Tortorici:* You know, it's a common saying; different strokes for different folks. There may be people reading this that are very much against eating animals and there are other ones that are into eating animals. So, because of such a variation, here is the one simple thing that I would recommend to get people off the processed sugars and starches and start implementing more healthy fats.

So what do I mean by that?

Very simply, in the morning, you can (if you are in the state where you have access to raw dairy), start implementing some raw milk into a smoothie, or raw kefir, which is basically yogurt. Kefir is fermented milk. For lunch, you can always throw avocados in there, whether you are eating a salad or sandwich, or you are eating sprouted grain bread. You can have the avocados, olives or raw cheeses that are imported from Spain, France or Italy. You can also have any types of raw nuts and seeds. Also get acquainted with coconut meat and coconut water, and I mean <u>real</u>, raw, fresh coconut meat and coconut water.

We are in a society right now where we are so fat and nutrition deprived and we are bumped up with sugar and starches — and that just sends glycemic index levels all over the place. When your glycemic levels are all over the place, you cannot function properly because of the sugar crash that takes place (which <u>always</u> happens after your sugar levels spike). So in order to prevent that crash, we want to see more fat added to the diet. By adding more of these healthy fats to the diet, we are sustaining those glycemic levels and we are giving our metabolism fuel to burn properly, which gives us the proper energy throughout the day. You must give your brain healthy fats because it's made up of 80% to 85% fat. If you look at a walnut, that's food, it looks like a brain. Those types of Omega 3 fatty acids help nourish the brain. If your brain is nourished, you're functioning at optimum levels, you're losing weight and you're keeping the weight off. But that can only be done through a high alkaline diet, healthy fattening foods and low levels of the processed sugars and starches.

## WHAT ABOUT WATER?

*Scot: How much water do you recommend for the average person, and what type of water?*

*Frank Totorici:* We are seeing such as boom of different types of waters — reverse osmosis, ionized water, distilled water — all of which I feel serve a tremendous health benefit to every person. I always tell my clients, drink anywhere from sixty four ounces to a gallon of water a day — and that range is dependent on your athletic output and how much you are sweating. If you are eating foods that have a high density of water like watermelons, cucumbers or grapes, you are getting hydrated from those sources as well. When it comes to drinking water, if you aren't eating all these fruits and veggies (and you are not able to get your hands on fresh juices), then I'd say you definitely need up to sixty four ounces to a gallon.

And then what type of water should people drink? I think they all serve tremendous benefit. For me personally, I feel the best when drinking ionized water. And why is that? Again, I am a big believer in the whole acid and alkaline principles. The bottom line is (from all the research I have done); disease cannot thrive in an alkaline system. So I personally like the ionized water because it is high in alkalinity. It is purified and it is alkaline. You also want to be careful purchasing alkaline water in retail stores because when you are buying bottle water that claims to have alkalinity and a PH level of nine-point-five, because after the water is ionized (twenty-four to seventy-two hours), it really stars losing those high alkaline properties. It is still filtered, but it is losing the high alkalinity.

I recommend purchasing an ionizer machine, filling up a big glass jug for the day and keeping that with you at all times. That way, you can see how much you are consuming. But if we are under high stress levels, if we are eating animal proteins, those conditions make our bodies acidic. If we are rushing, working and stressed – all of those situations they make us acidic. So whatever we can do to get our blood to an alkaline state, whether through the water or through the food, I think it's a beautiful thing.

## THIS IS NOT A DIET – IT'S A LIFESTYLE

*Scot: What's the best lifestyle we can have for us to have energy and high production? Is it a smart thing to go ahead and pack your food for the day? Isn't it best for me to go ahead and pack all the food I'm going to need for that day and take it with me?*

*Frank Tortorici:* I think it is great to plan, because if you are one of those people who is in a meeting, there is nothing around to eat and you feel your stomach growling while your blood sugar is dropping, then you will end up grabbing that processed lunch meat on white bread that the company purchased for lunch that day, which is bad for your energy and production. So, if you are one of those people, planning ahead is crucial. If you live in a city where you have juice bars on every corner, you have markets that are serving organic food like I have in Los Angeles, then maybe packing your food is not so critical because have access to the kind of food you should eat.

Even though I live in Los Angles, I am bouncing around every day from client to client, so I pack my cooler for the convenience of having the food I want to eat on hand. I think it really depends on your lifestyle and your work capacity throughout the day. All in all, I think it is important to plan ahead. When you are trying to live a lifestyle that centers around high alkalinity from real food, it requires planning. Whether that's packing it ahead of time or mapping out your day and seeing where you are going to be and seeing what restaurants or markets are nearby that can give you access to real food while on the road or throughout your work day, it's important to plan your eating.

## EXCERCISE

*Scot: Why is exercise so important to the human body?*

*Frank Totorici:* Exercise is so important to everyone for so many reasons. It de-stresses you. It builds bone density, more muscle tone and helps to burn fat even when you are resting. It increases hormone production, especially the "power lifting" type of movements like squats. Weight lifting, walking, functional fitness — any exercise that is done at a level of moderation has tremendous medicinal benefits. And when I say at moderate levels, it's because I want to be clear. People who are on a search for health and wellness and people who are athletes are on two different levels. Athletes have to put their bodies through a tremendous amount of abuse to perform at the top optimum levels. People who are searching for health and wellness should not.

Exercise itself is so healing, so anti-aging, that no one can dispute the health benefits of it. For an individual who is eighteen or an individual who is eighty-five years old, exercise will reap benefits for ages all across the board, both male and female.

# ROAD WARRIORS AND DESK DWELLERS

*Scot:* You train all body styles and people in all types of professions. What do you recommend to your sales people or executives who have to travel regularly? How do you recommend that they get their exercise throughout the working week?

*Frank Tortorici:* I train those types of people all the time and I think it is the easiest way to workout—when you are traveling. And the reason why I say that is, whether you are traveling or whether you are in your office, there are so many ways to have a killer workout in twenty to thirty minutes that only requires your body weight and a yoga mat, at most.

I teach my clients that all they need to exercise "on the go" is a yoga mat, a bottle of water and a stopwatch. With those tools, you can accomplish a lot of great results when you are working out. At the end of the day, for an individual who is on the road and working, if they want to be fit, that requires them learning how to use their own body weight and maximizing it during exercise. There are so many things we can do with just our body—body weight squats, push ups, seat ups, plank holds, jumping jacks, jump squats, lunges, pull ups, dips—the list of "body weight" exercises goes on and on.

They key is hitting higher repetitions, which then helps burn the fat.

So, say I am working with the client who is going to be in China for two weeks on business. I'll have that client commit to exercising at least three days a week to start. For the first week, they'll exercise three days and in the second week, three days, and within those days, I just tweaking their workout. On day one, I have the client work up to a couple of push-ups, squats, and sit-ups. How would I break that down? Depending on where his or her level is, the amount of repetitions that I would have them do for each movement would change.

Let me just give you an example regarding the push-ups, sit-ups, and squats. I would have my client do a set of ten push ups, do a set of twenty body weight squats, and then a set of thirty sit-ups. They would do a set of push-ups; a set of squats, a set of sit-ups and then that would be one complete round. So within that round, a client may be doing twenty push-ups, forty squats and sixty sit-ups—that's just within one round. Then, he may be able to do ten rounds of those. That's thirty to forty-five minutes! Add that up, look at the volume there—he is doing 200 push-ups, 400 squats, and 600 sit-ups. That's a lot of volume there. And the key is he is going to be sweating his ass off, burning a lot of calories, detoxifying the body, draining the lymphatic system, and his risk of injury is close to nothing because he is just working with his body weight. And he's getting those high repetitions in those rounds that are the equivalent of being in a spin class. So there are so many simple ways to maximize and see results with just the yoga mat, your own body and a stopwatch.

*Scot: If someone travels extensively, or they have to sit at their desk for eight to ten hours a day, what type of stretches do you recommend to make sure that back injuries don't come?*

*Frank Tortorici:* As a trainer, I see this all the time with my clients. When you sit at a desk all day long, you need to ask yourself: Is my posture is hunched over? Most peoples' posture is very "trap dominate," which refers to the muscle in between the shoulder blades. People who have this type of posture have a lot of lower back issues. So what that tells me is there is a lot of weakness within a lot of people's core, which is the stomach/lower-back area.

So for clients like that, I always tell them to try standing up instead of sitting, throughout the day. When you are standing up, you really want to loosen up those hamstrings. Bend over and reach down to your toes; that's one way to loosen the hamstrings. Another great way is by lying on your back and just taking your right leg straight up in the air with it locked out, and bringing it over across your body to the left side. That's going to pull the hamstring and also open up that lower back. Another great one is to lie on the floor, pulling your knees all the way into your chest and all the way back until your head touches the floor. And that's a great way to just get the blood flowing, draining the lymph system, but also while you are pulling those knees, you are giving a nice stretch to the lower back.

So it really comes down to keeping the hamstrings and the lower back loose for the individuals that are sitting at a desk all day and in meetings, or even the clients that are travelling or flying a lot on long flights. Stretching the lower back and the hamstrings is crucial.

The other critical thing to do is building core strength within the abdominal area. Nine times out of ten, a person who always has a tight lower back, or a lot of shooting pains in the lower back, or a weak lower back, is because they have a poor abdominal strength or weak abs. Your abs work in conjunction with your lower back. If your lower back is bothering you, nine times out of ten you have weak abdominal muscles and they need to be strengthened immediately. Within that process of building and strengthening the abs, you can also work on stretching the lower back.

# THE SIX PACK YOU DON'T PURCHASE
# AT THE STORE

*Scot: What are some exercises you give people to strengthen that abdominal region?*

*Frank Tortorici:* I would say basic crunches, basic sit-ups and plank holds are very effective. I have a saying that I use with all of my clients—"navel to spine." So when I say "navel to spine," it's just simply a reminder to pull your belly button in through the spine area. You are not flexing your abs and you can still breathe in through your lungs. You are just pulling the navel to the spine and holding those muscles inward. What that does is engage the core muscles. A lot of people just have weak ab muscles because their brain is not even connected to those muscles any longer. The brain is always realigning to their lower back to do the work.

So the first step is really becoming aware of "navel to spine." Sitting at the desk, driving, in the kitchen making food, walking—for women, I see that is needed tremendously. Since women are naturally top heavy in the front, and their shoulders tend to come forward.

Once you start learning that "navel to spine" trick, your shoulder blades are now pulled back, and your posture becomes more in full alignment. So once you start working the navel to spine, then we start going into the crunches, the plank holds, and other exercises like that. Whenever we are doing any other exercises, it is worth focusing on again that navel to spine concept. You'll be surprised when you are working squats and lunges and you can hold dumbbells over your head while you are doing your lunges - all of that activates the core tremendously.

There are various ways of strengthening up the core, but the start of it all is being aware of that navel to spine idea – that's the key.

## WHAT ABOUT A PERSONAL TRAINER?

*Scot: If I'm someone who's not an exercise expert and I've decided to use a personal trainer, tell us the best way to select a trainer, since you are one yourself.*

*Frank Tortorici:* If you are going to hire a trainer, you need to do a background check on them and make sure that they are living what they are teaching. That's my biggest piece of advice that I can give to anyone hiring a trainer. There are way too many people out there that just have the certifications, but have no true genuine history of living what they are teaching. They are just getting information out of a book. So I would look at what types of certifications they have. There are a lot of certifications out there now that are fully accredited and not fully recognized by a lot of the big conglomerate certifications within the wellness industry.

What are some of those certifications? The American Council of Exercise, AFAA, ICSM, Crossfit, as a whole, provide a lot of great certifications as well. I am certified through Crossfit, American Council of Exercise (ACE) and I am certified as a Functional Diagnostic Nutritionist (FDN).

So you really want to do the background check and see where your trainer and what association they are certified through, and then also see and talk to some of their clients. See what kind of feedback you get from their clients, or checking out the trainer's health page is very helpful. You can tell what's going on through their health page and seeing what type of content that they are putting on the web.

You want to hire an expert. You don't want to hire somebody that's just doing this as a part time gig or because the money is good. If you are going to spend your hard earned money spend it, you can be in the midst of an expert within that profession. It is no different than you wanting someone to train you to become a millionaire. You want to learn from an expert who has done it, not through somebody who is just reading it out of a book. The same holds true for hiring a trainer as well. You want to have someone that can get you healthy, get your vitals and get you in great shape at the lowest possible risk of injury. That's the key to hiring a great trainer.

*Scot: Do you find that the need for a personal trainer is higher because there are now so many different ways to work out?*

*Frank Tortorici:* Absolutely. I am not just saying this because it is my profession, but I truly believe that. I have been a certified trainer since 1997. I have been in the gym almost my whole life and did my first natural body building contest when I was in ninth grade. There are so many approaches to getting in shape. There is always new fitness training, but I think for the individual who runs or owns a company, it is major benefit to have someone who is going hold you accountable, because all day long, you are holding everyone else accountable.

I think it is important to hire a trainer because there's always new technique. I see a lot of trainers and it's like they are stuck in the 80s in terms of how they work out. Most people think that just going to a gym and lifting weights is "fitness". We are now seeing the boom of this "whole function of fitness" movements — P90X, Crossfit, the boot camp classes — there is a reason why that stuff is booming, and there is a reason why trainers like myself that use these types of principles are doing well, as opposed to the other trainers that are just stuck in the whole "body building" mechanism are not doing well. When you are dealing more with functional fitness and getting the whole body to work every work out, you are going to see results that much quicker because you are not just isolating muscle, you are working every muscle.

When you are working every muscle, your risk of injury could become much higher if it is not done properly. We all need teaches and mentors in our lives to achieve greatness. And personal training and exercise is no different. Hiring a personal trainer if you are somebody who wants to achieve health and wellness is key and is crucial to show how to do it and to help you make reasonable goals to achieve those goals. If you are not born and raised in this field, everyone and anyone should hire a personal trainer.

## FRANK'S 3 TIPS FOR BUSINESS OWNERS

*Scot: Give business owners three tips to help them and their employees maximize profit and performance.*

*Frank Tortorici:* My number one tip would be to encourage business owners to understand the alkaline and acid charts. Business owners need to understand why they are doing what they are doing—they shouldn't take action because they are hearing it from me or reading it online. Owners need to have a complete understanding of this concept and how powerful it is. When they start living their lives that way, then their eating habits have a clear purpose and intention. What I mean by that is that you are not eating simply because the clock says its time for breakfast, lunch, or dinner; you are eating because you know that for this particular meal I need these certain nutrients because I'm feeling a certain way today.

For example, if you have a sore throat, you'd want to have a meal that contains garlic, ginger, onions, spice and peppers. These items help the body kill types of bacteria that cause infections like sore throats. So that's what I mean by eating with a purpose and intention.

My second tip to business owners would be to encourage them to promote weight loss contests within their companies. Human beings are completive by nature, and I have seen a lot of success with corporate events like this. A couple of weeks ago, I did this type of event with some Universal Studio employees. While implementing these types of weight loss challenges, I noticed that it really works because the employee energy is high (from eating the correct foods) and people are feeding off one another's energy. They are inspired by each other while being competitive. I think it is crucial to give that to the employees to keep them on track and have them focused on a target of where they are starting and where they are going in regards to their weight and health. If you'd like more information on this, you can consult my website, Facebook page or I can talk with you directly about creating a customized program for your company that will increase productivity and profit.

My third tip involves creating a "cooking competition" between employees of who could cook or bring in the healthiest and tastiest food. Since many offices have "casual Fridays", I recommend this day to have these types of "cook and eat offs." Each Friday, employees can bring in certain dishes, whether it is a raw vegan dish, a gluten free dish, or a micro-biotic dish. Then, allow the employees to taste all of these different foods. So, you are bringing these healthy concepts into the workplace and also the homes of your employees, which will positively affect their families as well, making happier and more productive employees.

We've got to get rid of the mindset of reading the nutrition labels on products and start focusing on the ingredients. When you go through your grocery store, you'll see a lot of things on labels—no fat, no cholesterol, etc.—but when you read the ingredients, you cannot pronounce half of them. And if you cannot pronounce half of the ingredients, which means your body cannot recognize them either! If your body cannot recognize them, again, we are probably taxing the body's adrenals, wreaking havoc on our system.

I've seen this three point formula work time and time again in corporate settings and it is a win-win situation for everyone involved—even for the families of the employees!

# DR. SONZA CURTIS

Dr. Sonza L. Curtis, MPAS, PA-C, ND, NWC, IFMCP, received her Master's of Science in Physician Assistant Studies from the University of Nebraska Medical Center in 1996 with honors. Her diverse medical experience includes extensive training in otolaryngology surgery, plastic surgery, pain management, family practice, clinical medical research, community health, and integrative medicine.

She later went on to complete her Doctorate of Naturopathy for Health Care Professionals with honors in 2010. Her decision to choose the field of Naturopathy allowed her to break away from conventional medicine, which she felt had been somewhat fragmented and "missing something". She believes finding the underlying cause of an ailment should be the first step in treatment rather than immediately masking the problem with pharmaceuticals. She currently utilizes her expertise in holistic medicine for weight loss and proper nutrition by using HCG and other natural hormonal therapies.

Dr. Curtis' philosophy is educating patients about disease prevention and modification within the integrative model of medicine. She believes there can be many elements or influences that can affect a person's overall health. In order to understand what they are, she begins by evaluating a patient's mind, body and spirit. She feels optimum health can truly be acquired through the integration of all systems after each are individually assessed and healed.

# HORMONES AND THEIR EFFECTS ON THE BODY REGARDING PRODUCTIVITY

*Scot: Sonza, I know hormones are a big issue right now, with men and women, but so many only think about it concerning their personal lives, not their business or professional performance. In your practice, you're seeing men and women with many issues associated with hormones. What are some the general symptoms that might lead you to believe that there's a hormone issue with either a man or woman?*

Dr. Curtis: Scot, the main symptoms I see people come in to my office suffering from are chronic fatigue, "foggy thinking," and just a general lack of energy.

*Scot: What is "foggy thinking?"*

Dr. Curtis: Basically, you kind of feel like you are daydreaming during the day or you kind of feel like you have early signs of Alzheimer's. Patients complain that they can't remember where they are going, can't remember where they wrote something down, or sometimes people will feel like they're looking out of textured glass that you can't see through clearly.

## PRODUCTIVITY'S BIGGEST ENEMY — FATIGUE

*Scot: If I've come to you for what I would call "chronic fatigue syndrome," or some type of fatigue, what are my overall symptoms?*

Dr. Curtis: When women have progesterone deficiencies, a lot of time you'll see "frozen shoulders," fatigue, foggy thinking, and lack of energy. They usually say things like, "I'm a certain age, I'm eating the same, I'm exercising the same, but I just can't get out of bed," or, "I just feel like when I get home from work, I am just wiped out."

Most women of them come in when they are very frustrated because, as they express it, "I can't get it together." And they're very irritable, whether it's at work, or home. A lot of them say, "I'm just a witch. This is not the person that I used to be and I don't understand the person that I've now become. Can you help me?"

*Scot: So, basically men and women with hormone issues are saying things to you like, "I'm always tired, I can't remember anything, it feels like I am losing my mind, I go to work and when I get there I can't remember anything I'm supposed to do that day, I'm too tired to get through the day, I've gone through an entire business day and I'm not properly servicing my clients, I'm not really getting along well with my co-workers, and somehow, someway I've still got to go home that night, be a mother, be a father, work with the kids, handle those demands, all at the same time when all I want to do is lay down." Does that sounds pretty accurate for what your patients will tell you?*

*Dr. Curtis:* Pretty much.

*Scot: Here's a scenario for you: A woman comes to see you; she's just described all the symptoms that we've gone over, she has no energy, there is memory fog, a lack of sexual activity, she doesn't feel sexy anymore, she feels like she's losing her mind and/or she has no patience for the clients, kids, or husband. What are the areas that we need to specifically look at to help her?*

*Dr. Curtis:* First of all, I take a pretty thorough history to figure out what's the root cause of the problems. And then I do a complete female hormone panel to see if there are any deficiencies.

# THE EFFECTS OF "WHACKED OUT" ADRENAL GLANDS AND THE THYROID

*Scot: So, women tell you that they've gone from being this one person that they knew they were, and now their husband, their co-worker or their clients have started to comment, "Where did you go? What has happened to you? Did a body snatcher come and take your place?" So she's in your office, she's probably upset and you are getting to the physical issues. What type of testing do you do to go ahead and handle this issue immediately? What are some of the root causes of the problems that you find?*

*Dr. Curtis:* First of all, when I address hormone issues for every male or female, I always look at the adrenals first, and ask if they are under a lot of stress. If they are a CEO of a company, or an executive and they are traveling a lot, that's going to be a direct impact (on the adrenals and hormones), because some of the hormones are made in the adrenal glands. I'm going to look at the thyroid, because all of the hormones work together like a symphony orchestra. So if one's out, then the other one isn't working so well. So I address the adrenals and the thyroid.

*Scot: Now when you say thyroid, what are the components of the thyroid? I hear so much in the media; I don't know what information from the media is real and what's not. Can you describe what "thyroid" really means?*

*Dr. Curtis:* Basically, I do what I call a complete thyroid panel. In the results of this test, I look at the TSH levels. There are various different components of TSH levels. I look at the Free T3, Free T4, reverse T3, the thyroid antibodies, and the TPO levels, which tell me if anything is out of balance.

*Scot: Why are these TSH levels such a big deal? Is there a specific way, once I get the test results, which I need to look at this test to make sure I get my maximum treatment plan?*

*Dr. Curtis:* That's a great question. People can come into my office with "regular" TSH levels, but you look at the conversion data from T4 to T3 and the conversation is off, then the patient is not going to be feeling so well. There for things that can affect these levels, like zinc, selenium and iodine. A lot of time I have to treat my patients nutritionally to help with that conversion.

So when you look at the TSH levels, it can be a wide range. It's like going into a shoe store and saying, "I want the average women's sized shoe. What is that? Is that an eight, is that a nine, or is that a ten? Or is that a seven and a half, or is it a six? When you look at the TSH range in most glands is from 0.4 to 4.5. That's a huge range difference. A patient could have levels measuring at 3 and still be having symptoms. Usually, a patient with TSH levels above 3 exhibiting symptoms, you don't want to wait until their levels get to 4.5.

I also look at a patient's thyroid history. If they're levels have been at 2, and all of a sudden they've gone to 2.5, then they've gone to 3, then they've gone to 3.5, you can bet they are having thyroid issues. I don't like to wait till problems manifest; until the levels get to 5 or 6, and above. You might want to start treating the condition early with supplement or a natural form of thyroid medication.

## CORTISOL AND DHEA

*Scot: I had the adrenal, hormone and the thyroid issues myself. Obviously, I am not a woman, but the some of the symptoms seem to be the same for men and women. What are the hormone tests people need to perform and what would the treatments be?*

*Dr. Curtis:* The two hormones that we measure with the adrenal levels are the cortisol and DHEA levels. First, however, let me explain about cortisol.

If I have a tiger coming after me, I want my cortisol levels to go up, so that glucose will go to my muscles so I can run away. Cortisol helps me to try to get away from the tiger. If you are under that type of persistent stress at all times, you will see some of the same symptoms I've outlined previously. These are the symptoms you exhibit with adrenal "adaptation" or adrenal "fatigue".

At "adaptation" level, when your cortisol levels go up, your DHEA may stay the same. You also want to measure your DHEA sulphite, not just your DHEA levels, because that makes a big difference.

The best form of testing that I use is the salivary four-point cortisol test. This test allows me to do a "spot" cortisol check in the morning and then at other times throughout the day. Your cortisol levels may be fine in the morning, and then, as you go on during the day, as a practitioner, through this test, I can interpret where your levels change, which allows me to see where your problem is. Your levels may dip at noon and then I can give you something to take during that noon hour or prior to the noon hour to keep your levels from dipping.

*Scot: Why is that such a big deal?*

*Dr. Curtis:* It's a big deal because people are trying to use "artificial means" of fixing the problems instead of looking at the root causes of them. Now there are commercials about it. They always talk about the "two o'clock feeling," like you mentioned earlier.

What is that two o'clock feeling? Is it stemming from hormonal, adrenal or thyroid issues? What's causing you to take that dip in energy somewhere in the morning, afternoon or evening? That is the question we have to answer. The four- point test helps us answer part of the question.

*Scot: Here's the typical employee's life from their perspective: I am tired all the time, I'm at work, I'm drinking twelve cups of coffee a day, I am out making sales calls, I'm meeting with clients, and I am trying to be super man/woman. Is this cycle having an effect on their cortisol levels and why?*

*Dr. Curtis:* Since caffeine (from the coffee) is in itself a stimulant, once you have that stimulant rush, you are going to have a "rush" of energy as you consume and increase consumption, but then, your energy levels are going to fall back down. You are eventually going to crash and burn. So, you are basically self-medicating with caffeine. Then, you are going to become more irritable as well. This is what I call "adrenal flat line"; your cortisol levels are low and your DHEA levels are low.

*Scot: If I get my hormone, adrenal and thyroid levels tested, what happens next?*

*Dr. Curtis:* Of course, each individual has differing treatments because each person has differing contributing factors such as sleep issues, too much caffeine, fluctuating cortisol levels — that's all individualized. With my patients, I sit down with a very in-depth history to try to figure all of those factors out. I also review the results of various functional medicine testing that I use and we put all those pieces of the puzzle together and come up with a plan.

# HORMONE TESTING

*Scot: Now let's address hormones. What are the hormones that you normally look at and what kind of tests could someone anticipate in order for you to check those levels?*

*Dr. Curtis:* Testosterone, progesterone, estradiol, and estrogen — those are the main hormones that I look at when I am working with patients with hormone issues.

*Scot: Is this a blood, saliva or urine test — all of the above, none of the above or a combination of them?*

*Dr. Curtis:* You actually can do all the above. I like to monitor my patients on natural hormone replacement therapy closely, which means multiple testing cycles. Since the cost to my patients for urine testing is usually a lot cheaper than saliva testing, I usually use urine tests. However, we are seeing the costs for saliva testing coming down.

*Scot: Is there a special testing protocol for women to match their hormonal cycles? How about post-menopausal women? How about men?*

*Dr. Curtis:* For a female, if they are menstruating, I'll test them between days nineteen, twenty, and twenty-one of their cycle because I want to test them at the peak of their hormonal activity. For men or post-menopausal women, the timing of testing doesn't matter.

Because hormones do fluctuate, testing is like hitting a moving target. There's not really a 100% guarantee of accurate results because of that fluctuation. If a patient is stressed out, that may affect the hormone levels. If patients aren't getting enough sleep, that may affect their hormone production.

So I always keep a very close eye on hormone levels in my patients. If I do saliva tests, I'll check for to see that they are metabolizing their estrogen, and then I'll do the two 16-hydroxyl ratio test. This test helps me protect my females from breast cancer, making sure that the estrogen goes down the right pathway.

No matter whether I'm testing men or women, I usually do not use a combination of salivary and blood testing. When you do that, you are measuring apples and oranges, so to speak, so you have to stay with either blood or saliva testing modalities.

*Scot: After the tests are completed and the plan is begun, how quickly can I expect to just feel better?*

*Dr. Curtis:* That all depends on the individual, Scot. I have some women who, after getting progesterone, say that they sleep like babies from the first day of treatment. Some women came back and tell me that they still need to tweak the hormones a little, so that they can continue to feel a little bit better. So, results can be felt immediately or it may take some time until we get a patient's hormone levels up higher. Usually, you have about four weeks before you start to see some overall improvements.

*Scot: There is no one-size-fits-all solution. However, there is a solution for each individual, right?*

*Dr. Curtis:* Correct. It's based on that individual's personal biochemistry.

## HORMONE IMBALANCE AND MEN

*Scot: Now, you've shared that it usually takes about four weeks to see some results in female hormone level adjustment. Is there a difference between women and men? Because we know the symptoms are very similar, but we know that women go through menopause, but do men go through menopause as well? If they do, what is it called?*

Dr. Curtis:  Men do go through menopause and we call it andropause and now, you are seeing more and more men going through this at an earlier age because of stress. That stress is the stress to produce at work and at home. One example of a condition of stress many people never consider is the effect of travel. Men are traveling for work, and are being exposed to environmental toxins, such as jet fuel, believe it or not, which can be an endocrine disruptor. There are a lot of environmental toxins that can also interfere with hormone production in men and in women, in addition to our horrible American diet.

Scot:  *What are the reasons men need to see a functional medicine practitioner concerning their hormone production?*

Dr. Curtis:  The most common complaint I get from men when they come into my office is a decrease in sexual production. They are not able to perform like they used to when they were younger. That's the main issue I hear from men? They want Cialis or they want Viagra and they are having issues they need answers for in regards to their sexual performance. They will describe their hormone troubles as "man issues." Usually, they will not come right out and tell me that they're having decreased libido or performance issues.

Scot:  *What are some of the physical signs of lack of proper hormone production you look for in a male? Is it belly fat, lack of muscle mass or an inability to sexually perform or all of the above? What are some of the things that you would look for in a man who has a decrease in his testosterone?*

Dr. Curtis:  The first thing a man will display if he has low testosterone is "man boobs". More than likely, they are producing more estrogen than they should. In the horrible American diet, we are eating a lot of different foods that aren't necessarily good for us — products containing GMO (genetically modified organism), soy, and other unnatural chemicals and additives. Sometimes you can see the diet reflected in the bodies of males. I'm also starting to see obesity with younger men, because diet becomes an endocrine disrupter, which creates weight issues.

*Scot: Now with males, they're experiencing low testosterone, belly fat, decreased libido and a decrease in energy, which leads to a decrease in production at work, at home and in life in general. Are there any cardiac problems that could come with it? Are there heart issues, brain issues, lung issues, or any other type of organ issues that come with male hormonal imbalance?*

*Dr. Curtis:*  There are theories out there now that feel that estrogen is to females as testosterone is to males, because if your testosterone is low, you are going to have low muscle tissue mass. Add to that, decreased cardiovascular output and you're going to get cardiovascular issues as well. Many times men come into my office and tell me that they are very irritable. I also want to make a point to say that men also come into my office complaining about their struggle with anxiety. Sometimes they'll just come in with elevated cholesterol and that can signify that there may be some other issues going on. Another issue that complicates this entire situation is that various medications can also decrease hormone production.

I've had many male patients who don't process B vitamins very well. And you need to be able to process B Vitamins for energy production, detoxification and methylation. By giving them the right form of B vitamins sometimes that can also increase hormone production, energy and detoxification.

Another symptom in men (and women) I've seen is low levels of Vitamin D. I have seen patients I've treated for deficient Vitamin D and once the Vitamin D levels are higher, their testosterone goes up and their energy production goes up.

One other symptom of low testosterone I see in men is infertility.

*Scot: If I am a man and you need to check my testosterone levels, how is it done? How long before I can see results from my treatment plan?*

*Dr. Curtis:* First of all, with males and females, I would start with a thorough physical exam.

For male patients, I look at their PSA levels, because if they have a history of prostate cancer, you don't want to put them on any hormone replacement therapy.

For men, I would also check Vitamin D levels, check their testosterone, and check the estradiol in their systems. I like to check the cortisol, thyroid and DHEA levels. Testosterone can actually become estrogen, so many times; I have to put May male patients on estrogen blockers in addition to testosterone therapy. If a man has "man boobs," I usually have a high suspicion he is estrogen dominant or his body is converting his testosterone incorrectly. Sometimes male baldness is also a symptom you'll see with low or high testosterone levels. Too much testosterone can also give you the same symptoms as low testosterone. So there is a balance that men need to achieve.

*Scot: For men, once they've started their treatment plan, their results could be immediate or it could take a few weeks, but if men get this done immediately, they will begin to recover memory function, their muscle mass will increase and their likelihood of heart issues has gone down. Their anxiety is going to go down, their sexual output is going to go up and naturally, their self esteem will increase because they now feel good about who they are, and they can perform better, not only at work, but also in life. Is that an accurate statement?*

*Dr. Curtis:* Very accurate.

## HORMONES AND SLEEP APNEA

*Scot: In addition to hormones, the next huge issue in employees performing at high functioning levels is sleep. In my own case, it was my wife that got me to a sleep centre and involved in sleep research because she said in five years, I had not slept for a full night. I was out of gas, I couldn't work at a high performing level, I couldn't produce, I couldn't work with my clients or participate with my family at a high level. I felt like I just couldn't do anything. Your clients come to you all the time complaining about being tired — they can't produce where they work, they have hormone issues, their cortisol levels have increased, they are depressed, they are anxious, they can't concentrate, they've started to gain weight, and a lot of time we can trace this back to sleep. Why?*

*Dr. Curtis:* In my practice, I have found that many patients have what we call obstructive sleep apnea. Sleep is where your body restores and repairs itself and by not getting a good night of sleep, your body can't do that. What's even scarier is if you have a disorder called obstructive apnea, basically you stop breathing, decreasing the amount of oxygen supply to the heart and the brain. That's why you have a foggy thinking; your heart is working overtime, increasing your risk for cardiovascular issues.

Increased cortisol sometimes leads into diabetes, or what is called metabolic syndrome. You also have a decreased production of testosterone. So if you don't correct the underlying problem of sleep apnea and if I'm giving you testosterone, the testosterone only acts as a band-aid to the situation. It won't be until you actually treat the apnea that you will see total overall improvement.

*Scot: When I finally decided to get a sleep study done, I was working sixteen to eighteen hours a day, and, on average, was drinking hours cups of coffee just to stay awake and do what I thought was productive. What I didn't realize was that I really wasn't servicing the people I needed to take care of. I wasn't who I needed to be for anyone, including myself and I always felt awful.*

*I did the sleep study and I got my machine within forty-eight hours. After the first night, I had energy again. I had not seen "the real me" in about seven years and now I did again — all because I finally went to sleep. The sleep I got I felt better.*

*The one thing that you said when I came to see you as your patient was that my life span was going to decrease if I didn't cut out the nonsense and get this study done. And I kept thinking that I could be the business guy, the family guy, the father, the husband and that guy who works sixteen hours a day. I'm sure a lot of my readers can relate. Until that day, I kept telling myself that I could wear the big "S" on my shirt and keep going without sleep. None of that is true at all and you finally sat me down and said my life was going to end very quickly if I didn't stop it. Why?*

*Dr. Curtis:* When you stop breathing during sleep, you are not getting enough oxygen to your brain, nor your heart, so your body feels like you have to work more and harder, and you are not even being productive. You are doing all these stuff for what? I always say it's like the hamster; you have to get off the wheel. Once you get off the wheel, you have to realize that you aren't sleeping, and that the "not sleeping" is a big part of the problems you're experiencing.

There are a lot of people who have died from untreated sleep apnea. And I will state that Reggie White was one of them, as well as my own father. He died at the age fifty with a massive heart attack secondary to untreated obstructive sleep apnea.

*Scot: For those of us who thought we could do the eighteen-hour days repeatedly with no "after effects" (and I had been doing it at least twenty years between business, coaching and teach), that's not going to happen. Since I got my CPAP (Continuous Positive Airway Pressure) machine, my whole career has blossomed. Most people's career and business ability is based on creativity, the ability to communicate, and the ability to perform and provide a service. All of that goes kaput if you don't feel good and you can't sleep. What I noticed is that all my creativity and ideas came back; I'm more imaginative, I can create, I am better with my clients, I do my radio and coaching shows more creatively, smoothly and efficiently and my personality and animation has been restored. The greatest thing is that everything is clear and I know that I can produce for my clients so much more if I sleep well, and when I am with my family they enjoy this version of me so much more.*

## DR. SONZA'S HEALTH RECOMMENDATIONS TO OWNERS AND EMPLOYEES

*Scot: Dr. Sonza, what would you recommend to this type of person: You've got a business person out there right now, and they are going through the days like I did. The twelve to eighteen-hour days, the coffee, the sugar substitutes, the American diet, no green leafy vegetables — we get all that we don't do the things we should. What would you tell the average executive, male or female, to do to make sure they get the optimal sleep, so that they can have the optimal production at work and at home?*

*Dr. Curtis:* I would tell them to see either an integrated or a functional medical practitioner so that they can look at more than one thing that's happening in the person's life so that the practitioner can put everything together and treat the cause of the problems.

You want to have a practitioner who has the mindset to look at everything that's happening in your body. If you are having decreased hormone production, they should look at treatment as more than just natural hormone replacement therapy. Your practitioner should try to find the root cause of the hormone issue. Is the problem lack of quality sleep or is it stress? They need to be looking at all types of root causes of problems.

Then, after a full physical examination, a practitioner should order the appropriate testing. The first thing I personally investigate is the adrenal function, and in addition to that, I also treat the gut.

Imagine you have a car with four wheels. Each wheel represents a bodily function — one wheel represents the gut, one represents the adrenals, one represents your sex hormones, and the other wheel represents your thyroid. If any one of those wheels are not balanced properly or don't have enough air in them, it's going to affect the overall performance of the car. It's the same with your body. So that's why I check all of those levels.

If you are eating a lot of processed foods containing gluten, I start with the gut as a natural path to back to a balanced system. I start having my patients eliminate dairy, sugar, and gluten from their diets. I also have them eliminate soy if they are having hormone issues because soy can become an endocrine disrupter.

Then I work on your lifestyle modification to reduce stress. I also add exercise to that equation. Sometimes I recommend that my female patients take just 10 minutes out of their day to take a hot bath with candlelight. I also recommend meditation. Many studies have shown that meditation is just as important as sleep.

Then I look at a full panel of the blood work addressing all the issues with the adrenals. I look at your DHEA and your cortisol levels. Then we get to the thyroid, and I look at your TSH, T3, T4, TPO, Reverse T3, and your thyroid gland. Then we get down to the sex hormones, and I'll look at your estradiol, estrogen, progesterone, and testosterone. If you are male, I'll look at the PSA because I want to make sure everything is fine there. For a female, I recommend that she has no history of any breast cancer, or we'll measure the 216 ratio to make sure that if I were to give her some estrogen that it won't go down the wrong pathway, converting to the wrong hormone.

Then, I would evaluate their sleep, if they are having any sleep issues, making sure they don't have any obstructive sleep apnea, or addressing their cortisol making ability.

I would recommend to all executives and employees everywhere to look for practitioners who will go through all of those types of steps to find the root causes for problems in the body.

*Scot: Can the human body solve most of these problems if it's given the tools to do it?*

*Dr. Curtis:* Yes! We were definitely made to heal ourselves!

# DR. HANK SLOAN

## THE AMERICAN DIET IS KILLING US

*Scot: Why are Americans having so many problems with their health?*

*Dr. Sloan:* The American diet is probably the worst diet in the world. The World Health Organization ranked 200 countries in health and the United Sates was number thirty-seventh in the world. Even the third world African countries are healthier than us. This study is based on the amount of disease, illness, and quality of life, and the main people who ranked the highest and best were people in all of the Mediterranean countries. When you look at food and how it affects the human body, their health was directly related to what they eat. These "healthiest in the world people" are eating fresh items; they are able to go out to market everyday and get fresh vegetables and healthy fish and chicken without steroids and antibiotics, and they eat a lot of big salads with a lot of different fats and oils — even their cheeses and their wines are healthy for them.

So knowing that food is directly related to health, you can see why America is thirty-seventh in the world in "healthiness," but number one in the world in spending for healthcare issues. Every day, I get to work with the sickest of America and I see how food makes people sick. And by the time they come see me, I actually have to treat their diseases. I have to treat autoimmune diseases, cancer, mental illness — nobody can have the right brain function if your gut is impaired and your food isn't correct. Food is supposed to be the genetic material that tells our cells how to run. Forget the taste; we are supposed to look at food and nutrition in that light.

In other countries, when they cook the food, they know the medicinal properties of the food. In India, they cook all these spices and herbs into food based on how somebody feels, or how their body is doing. In China and Asia, they do the same thing. One of the simple things in Asia that I can relate to your readers is menopause in women and breast cancer. They hardly have any menopause or breast cancer because they eat the fermented soy and sauces that give their bodies the ability to heal themselves.

In America, we don't have that kind of food. Women are supposed to get one to two milligrams of estrogen in their food and they don't get that from the American diet. So the receptor sites are hungry, which leads them to eat up anything that looks like estrogen. That creates breast, ovarian and hormone related cancers. So foods should be your medicine. In America, we definitely don't look at that correctly.

The food pyramid is actually upside-down. I love it when people say to me, when I tell them that they can't have dairy, "Does that mean I can't eat eggs?"

I always say to them, "Well, I have never seen a cow lay an egg."

*Scot: But it's on the food pyramid chart, right?*

*Dr. Sloan:* Right. It is on the chart. It doesn't seem to matter that it is incorrect.

*Scot: So, let's go into the dairy issue. Why shouldn't we consume dairy?*

*Dr. Sloan:* There are two different kinds of allergies in the body. The first one is an IGE allergy. We nickname it "emergency" because that's the allergy that your doctors test for through that skin prick that they do. The doctors doing this test are checking only for allergies that can create an immediate reaction, called an anaphylaxis — an "itchy, throat close up, can't breathe" kind of reaction. That's all they are checking for — the "emergency" reaction. Patients come to see me all the time and when I ask them if they have had an allergy test, they tell me that "my other doctor already did that." But generally, the only test that the other doctor has run is the test that's for the topical allergy. That's the "allergy that is going to happen quickly and it could kill you, so don't eat those foods" type of allergy test. By the time most of my patients get to me they know if a banana makes their throat itchy and they shouldn't eat it.

What I have to check is the delayed reaction that happens in the gut — that allergic reaction is totally separate from the "emergency" reaction. It's called the IGG reaction. We nickname this reaction "gut". So gut reaction can happen one to four days after you have the food. In addition, different combinations of foods make it even worse on those days after, so never can really tell what food is causing what reaction — you just feel like crap all the time. Your brain is foggy, you can't think, the reaction impairs neurotransmitters, it inflames your gut so your gut microvillus can't process properly, the holes get bigger, and now you've created "leaky gut" symptoms.

Any time you have an inflamed gut, you have an inflamed nervous system, because what happens in the gut in relationship to allergies creates a release that inflames your brain and your nervous system. If your skin's red, you have an inflamed nervous system, because that same histamine that makes your skin red makes your nervous system impaired.

So when we check blood for IGG reactions, then we are actually showing the patient what kind of food or reactions can affect their whole body from head to toe, not just IGE reactions that affect them in certain tissues in their body. So the IGG reaction is what we work on in my office. I have to take away the inflammatory foods that cause everybody to feel puffy in their hands, causing their rings fit differently, red cheeks and chest after they eat. They feel groggy after they eat, have a foggy head and can't think — there are so many symptoms that go with it.

When it comes to foods and what to eat, it is so much easier to do a food test and say everything that's "not red," you can eat, because your body doesn't react to it. And based on how many foods are on the "red list," I'll know if they have a leaky gut or not.

When a baby is born, it doesn't have any bacteria in its gut until they pass through the mother's vaginal canal. Typically, a woman gas more yeast than good bacteria in the canal, so the baby starts off its life that way. So that's the first bacteria they get in the gut and we're supposed to have up to ten times more bacteria in our gut than the number of cells in our own body.

Ninety percent of neurotransmitters, which are in the brain, are made in the gut. So when the gut is forming, and the mother is supposed to breast feed, so that the baby receives colostrum to start the immune system in the baby's gut. So many babies are born caesarean and they don't nurse, so they have missed both of the opportunities to start life on a note where they can have a proper immune system, which begins in the gut and is 70% to 80% of your body's entire immunity.

So as a baby nurses, the colostrum actually seals the gut of a baby in three days. There is a part of colostrum called Proline-rich *polypeptides* that we now know as the exact molecule of the peptide rich amino acids that seal the gut.

But, if you are like most American babies, before you are twelve months old, you are probably going to have your first round of antibiotics, and by the time you are three or four you are going to have three or four rounds of antibiotics, so there goes all that gut bacteria. The gut bacteria helps the intestinal lining, so if your gut bacteria is affected, your intestinal lining is going to be affected.

Our bodies are supposed to leak proteins (500 Daltons or less) through the lining of the gut, within an impaired leaky gut. Right outside the gut wall we have something called the Peyer's patches. The Peyer's patches are a vast immune functioning area around the gut that keeps all the bad stuff from getting into the body. Just because you eat something bad does not always mean it is going to get into your body and affect your cells. So the Peyer's patches are trying to keep those bad issues away from your gut. But sometimes, the attack is so great that things are going to leak through. That immune action outside the gut is going to leak through there and cause systemic problems. So that is what is considered leaky gut. Leaky gut is when larger molecules are leaking through the gut because of the cell wall integrity has been diminished or compromised.

I can eat the wrong food for a few days and in a short time, I look six months pregnant. I can swell like the best of them. I hate that feeling. So you feel bad in your gut, you're bloated, puffy, stuffy, have diarrhea or constipation or loss of appetite, yet you feel hungry, or you eat a little bit and then you immediately feel bloated; those are the leaky gut reactions that happen in your gut. But if it is happening in the lining and it touches the cell walls, the next layer it's going to touch is your organs and your cells.

Then you are going to have a sick cell or a sick body if you have things happening in the gut that leak out into the body, where they are not supposed to be. From that point on, you are affected head to toe, especially your brain. The protein from grains and dairy are called gluten. Of all the foods in the world, grains and dairy are the only foods that can actually have a direct neurological effect on a human body. They actually have the ability to cause the gut to change gluten into gluteomorphin. These molecules can leak through the gut and have a direct opiate or endorphin action in the nervous system.

Other foods don't have that exact neurotransmitter fit; they just break down to the vitamin, the mineral or the amino acid and do what they are supposed to. Gluten has a different effect on people. They can be too high from their gluten/opiate reaction and they can't focus or they can't concentrate, or they can be really zoned out or kind of too chilled. I see this especially in my child patients—they come to my office with their pupils dilated so big I can't see any color in their eyes, and they are just laughing at stuff and pointing at random objects—all effects of consuming gluten.

So those two foods—grains and dairy—can affect you the most. All of my patients that visit me, we advise them to eat a Paleo or a Mediterranean type diet.

## THE PALEO DIET

*Scot: What's a Paleo diet?*

*Dr. Sloan:* A Paleo diet is pretty simple. It's the concept of eating like you are a cave man. Whatever a cave man will eat, we eat. So we are going to eat meat, we going to eat proteins, anything you can catch in the woods that has a heartbeat or swims in the ocean. When it comes to fish, you have to eat the smaller fish.

Did you know that canned tuna is actually better for you than tuna filet? Because it's a bigger fish, it's been around longer and it has eaten more mercury. Swordfish has the highest mercury levels of all fish in the ocean, so don't eat swordfish.

You should eat clean, lean meat; bison, buffalo, deer, ostrich, wild boar, clean chicken and light white fish. Eat any vegetables you want and a moderate amount of fruit.

*Scot: What would be an example of the fruits, nuts and vegetables you would eat?*

*Dr. Sloan:* Low glycemic fruit, such as apples, pears, cherries, berries, beans or chickpeas would be a good start. Avocadoes, beans, nuts, oils, coconut or any oil that's not heated to an extreme point is probably going to be good for you unless it's genetically modified.

## WIRED & TIRED

*Scot: So what are the problems your patients are complaining about that are affecting their work lives the most?*

*Dr. Sloan:* Sleep issues are probably the main reason why people can't function well today in the work place, or any place—at home with their family, with their husbands or with their children. People get into a place of burn out. We are talking about men and women. People get into a place of burn out by not sleeping well and then drinking coffee and eating sugar to keep them going through the days. There is a rule of physiology in the body that you cannot ever get away from and that's simply this, "What goes up must come down."

The higher you try to push your body into energy phases, the lower you are going to drop off into your baseline. When you do this, and what people don't realize, is that you don't return to your normal baseline levels after you go through the sleep deprivation/coffee/sugar cycle. You actually return to "below baseline" levels and then you work back up to your baseline and it takes a long time to do that.

When you get into a tired mentality, you are tired all day long and you don't feel well and then you lay in bed and you are waking up at night and your body doesn't know whether it is asleep or whether it is awake. Your body has now lost your sense of energy surge and sleep hormones surge, so your body is completely out of balance.

When people came in here looking for answers to why they are so tired and why they have such intense fatigue, the first thing I ask them is how they are sleeping. It is impossible for me to try to pick up the daytime energy with thyroid and adrenal supplementation when they are not sleeping and recovering at night.

For me, helping my patients recover sleep has personally become an area of focus for me because I am now in my 40s and have an intense personal understanding of the problem. When I was in my thirties I was like, "Yeah, energy, energy!" Now, in my forties, it is like, "Got to sleep."

Lack of sleep is especially problematic with women that are going through menopause, and men who are going through andropause, which can happen in the late thirties to fifties. That's the first time women typically experience anxiousness or a pulsing heart rate for the first time in their life. Most of them tell me, "I am starting to feel anxious. My heart beats in my chest and I am waking up multiple times during the night."

When someone wakes up multiple times during the night,

for multiple nights a week, they are now in sleep deprivation mode. If you ever look at the symptoms of sleep deprivation, the first symptom that usually appears is short-term memory loss. You'll also see mood changes and mood disorders and then your nervous system goes into a fight or flight mode because you have now put your body into a mode where it is living for survival. So you have to break the fight or flight cycle, we have to get the hormones balanced, and have to work on the ability to sleep even before we can work on getting energy levels up.

For men, when they hit andropause, they actually have an increase in estrogen and a decrease in testosterone, so that makes them feel really crazy and more emotional. "More emotional" can also present itself as more anger, more weepiness, more emotional volatility or more temperamental-ness. It is just different for different people.

But the sleep issue is super duper important. Even though I usually advocate natural treatments, I sometimes recommend some non-narcotic and non-abusive low dose sleep medication for my patients. The important thing is that we've got to get you to sleep. I want you to take this, go to bed and not worry about falling asleep. Because many people who can't sleep get stressed out about sleeping, increasing their heart rate at bedtime, we have to be able to break that vicious cycle. There is no such thing as trying to sleep; that means you are putting effort into sleep and that doesn't work. You have to fall asleep. You have to drift away easily.

You can do deep breathing and meditation techniques. There are even plenty of app meditations you can listen to on your phone where people take you through breathing exercise and there is even the FitBeatz watches now that can track your sleep at night, and can tell you how much quality sleep you are getting. I actually like that people can bring their data in my office with the new technology that's out there now.

## ADRENAL AND THYROID FUNCTION

*Scot:   Let's talk about adrenal and thyroid functions, why it so important and why it affects so many people on the work place.*

*Dr. Sloan:* Underactive thyroid issues are just as big as adrenal issues. The American Endocrinology Association now has new standards for where we want our thyroid numbers to be, yet on that piece of paper you get from your doctor when they test your thyroid, the old values are still listed, so people's doctors are looking at the old values and they're not compatible with the new standards anymore. Doctors are not checking the thyroid down to that free T3 molecule, and that's really all that counts.

Most people have driven themselves for so long and so hard, that caffeine doesn't "give them energy" anymore. If you can drink caffeine and go to bed, you have no adrenal function remaining. Remember, caffeine doesn't give you energy; caffeine mimics a hormone that your brain that releases to stimulate your adrenals to give you adrenalin. So, caffeine energy by nature is actually the wrong energy to pursue. The way to get the proper adrenaline and the proper thyroid function is to consume proper foods that will help you get the proper type of energy.

So when you drive yourself and you push yourself and then you are not sleeping well and then your body goes into fight or flight mode, you start feeling anxious and depressed. In my office, we call that "wired and tired." You feel like you are never really awake and you feel like you never really get good sleep.

You feel like you are in a flat place, buddy. You are not going to have your nice little happy times, you are not going to feel happy — you are going to feel blue.

In the workplace, everything is going to be affected. There is no way that somebody can perform up to their normal level when they are not even the person that they are supposed to be.

When you push yourself and you drive yourself and caffeine doesn't work and you get worried and tired, you start to feel anxious, you start to feel depressed, your mood changes (you can definitely develop mood disorders on sleep deprivation mode), you're eating bad food, taking no supplements and nothing good is going in your body.

How in the heck do we think we are supposed to function normally? Really?

We have to break the fight or flight cycle, and that typically means that I have to force someone into a sleep pattern again. I use a saliva test that checks for functions of adrenals over a twenty-four hour period, so I can graph the results to see if their adrenal functions are going back up or down at night. There are ways I can help their bodies calm down and get that good quality sleep. Melatonin usually helps, magnesium helps, and valerian are different combinations that people can pick up from a health food store.

## THEY CAN BE FIXED

*Scot: So you are saying, basically, these symptoms are not a lifelong problem; they can be fixed?*

*Dr. Sloan:* It can be fixed, yes. It has to be fixed or you will go crazy. When I see a patient suffering from this condition, it's usually after they've crashed out of fight or flight mode, and now they are in absolute "flat land." They have no energy and are not sleeping or maybe now they are sleeping too much and they can't wake up, but they never feel rested. That's when everything in their metabolism slows down so much that they are going to feel blue, depressed or even anxious because they can't do the things they used to do.

I then have to focus on getting the body out of what I call rest and preservation. You get from fight or flight to rest and preserve and that's when you gain weight, your chemistry is not moving fast, your metabolism is not moving fast and you feel awful. So we have to get patients out of rest and preserve into normal metabolism mode.

In each one of these phases, I have to help patients understand that the brain is shifting to find what normal is again and it might feel weird, it might feel different, but we are going in the right direction. That's the interesting perspective of what each person thinks is normal. We all have a different perspective on that.

In over fifteen years of working with around 100,000 patients, about 80% walk around in a state that isn't their optimal state. Most of these patients are women. You'd call it a zombie state. They are in state of sleep deprivation and low hormone function...

*Scot: Sort of a state of limbo?*

*Dr. Sloan:* Yeah, you are stuck in the middle — flat, flat lined.

With the American diet and so many people consuming sugar, gluten casein has a direct effect on the brain. It's a direct cause of inflammatory state in the brain and yeast releases what we call false neurotransmitters.

False neurotransmitters look like they should fit in the nerve synapses, but there is no information in it. So when your brain begins to process that movement, thought or word, poof! There is nothing there due to the false neurotransmitters.

These false neurotransmitters, manufactured from the consumption of gluten and caseins, produces the effects of Tourette's, short-term memory losses, or mood issues.

We must repair our hormones, fix the thyroid, sleep better, eat the right kind of foods and get rid of pathogens in the body that shouldn't be there. When we do those things, we begin to uncover the brain's ability to allow neurotransmitters to work as they are supposed to.

*Scot: So I really don't have to be worried, tired and always angry, anxious, depressed or fatigued?*

*Dr. Sloan:* Right.

When I see a patient and I'm trying to recover their endocrine functions, it is usually about a three-month process to get to a point where they feel good again, and then another three months process for optimal health and energy. Results may vary, of course, dependent upon the individual's state and lifestyle. But, generally speaking, my patients are feeling good after three months, and if they are not better in three months then I am not doing my job, or we simply haven't found the underlying problem yet.

When it comes to people trying to find help from a traditional doctor, they're probably going to explain that they feel tired and depressed. For most people, this condition isn't depression; its chronic fatigue. Very often, it gets misdiagnosed because the symptoms of those two are just the same. I have never met an energetic depressed patient, so typically, when I get a patient's vitality restored, the depression goes away, unless it is a situational depression brought on by a life event such as the death of a loved one.

So thousands of patients go to the doctor every day and they are going to only get offered anti-depressants, and sleep medication. If they stay with that treatment plan, that patient will stay there for the rest of their life, going around in a zombie-like state. The anti depressants may seem to work in the beginning, but eventually, they are going to eventually make them feel so flat that they can't find happiness, and they can't cry at commercial and sad things, which is a natural thing humans need to do.

So the best way that we treat these conditions is to actually look at the food we're eating, the sleep habits, the adrenal and thyroid function, possible toxins in the body, the endocrine functions, the state of the spirit of the body, their outlook, and try to encourage, coach and mentor them back to see hope and a light at the end of the tunnel. Putting all of these together can give a better health outcome.

*Scot:  All of these conditions can be tested scientifically, correct?*

*Dr. Sloan:*  Yes.

*Scot:  This is not guesswork?*

*Dr. Sloan:*  Absolutely not. It is not guess work.

*Scot:  You scientifically pin point what's wrong and fix it?*

*Dr. Sloan:*  Yes.

*Scot: And the human body has the ability to fix itself?*

*Dr. Sloan:* If something does show up on labs, then we use what's called common sense. You can't look at the labs completely just by themselves; you actually have to look at the patient. Sometimes the thyroid may look okay, but they have all the symptoms of having low thyroid, so we give them a small dosage of thyroid medicine, and if they feel better, we know that they needed it. If they feel nothing, they need more. If they feel too much then we can back it off. So that is our common sense approach.

*Scot: This is encouraging, thinking that, regardless of age, you can still have a vital, healthy, active and maximized life. If there were three things you could tell my readers to do to maximize their performance at work, what would they be?*

*Dr. Sloan:* So to maximize performance — the same thing I would want for my employees here in my own office to practice — the three things I would encourage employees to do for themselves would be to get good quality sleep, practice healthy habits in their diet and to exercise. These three very simple things that anybody can do need to be dealt with immediately. If you can balance your work, your sleep, your exercise and eat good food, you are going to have a win-win situation on every level of your life.

# Conclusion

I like to say that results have no feelings.

Your business' balance sheets provide a non-emotional, crystal clear view of your results. Each month, a simple spreadsheet can tell you if you achieved your desired goal. A spreadsheet can tell a magical story when it pertains to results based on dollars.

Spreadsheets tend to break down when measuring results based on character, integrity and wisdom.

The fastest way to measure a man or woman and who they truly are as a person is to interview their employees and their family members. These two groups give you a glimpse of actions that are based on observable habits and behaviors that are displayed on a continual basis. The observed behaviors are a human balance sheet and will be used on a daily basis to measure you, not only as a businessperson, but also as a man or woman.

In life, as in business, **it's not them, it's you.** The environment in your home and the environment in your business is based on your previous programming, your thoughts, your feelings and your actions. Realize that you do live in a glass house and everything you do will be seen, heard or felt by someone. Knowing that every single action that you take in your life affects every person connected to you, you have an overwhelming responsibility to your family, your business and your community to choose your actions wisely.

As a family member, leader and business owner/CEO, you have an opportunity to take your character, integrity and wisdom and bless not only the individuals in your daily life, but generations to come. Success is not a "by chance" proposition, but a daily, systematic, thought-out method that provides guaranteed results. As the role model for your family and company, it is your job to teach the right people proper leadership, how to function as a competent unit and why results matter. It's not them, it's you.

Life has an expiration date and the joy of life is getting to live on a daily basis, making decisions based on unguaranteed outcomes in time. Because we, as humans, do not know the date of our death, we are forced to acknowledge life as a finite being and if we need to change course, we must do it immediately.

If tomorrow was your last day on Earth, is this how you want your story to end?

In business and in life, return on investment is at a premium. Your CPA, your CFO, your spouse and your kids will all agree.

Personal and business lives are not and cannot be separated.

You are the common denominator in each.

If legacy is a reflection of a lifetime, what will your lifetime mirror reflect?

I leave you now with one question:

If today were your last day, what would change?

Now, go and change it…because **it's not them, it's you**.

# *Next Steps*

If you're holding this book in your hand and you have read it to this point, I'd like to gift you a free Rock Star Executive Mentoring Session for your perseverance and interest in my work with business behavior.

On that call, we can work on any of the topics listed in this book, such as:

- How you got to this point in your career
- Rewriting your programming
- Your leadership abilities
- Your hiring and firing processes
- The unit you've built within your company
- Your business behavior rules
- Your corporate environment
- The personal role you've played in creating your company
- My executive coaching

Upon the conclusion of this call, I will give you strategies that you can put into place immediately to begin the behavioral changes you need in your company and in your life.

Go to my website at www.ScotFerrell.com and send me a message through my contact page. Include in the Subject Line of the Message the phrase "Rock Star Executive Mentoring" and I'll know to gift you a free session.

## I LOOK FORWARD TO HEARING FROM YOU

95858075R00191

Made in the USA
Columbia, SC
23 May 2018